# OPERATION INSANITY

'As the SAS Operations Officer in charge of formulating a plan to get Richard and his men out of Bosnia, I know just how hopelessly trapped they were.

'Thrust into an operation that started as peacekeeping and ended with the most protracted combat for British troops since Korea, their plight seemed almost inevitable.

'This is an important book. Britain's Muslim community should know how these brave men put their lives on the line to save thousands of Muslims from a Srebrenica-style massacre.'

COLONEL TIM COLLINS, OBE
Former Commanding Officer,
The Royal Irish Regiment

Richard Westley was educated at King's School Worcester, where he played in the same rugby team as his ghost-writer, Mark Ryan. He served with the Sultan of Oman's Armed Forces and attended the RMA Sandhurst before being commissioned into the Royal Welch Fusiliers, serving in Northern Ireland, the Falkland Islands and Berlin before undertaking a surveillance role in Northern Ireland.

In 1995, as an acting major, Westley served as a rifle-company commander with the Royal Welch Fusiliers in Bosnia. For his gallantry and operational leadership in and around the besieged town of Gorazde, he was awarded the Military Cross by Her Majesty the Queen in 1996.

He returned to Northern Ireland before moving to the Rheindahlen headquarters of Allied Command Europe and their Rapid Reaction Corps, NATO's high-readiness deployment forces. From there he served as an intelligence officer in Greece, the former Yugoslav Republic of Macedonia, Kosovo, and Albania. He was then chosen to be a company commander at the RMA Sandhurst until 9/11, when he was posted to Afghanistan on operations with US Special Forces and then with 3 Commando Brigade. He also deployed to South America, Côte d'Ivoire, Sierra Leone and Beijing.

After being selected to be an instructor at the Joint Service Command Staff College in Shrivenham, Wiltshire, he was chosen to command the Worcestershire and Sherwood Foresters Regiment. He assumed command in Masar-e-Sharif, Afghanistan, in 2005 and led his Battle Group in Helmand Province in 2007. He was awarded an operational OBE for leadership and vision during this tour. On his return he was promoted to colonel, and assumed the post of commander of all operational training for the armed forces. He retired from the Army in July 2010.

# OPERATION INSANITY

## THE DRAMATIC TRUE STORY OF THE MISSION THAT SAVED 10,000 LIVES

## COLONEL RICHARD WESTLEY, OBE, MC
### WITH MARK RYAN

JOHN BLAKE

Published by John Blake Publishing Limited,
3 Bramber Court, 2 Bramber Road,
London W14 9PB, England

www.johnblakebooks.com

www.facebook.com/johnblakebooks ⓕ
twitter.com/jblakebooks ⓔ

First published in paperback in 2016

ISBN: 978-1-78606-137-9

British Library Cataloguing-in-Publication Data:
A catalogue record for this book is available from the British Library.

Design by www.envydesign.co.uk

Printed in Great Britain by CPI Group (UK) Ltd

1 3 5 7 9 10 8 6 4 2

Papers used by John Blake Publishing are natural, recyclable
products made from wood grown in sustainable forests.
The manufacturing processes conform to the environmental
regulations of the country of origin.

Every attempt has been made to contact the relevant copyright-holders,
but some were unobtainable. We would be grateful if the appropriate
people could contact us.

I would like to dedicate *Operation Insanity* to the memory of Fergus Rennie and Wayne Edwards, who gave their lives in a foreign country for other people's freedom and safety; and to the fighting men of the Royal Welch Fusiliers Battle Group, who ceased to believe in fairy tales and fought to prevent a Bosnian town from suffering a hideous fate.

# CONTENTS

# LIST OF MAPS

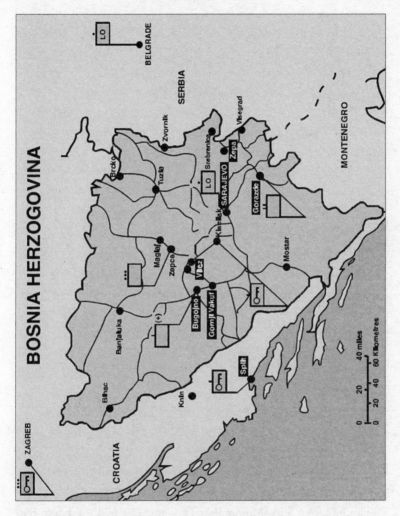

The lay-down of BritBat2 (Royal Welch Fusiliers) on deployment in March 1995. D Company in Bugojno; A, B and C Companies in Gorazde; with administrative echelons at Split and Kiseljak and a liaison office (LO) in Sarajevo.

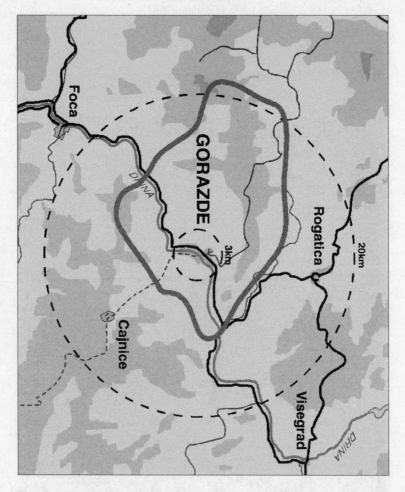

The Gorazde Pocket, March 1995. The heavy grey line represents the Muslim BiH front lines. Muslim fighters numbered 8,000 – although they had weapons for only 6,500. The thinner black line represents the front line of the Serb forces, who had surrounded the Muslims with over 40,000 troops from three Serb Corps.

# INTRODUCTION

# GORAZDE ISN'T SEXY

'**G**orazde? Where the hell is that?'

Few people have ever heard of the place; even fewer care about the terrible things that happened there. Sure, a couple of Hollywood film stars have visited Gorazde as UN ambassadors in the last few years. It doesn't get much more glamorous than Angelina Jolie and Brad Pitt. Gorazde, set in a beautiful valley with a fast-flowing river running right through it, was once pretty too, though it never did get very glamorous. I wonder if Angelina and Brad truly understood the horrors that unfolded there.

When we first set foot in Gorazde, more than twenty years ago, we were with the UN too. We tried to save its Muslim inhabitants from a massacre. Things got messy. Try to talk about it now and people start to look uncomfortable. I can almost hear them thinking stuff they don't have the guts to say. Not to my face anyway. 'What did you really achieve?

Don't you know that some of the most fanatical Muslim fighters in the world today hail from Bosnia, precisely because of what happened there during the war? They hate the West. Is that partly your fault? Didn't UN soldiers refuse to fight and protect those poor people in the enclaves?'

We British fought. I should know because I directed the battle. We abandoned our neutrality to try to stop a murderous Serb general named Ratko Mladic – a man they later branded 'the Butcher of Bosnia'. The British Queen and Prime Minister became involved when some of our soldiers were taken hostage. Awkward. The SAS had already been warned that some of the British officers in Gorazde might be cracking up because it was getting so ugly there. Imagine. Our own elite forces, observing us carefully, to see if we were losing the plot – you couldn't make it up.

Just as well we were still combat-effective. Before long we had to defend ourselves against some of the Muslims we'd first been trying to save. And I was accused of being a war criminal – even though it wasn't supposed to be 'our war'. Believe me, it felt like our war and it was.

Civilians often struggle to understand what soldiers go through and some think we deserve the worst anyway. 'Sorry most of your men came back with some form of Post-Traumatic Stress Disorder, sorry they'd spent a summer in a place where children were murdered for fun. But you signed up for that life, you're paid to get on with it. I don't want to hear the gory details.'

We did get on with it but there was a price to pay when we came home. And the lessons learned in Gorazde directly influenced the development of the current Trauma Risk

Management (TRiM) programme, designed to prevent or at least minimise PTSD among Britain's armed forces.

So Gorazde and its legacy do matter. If we're to enjoy a closer relationship with Muslim communities in Britain and beyond; if we're to help prevent war veterans from developing severe PTSD; for these reasons and more, Gorazde should not be forgotten.

'Gorazde. Where's that again?' Even as people ask you the question, they hardly seem to care.

Angelina and Brad might recall an ordinary town. But let me take you to the Gorazde I knew. Get ready, though, because this isn't the movies; this actually happened. For me, it's still all too real.

# CHAPTER ONE

# THE BOY ON
# THE BIKE

The sniper didn't realise how good his first shot had been. The boy was twitching, so the marksman thought there was still work to be done. Although two more bullets bounced off the road next to the child's body, accuracy no longer mattered. The twitches were just death throes and part of the boy's chest had already been shot out. I saw the damage as I scooped him up in my arms.

He couldn't have been more than ten years old. Even though I was an experienced soldier, this was the most cold-blooded piece of nastiness I'd seen. We were in a war zone but what I'd just witnessed wasn't an act of war. This poor kid hadn't been caught in crossfire; the marksmanship told a very different story. This was deliberate; a murder, right in front of a British UN peacekeeper. They'd picked the wrong peacekeeper to taunt with their casual savagery. They should have killed me when they'd had the chance a few days earlier.

Tensions were already close to breaking point by early April 1995. The Bosnian Serb forces of General Ratko Mladic were gathered around the enclave of Gorazde, hoping to carry out a massacre. A NATO air strike had prevented one a year earlier. Now the infamous Butcher of Bosnia's men were back – and we weren't exactly well equipped to stop them. In the previous twelve months, the British had doubled their UN peacekeeping contribution to two battalions with associated logistics. The UN called them BRITBAT 1 and BRITBAT 2. Strangely, BRITBAT1, the heavily armoured battalion, was sent somewhere less dangerous. BRITBAT 2 had much less firepower but we were based in an enclave where extreme violence was the norm. I soon realised there was little point in trying to apply logic to our predicament in Gorazde though. Suffice to say it was unusual for one battalion to be sent so far behind the lines of the most powerful aggressor in a war, with so little support. We were effectively surrounded, we were fast becoming cut off and yet we had been charged with preventing genocide with only 'peacekeeping weapons' to help us.

The situation had begun to deteriorate both regionally and locally. The Bosnian Serb Army and their Muslim enemy, the Bosnian Army known as BiH, were preparing for the fighting season. The Cessation of Hostilities Agreement – a temporary truce brokered by the Americans – was drawing to a close. With winter over, the British soldiers in and around Gorazde were seen as soft targets. Attacks on us had increased in intensity and frequency; meanwhile Bosnian Serb restrictions on our resupply had turned into a stranglehold. We'd already had to reduce our rations by a third and before long we'd have to reduce them by another third. But the danger was gnawing away at my soldiers just as much as the hunger; you could see it in their eyes. Every day was becoming a challenge. One young Royal Welch Fusilier confided this to me: 'Six months is a long time when every day you wake up and you're scared.' Fear or no fear, we all had to carry on because we had a commitment to the humanitarian agencies. Each week we had to escort their vehicles from Gorazde to the outlying villages.

We were never under any illusions about the perilous nature of our mission. Lieutenant-Colonel Nikolai Batalin, the short, squat Ukrainian UN Commander who'd departed the camp as we arrived, had explained the risks clearly enough. Our commanding officer, Lieutenant-Colonel Jonathon Riley, had told Batalin precisely what we intended to do around Gorazde; how we were going to stand up to the Serbs and show them we meant business. Batalin looked at Riley and said, 'You're all going to die.' Then he got up and left. It seemed melodramatic at the time but I soon understood why he'd said it.

There was no warning shot. A huge burst of automatic fire hit the bank just to the right of our position. I heard the buzz of the bullets, telling me they were no more than five metres away, close enough to spew dirt and rocks over people in sharp sprays and cut them. This was clearly the work of a heavy weapon and, if those bullets struck flesh, they were going to do some serious damage.

It was 5 April 1995 and we'd pushed into the unknown in our determination to make our presence felt beyond the confines of Gorazde. It was an important part of the mission as I saw it. If we were going to reach out to the Serbs, we knew we'd have to venture outside the 3-kilometre buffer zone around the town. It might put lives at risk but what were we supposed to do? Stay where we felt safest and watch the chaos unfold from there? If we were going to take that approach, we might as well have stayed in Britain. So every day I led patrols on the east bank of the rushing River Drina, a natural boundary that separated most of the besieged town from any hidden Serb positions in surrounding hills, which rose to 3,000 feet above sea level.

On this particular day, we were still only five kilometres from Gorazde when we went over one ridge line too many. We hadn't told the Serbs we were coming but, then again, we didn't feel we needed to. The high-profile UN flags on our radio antennae and the blue berets on our heads told them exactly who we were. We made nice clear targets, I suppose. The moment the bullets buzzed and thudded and spewed fragments at us, I gave the order:

'Take cover!'

We tried to identify the source of the gunfire but it was well concealed. Even when we finally picked up the Serb position, we realised it was outside the range of our individual weapons. Try as we might to concentrate our fire to give us range, we could see it wasn't arcing far enough. To be outgunned was one thing; we could just about handle that. To be outranged was another because it meant our weapons were effectively useless. We were going to need help – and fast.

I called Battalion Headquarters in Gorazde to request close air support from UN aircraft, using the code words 'Blue Sword'. It was going to be difficult to guide them onto the target because I didn't have any Forward Air Controllers with me. Either I'd have to talk to the pilot myself on a VHF radio, which would be tricky but not impossible, or else relay everything through headquarters. We could cross that bridge when we came to it. For now we just wanted to hear the good news that the air cavalry were on their way.

After half an hour of being pinned down under fire, with not so much as an acknowledgement from the UN, I made the request for Blue Sword again through Battalion HQ. We were told there was still no word from the UN's Bosnian HQ in Sarajevo. We waited for that air support... and we waited some more. Another hour passed. Still pinned down, I called again.

'Give me an update on Blue Sword.'

'Blue Sword non-viable, over,' said an embarrassed-sounding voice from Gorazde.

'Why?'

'We'll explain when you get back.'

'If we get back,' I thought.

There was only one way out. Wait for darkness, extract back through the Muslim lines and hope they didn't shoot at us too. I asked Battalion HQ to tell the relevant BiH commanders that UNPROFOR (the United Nations Protection Force) would be coming back through them. We could only hope our HQ would manage to speak to the right people this time.

The sun went down and we made our move. It was a nervous journey, feeling our way through the night. Every time we came close to a Muslim position, we warned them we weren't Serbs trying to sneak up on them. 'UNPROFOR! UNPROFOR!' It would only take one jumpy guard to start shooting and they all would. Fortunately, they must have heard our cries and believed us. Somehow, we made it back into camp in the early hours and knew we'd been lucky.

There was only one question I wanted answered when we reached the Battalion Operations Room.

'What the fuck happened to the close air support?'

'We forwarded your request, sir,' said the Operations Warrant Officer, who was fuming as much as I was because he knew what we'd been through. 'But Sarajevo said they needed clearance from New York.'

'So what happened in New York?'

'Nothing. It's the weekend, sir.'

'What?'

'They said there was no one in the New York office, but rest assured our request for close air support would be top of the in-tray on Monday.'

Not knowing whether to laugh or cry, I whispered, 'Do not share that with anyone.'

I didn't want my soldiers to know that the key to getting them out of life-threatening situations was probably not viable. The UN didn't want to bomb anyone, no matter how much danger their own soldiers were in, and that was already becoming abundantly clear. Why share my sense of abandonment with the men? It wouldn't do them any good and it wouldn't change anything – even though it was easy to see the solution. While the UN needed to be in charge of the peacekeeping mandate in order to give legitimacy to the mission, they should not have been commanding the mission itself. The UN was not designed for commanding operationally. I realised that now more than ever. We were wearing their blue berets and, instead of empowering us to carry out our mission, in return they were leaving us in the shit. There were going to be tragic consequences before the end of the summer. For the moment, we just knew we were going to have to adapt our strategy daily and use our own initiative in order to make a significant impact on the chaos around us.

The very next day I was in the Ilovaca Valley, about twenty kilometres out of Gorazde. It was BiH territory but also directly across the River Drina from the Serb front line. I'd been trying to see one of the Muslim brigade commanders, who had refused to meet anyone from the UN before. His name was Sefik Drkendra and you might have thought he'd be more helpful because he had rescued a British pilot from a Sea Harrier shot down over Gorazde the previous year. Having reached the pilot before the Serbs got to him, Drkendra had then handed him over to a British SAS team, who completed the extraction. He'd done the Brits a massive favour.

However, Drkendra didn't hold the UN in such high esteem anymore and it soon became clear he wasn't going to make an exception for me, whatever my nationality. Reflecting on a wasted journey, my driver, 'Scud' Jones had just begun to take us back to Gorazde when we came across two wounded soldiers on the side of the road. It looked as though they'd crashed their car under fire and now they were going nowhere. A UN directive had warned us to avoid picking up troops from either side in a UN vehicle because we'd be accused of favouritism. But one of these soldiers, who was tall, thin and losing his dark hair, looked in a lot of pain. A bullet had forced his forefinger right back into his hand. The other man, a little younger, had a clean entry and exit wound in his thigh.

Confident no one was watching, we put these Muslim

soldiers in our Land Rover, drove to Gorazde hospital and took them in through the main entrance. As we did so, the guards stood to attention. 'We've got somebody here,' I thought. It seemed to be the older guy with the horribly distorted finger. The doctor asked his name.

'Sefik Drkendra,' he replied.

I visited him over the next few days, took him fruit and cigarettes and generally made sure he was all right. Drkendra was a nervous, ferret-like character but he seemed to be warming to me, which made it all the more disappointing when I arrived one day and he wasn't there anymore. No matter, because he had left me a message to say he was back in his headquarters and would I like to pay him a visit there? Perfect!

We received a much warmer welcome next time we went to the Ilovaca Valley. Drkendra greeted me with a smile and said he would show me all his front-line positions. If I came back the following night, under cover of darkness, he would even show me all the Serb positions as well. Brilliant! Mapping out the front lines was a big part of our job for the UN. What a stroke of luck.

As 'Scud' was taking us back to Gorazde in our UN Land Rover, I was still feeling jubilant that Drkendra was going to play ball at last. We reached the edge of Vitkovice, a village in the river valley. We were soon driving smoothly along a good piece of tarmac road and all was quiet. The high ground to the left, Muslim-held, was dotted with a few harmless buildings, while to the right we noticed the turning for a factory complex, which had become the Ukrainian UN contingent's latest base. The only sign of life on the road ahead was a boy, cycling in the same direction, about ten metres in front of us. He must have come from the school we'd seen about six hundred metres back and now he was on his way home. The main part of Vitkovice was only four hundred metres away, so he didn't have to pedal much further to reach safety and we didn't want to flatten him.

'Just slow down a bit,' I told Scud. 'We've got a kid on a bike here.'

As I said it, the boy just lurched off his bike, fell slightly forward to the left and dropped straight down onto the tarmac. 'Fuck me, we weren't anywhere near him,' I thought. Then I saw those two strikes on the road next to him, as he twitched. A Serb sniper was at work across the river; it was the only explanation.

'Put the vehicle between the Serb position and the boy,' I told Scud.

The Land Rover wasn't armoured but at least it could provide a bit of protection from further sniper fire. We jumped out. We weren't wearing any body armour below our camouflaged smocks, and nothing more than blue berets on our heads, but you react instinctively and I ran to the boy to try to give him first aid. He was wearing a red woollen jumper – what was left of it – brown nylon trousers and cut-off Wellington boots. The UNHCR (United Nations High Commission for Refugees) people gave the local children boots for the winter and then their parents cut them down for comfort when it grew a bit warmer, because the kids had no shoes. This child wore no socks. And he was dead.

The twitching, his death throes, had stopped by the time I got to him. I rolled him over and saw he was about nine or ten. He was thin, had cropped brown hair and a little mole on his left cheek. He would have had an olive complexion but the blood had drained very quickly from his face. A tooth was missing at the front of his mouth; only one, which was surprising for a Muslim child in this harsh environment. Although his brown eyes were open, within seconds the corneas were crenellating, like cling-film starting to crinkle. When corneas do that, flickers of other colours can be seen in them. This is not a good sign. I did all the vital checks but he was gone.

The round had come in through his shoulder blade and must have gone on to hit his spine or rib cage because it took out fragments of bone along with pieces of vital organs as it exited his chest. The big exit wound told me that death had, at least, come quickly but why had it come at all,? What was the point? An anger rose inside me, more powerful than upset. I was thirty-three by then and I'd done a lot of soldiering, from fighting in Oman as a youngster alongside the Sultan's Special Forces, to some difficult tours of Northern Ireland. I'd held many ranks and commanded forces in all kinds of operations in various theatres. I'd seen people killed before but never anything like this. I mean never. It was an appallingly nefarious act. It was also a hell of a shot. A single shot from at least five or six hundred metres, way across the river, at a moving target. Putting everything else aside, that is an extraordinary shot to make. The murderous marksman was probably giving himself a pat on the back and telling his friends what he'd just done. But what had he just done? Taken an innocent child's life away from him for no reason. Congratulations.

We had to take the boy somewhere, so I thought we'd take him to the hospital anyway. I didn't want to drift around the neighbourhood and ask every local we saw, 'Does anyone know this child?' Given the state he was in, it would be too distressing. If we took him to the hospital, at least they could clean him up a bit and then bring someone down to identify him. In these first desperate moments, no one from his community, let alone his family, knew he was dead. Although his life had ended on the road between his school and his village, the scene was deserted. Some minibuses had already turned up and taken most of the children home, we heard later. Safety in numbers, they probably thought, or at least a safety of sorts.

Other children had been shot at outside the school during the preceding weeks. It was chilling to imagine how the Serbs had developed their habit of trying to murder Bosnian children as they came out of school, either for fun or simply to inflict maximum hurt on their parents, the real enemy. This boy must have been a bold and independent little chap because he'd chosen to cycle anyway, despite the violence and intimidation.

I picked him up, wrapped him in what remained of his own upper clothing, which was a horrible mess, and laid him on my lap in the back of the Land Rover. He didn't weigh much; none of the enclave's hungry children did. So it was no physical effort to carry the boy into Gorazde hospital, my camouflage smock covered in more than just blood, and hand him over to an orderly at the triage point.

He looked at me as if to say, 'What the fuck do you think I'm supposed to do with this? Why have you brought him here?'

What he actually said was, 'You need to find his parents.'

'You find his parents!' My anger had been simmering under

the surface and now I was taking it out on the wrong person. Having told the orderly more calmly where the murder had taken place, I left the boy's body with him. Surely the hospital had a system for tracking down a bereaved family in a case like this? I'd done all I could for now.

I wanted to wash some of the poor child's remains off me and knew where to go. The offices of Salko Osmanspahic, the charismatic commander of 801 Brigade in the BiH (Muslim) army, were only just around the corner from the hospital. He'd want to know what had happened anyway.

Although his menials told me Salko wasn't there, I insisted he be called. In the meantime, 'Riso', his second in command, would do. Sure enough, Riso came out, his eyes swivelling wildly as they always did. Slim, with a dapper-looking Erroll Flynn moustache, Riso may not have looked the fighting type but he had seen plenty of action as a field soldier. Perhaps that was why he didn't look too surprised by the state of my smock and simply invited me to sit down. 'I'll get you a coffee and a slivovitz and you can tell me what's happened,' he added.

If ever I needed a slivovitz, a shot of the local plum brandy, it was now. While he went to fetch Salko for me, I had time to get cleaned up as best I could in the toilet. It wasn't easy because in Gorazde running water was a rarity and people used buckets instead. I found one there, poured some water into a little plastic tub on the basin and tried to wash. I scrubbed as much gore off me as I could, washed my hands and returned to Salko's empty office, where there was still a moment to reflect. I had a two-year-old son at home, George. How could anyone do this to a child? I tried to calm down and make sense of the barbarity I'd just witnessed because in a moment I was going to have to explain the incident objectively to a high-ranking officer. Close your eyes. Try to erase some of the images. Try to tell yourself this is going to happen, it comes with the territory. Try to rationalise the irrational. I did my best.

Salko entered, tall, confident, always giving the impression that he was in control of a situation. Fury flashed across his face for no more than an instant when he heard what had happened and then was gone again. He was unsurprised, essentially, and that probably helped him to keep his emotions in check.

'This is not an isolated act of savagery,' he said after I'd given him all the details. 'This is what the "Chetniks" do for their own amusement.'

'I'm going to try to do something about it,' I assured him.

For a moment he looked at me as though I were some mad idealist, trying to cling to my own little fantasy world. Perhaps there was an element of truth in that but it was still important to let him know that the British UN forces didn't intend to sit back and let this kind of thing happen, not like our Ukrainian colleagues seemed to have done until then.

Back outside I glanced to my left. I could see all the way up the road to Cemetery Valley, a bleak yet strangely beautiful spot on the edge of town. It was the final resting place for many of Gorazde's inhabitants. The vast River Drina flowed uncaringly past the cemetery on one side while, on the other, steep limestone stretched up and turned into mountains that rose to 3,000 feet. It was a spectacular setting for a cemetery, though, to me, those imposing limestone cliffs gave the place a slightly sinister feel.

'That's where the boy's body will probably end up,' I thought. 'Hope they can find his parents in time to organise a decent funeral.'

At his tender age it shouldn't have been necessary and the anger was still simmering away inside me as I rang up the British liaison officer at the local Serb headquarters.

'Arrange a meeting with Kepic,' I said. 'There's been a murder.'

Captain Kepic was the Serb liaison officer, the man we went to on a variety of issues, though we rarely received a satisfactory response. Predictably, a message came back saying he wasn't available until a week on Tuesday; a typical tactic.

'Okay, in that case I'll see Lieutenant-Colonel Fortula,' I said. The mere mention of the Bosnian Serb Army's area commander would help to focus Kepic's attention.

'Captain Kepic will see you at eight o'clock this evening,' was the fresh message. Rather than suffer the humiliation of having me go over his head, he'd had a change of heart. Nice of him.

There was still time to go back to the camp and get cleaned up. Queasiness began to take over from anger, as often happens when your adrenalin levels start to drop. I hoped a shower would help. We'd created some makeshift showers with pump handles, so you could draw the water up from a Burma oil drum after it had been heated over a fire. Normally you'd be in there for just as long as it took you to get wet, soaped up, washed and get out again. This time I asked the soldier waiting outside, 'Please just keep pumping the water.' Although he patiently obliged, I couldn't make myself feel clean. Eventually I gave up, got dressed, went back to my room and lay on my bed. I had about half an hour before the evening conference and my left leg was rocking back and forth, as though I were operating one of those old sewing machines. What was going on?

A hundred blokes from the Royal Welch Fusiliers were waiting out there for me to talk to them about today's incident. You have to be careful how you deal with your emotions when you have a job like that to do. You can freely admit, 'I'm really quite angry this has happened,' but you can't show how it's affecting you. You have to play-act a little, show you're in control, try to contain it all, lock it away if you have to. My way of taking control, of my own body at least, was to go through a series of tensing and un-tensing exercises. I could have locked myself away in one of the cubicles and cried my eyes out to release the tension. There would have been nothing wrong with that, except that it would have complicated things, unsettled my audience. This little speech was going to require a degree of composure. Standing up and speaking in front of a large crowd of people had never fazed me in itself. But I didn't fancy going out to talk to the blokes with red eyes, because they weren't stupid and they'd have known immediately what I'd been doing. As a company commander, you're supposed to be stronger than the men in your company. So I didn't let myself cry before I faced them.

We went through what we called an 'after-action review', a sort of debrief, coldly objective but necessary. The murder of the child showed that our initial concept of operations didn't tally with what actually happened in a place like this. In short, we needed to get real. We ran through the incident and asked ourselves how we might prevent further murders. I reminded them why we were there and this was where I could allow some emotion to show. We had to learn from this dreadful murder because who would protect the children of Vitkovice and Gorazde itself if we didn't?

'Although this poor boy's death has changed nothing in the general scheme of things, it has to stand for something. It has to strengthen our resolve to protect the people caught up in this conflict and not allow ourselves to be pushed around while we do it.'

The men listened and I sensed they were with me because they knew I meant it. That Serb sniper had made a big mistake because I'd always hated bullies and I'd always done something about them too. Though it seemed so superficial in comparison to what had just happened, my mind went back to my school days for a moment. I remembered how a friend had been bullied by someone two years above us and how his life had become a misery. It had prompted me to march into the older boy's study, where he politely told me to sit down and put my feet up. I tried to remain calm and explained what the problem was and he responded by kicking me hard in the back of the leg, which was why he'd asked me to put my feet up in the first place. I got up and floored him with one punch. I was punished, of course, but he didn't bother my friend again.

Even now, almost twenty years later, there was still no place for bullying in my world. Gorazde was a far more savage environment than mine had been as a boy and almost all respect for human life had evaporated. The Bosnian Serbs weren't just bullying young children; they were casually taking their lives for fun. But that sniper had a problem now because his world had just collided with my world and I was determined to make him regret it. As a UN peacekeeper, I had one arm tied behind my back but I was still going to apply my own moral code to this madness, whatever colour beret I was wearing. And the sniper wasn't going to enjoy it.

The anger still simmered inside as I drove out to meet Captain Kepic at the Kopace wire factory, the Serb headquarters on the other side of the front line, a couple of kilometres out of Gorazde. The confrontation line was nearby, complete with a no-man's-land of about two hundred metres.

Selma, my favourite interpreter, was with me and I told her what had happened to the boy on the bike. Like the dead child, she was Muslim, so maybe she had even more reason than me to feel outraged by the incident. While saddened by the news, she was more used to the callous killing of children in her town though.

'He's probably better off where he is, Major Richard,' Selma said.

Three years of atrocities had toughened her to tragedy. Although you sensed the murders had never stopped hurting her deep down, she'd found a way to block them out, or, at least, those killings she didn't witness personally. To an extent, the entire town had done the same. A place that could have been a picture-postcard tourist trap in peacetime had assessed the hopelessness of its predicament and smiled bitterly. Someone with a dark sense of humour had created a postcard, which had been printed in the town.

The message read, 'Greetings from Gorazde – where only the dead are lucky.'

So Selma had only echoed the grim sentiments of the postcard. The boy was now at least at peace, whereas, in life, he'd probably never known any. Death seemed to be the only realistic way out of this hell for many of Gorazde's 45,000 inhabitants. You ended up in Cemetery Valley, between the beautiful River Drina and the mountains. Sure, you were in a cemetery but there was that striking view, if you believed souls could see. Most important of all – and this seemed to be beyond debate – nothing worse could happen to you than had happened already. That's why people like Selma believed the dead were lucky in Gorazde. If you didn't believe it, you'd be crushed by the weight of your own sadness.

You could dream of escape to a better life in this life, of course. Selma had a dream of her own – to go to Spain. The friendliest, sunniest, happiest place in Europe, she reckoned. Selma had never really lost her lust for life, despite what she'd sometimes have me believe. It bubbled away beneath a gritty exterior, waiting for lasting expression. It was fuelled partly by the danger she faced most days – because to cheat death makes you feel so alive – and partly by Spain, her idea of heaven on earth. You saw a twinkle in those brown eyes any time you mentioned Madrid or Barcelona.

For now, however, Spain belonged to another world. Here in Gorazde, she was used to children being murdered and she was used to being abused every time we crossed the Serb confrontation line too. That was why, even though I needed an interpreter to get through the Serb lines, I was always nervous about taking Selma because the guards would make disgusting comments to her. She was only just over five feet tall and still in her early twenties, though the war had made her look older. Selma was slim, like all the Gorazde women, because there wasn't enough food. She had dark hair, brown eyes and a

Cindy Crawford-style mole on her cheek. Her face was full of character and she had the heart of a lion. The Serb soldiers didn't see her like that. They saw her as an object; a target to taunt and threaten. At the checkpoint that evening, they made crude gestures as we slowed to go through the barriers. Then they shouted and glared at her with such malevolence in their eyes that I was shocked and offended by their treatment of her.

'What did they say this time?' I asked her sympathetically, once we were clear.

She looked at me and shook her head as though to tell me to forget it. 'The usual, Major Richard. I don't want to dignify it by translating it.'

I knew what 'the usual' meant because I had recently asked male interpreters what was shouted at the female interpreters by these Bosnian Serb guards.

'Wait until we take Gorazde, we'll bend you over a table and take it in turns to fuck you before we kill you because that is all you fucking Muslim whores deserve.' That's what they habitually yelled.

Selma just maintained her dignity and ignored them, though it must have been terrifying and humiliating for her. To add to her ordeal, she hated travelling in our UN Land Rovers because they made her feel car sick, so she was already feeling weak when she had to absorb these verbal assaults on her. Still she did her job uncomplainingly and she would do so again on this particular evening. She would translate for me and for Captain Kepic, the Bosnian Serb liaison officer.

Kepic looked like a pig. Small eyes, medium height, grey hair, no front teeth and an ugly, protruding nose fit for snuffling in the soil for truffles. He'd been an engineer before he joined the army. Now he was an apologist for the people who were terrorising Selma's town and laying siege to it with massacre in mind.

I sat down opposite Kepic and couldn't hide my distaste. 'I've been a witness to the murder of a child in Vitkovice,' I began. 'And he was murdered from a Bosnian-Serb position that was directly targeting children coming out of the school. I'm writing a full report. In most countries a child has a right to education without fear.'

Selma translated. Kepic still looked quite comfortable and said nothing. I tried to make it simpler for him, in case my message wasn't getting through. 'This child was cycling home from school when he was murdered by a Bosnian-Serb soldier.'

Kepic looked completely bemused. He sat back and said, 'What is it that you wanted to see me about that is so important?'

Selma translated again, trying to stay as detached and as professional as she knew how.

'I just told you what is important,' I said, seething.

Kepic almost seemed to think I was being childish. 'You threatened to go above my head because some kid got killed? Do you know how many kids get killed here in Bosnia?'

'I have no idea,' I said, refusing to be patronised, 'and, frankly, right now I don't care because this child was killed right in front of me by one of your soldiers.'

Kepic replied with more provocation. 'How do you know it was a child?'

'Because I picked him up and took him to hospital.'

'Well, how old was this "child"?' he enquired casually, with a touch of sarcasm.

'No more than ten.' Where was he going with this?

'In six years he would have been carrying a Kalashnikov and I wouldn't have expected any mercy from him.'

By now Selma was almost spitting these words out, as she translated them. Kepic was completely insensitive to the presence of a young Muslim woman in the room. In fact, if anything, he seemed to take delight in the fact that she had to repeat his warped message in order to do her job.

'We're going to put a stop to this,' I warned Kepic. Then I told Selma it was time to leave.

What had I learned from this meeting? Apparently, children were not really children. Because a child will no longer be a child one day, that means he isn't a child now. How do you argue with someone who thinks like that? This was when I began to understand the dehumanisation of a people. In my bourgeois little Western world, the death of a child was horrendous and an important happening. To them it was a daily occurrence of no consequence whatsoever. I'd made my complaint and had it thrown it back in my face. I left even more determined to try to do something. We were going to put a stop to children being killed outside that school.

Selma was very quiet on the way back to Gorazde.

'Are you okay?' I asked her. You feel a huge bond at a moment like that. You're going through extraordinary things together and your emotions are going up and down all the time. The only constant in all this is your relationship with your interpreter.

She looked over at me, almost as though she hadn't heard what I'd said.

'You okay?'

She shrugged and said, 'Who is okay in this place, Major Richard?'

She had a point. Who could possibly be okay while this kind of brutality was allowed to continue unchecked? She was tough and I thought I was too but how much of this should anyone have to take? The Bosnian Serbs had to be stopped and the children of Gorazde protected. Was there a way to take on the Serbs and stay within the UN rules of engagement, while making the point that we wouldn't be pushed around? Since we knew we could never beat the Serbs toe-to-toe, we had to box clever. Hit them hard if they attacked us but limit the engagement and quickly threaten to report their activity to the wider world. That's how we'd take a stand against atrocity in Gorazde and, if we did, it would make us feel a little less helpless as we witnessed the suffering of civilians on a daily basis.

Time to put the plan I'd been formulating into action.

It was called Operation Minerva. There was no special significance to the name; just one of those things they come up with at Battalion Headquarters. But after witnessing that little boy's murder, the operation itself definitely meant something. The plan was simple enough: to put vehicles in place to protect that school in Vitkovice and have some of my best men ready to respond to any aggression. Operation Minerva 1 went in the day after the boy was killed. Two armoured Saxon vehicles, Colour Sergeant Pete Humphries in charge of one and Colour Sergeant Dai Martin in the other, were to be placed directly between the Serb position – the one that was doing the shooting from over the River Drina – and the school. That meant that, if the Serbs opened fire, they'd have to shoot over the heads of my men to aim towards the school. Under the rules of engagement, that allowed us to return fire and I knew that, with Humphries running the show, he and Martin would react swiftly.

Humphries, 'The Silver Fox', a thirty-three-year-old from Caernarvon in north Wales, was a particularly cool customer whose sharp blue eyes gave nothing away. He was quiet but potentially ruthless. So, if the Serbs fired one round in our direction or the school's, they were going to get a hundred right back at them. The rules of engagement talked of 'appropriate and necessary use of force' and it could be argued that the response I was calling for exceeded that considerably. But I wanted to show the Serbs that we weren't going to mess about and, although we'd be guided by the rules, we wouldn't be bound and weakened by them.

On that first day, the Serbs didn't open fire and we couldn't exactly feel disappointed because it meant we'd had a good deterrent effect initially. However, we couldn't let things end there, so Operation Minerva 2 went in the very next day. Humphries and Martin weren't available for this second phase so I put two fresh corporals in the Saxons in their place.

Before they went out, these corporals were nervous about the rules of engagement. I left them in no doubt. 'One in, a hundred back, please, gentlemen.' That was the only language a bully would understand; that was the message my men were told to send the Serbs if they started shooting again.

Two rounds were fired over our vehicles that day, which should have meant two hundred rounds fired back over the river at the Serbs. Unfortunately, the corporals claimed they couldn't identify the precise point of fire and, since no one was injured anyway, they'd kept their powder dry. Although this was frustrating, it was only a temporary setback because I wasn't going to let this go. We would see what the next day brought.

In the meantime, I went back to the hospital and found a doctor who was familiar with the case of the boy on the bike.

'Did the child get to his parents?' I asked.

'Yes, Adem was returned to his parents,' he replied. 'Thank you for bringing him in.'

Adem. So now I knew his first name. I didn't want to know his surname. Emotionally it just wouldn't be good for me to learn more about him. I thought again of my two-year-old son George at home, being lovingly looked after by my wife Jane, the girl I'd met and fallen in love with back at school in Worcester. Suddenly I missed them even more. We'd only recently found out that Jane was pregnant with our second child and my army career meant I'd barely had time to get to know our first. I resolved to put that right if I got out of Gorazde in one piece. If ever there was a place to help you appreciate your own children, it was Gorazde. The irony was that you had to blank out your family most of the time, just to be able to function properly as a soldier. You only allowed them back in during a weekly phone call, if you were lucky enough to get one, or when you received a letter. Otherwise you trusted they'd be there waiting for you, safe and sound when the time came to return to that cosier world. In the meantime, you tried to come to terms with the far more savage world into which you'd been thrown.

How did parents cope with the death of their young child? I didn't want to go there; I didn't want to see the impact this casual killing must have had on Adem's father and mother. A lot of the guys did get emotionally involved in the lives of the kids around Gorazde. That was natural enough but, in the longer term, it gets to you, especially if it turns out that you can't do the things for those children that you wanted to do. Adem was gone and we couldn't change that. What we could do was try to stop the Serbs killing any more of his school friends.

Operation Minerva 3 went in the following day, led afresh by the unflappable Humphries, with the trusty Martin alongside. On this occasion ,the Serbs unleashed a burst of machine-gun fire over the UN vehicles towards the school, narrowly missing my men in the process. Big mistake. Humphries and Martin had time to locate the source of the fire and within seconds they were returning it with interest. Before long the exchange had turned into the mother of all gun battles.

I was in the Ops Room back in the camp. The first I heard was from Humphries. 'Zero Alpha, Charlie Four Zero Alpha, contact, wait out.'

The noise and frequency of the gunfire told me what my next move should be. 'Right, my blokes are involved in a heavy contact, so let's get the Quick Reaction Force down to help them. They're in a valley and we need to help them get out.'

You feel excitement but you're also thinking, 'Shit! Are they going to be all right?' because they clearly sounded under a lot of pressure. Luckily, Humphries and Martin thrived under pressure. They were in a massive fire-fight but, the longer it went on, the more of the exchanges were coming from them. Humphries and Martin fired six or seven hundred rounds back at the Serbs. They were absolutely hammering that Serb position on the other side of the river.

In the middle of all this they came back on the radio. 'Two Serb positions engaged. One destroyed. Second one is engaging us.'

More thunderous fire assaulted my headphones and then it went quiet. What had happened? Had Humphries and Martin been hit?

I soon had the answer. 'Second position neutralised. Moving back towards Gorazde. Confirm position of QRF.'

'QRF is at Green One.' (We used spot codes instead of grid references or place names because both sides were listening to our radio and UN radios weren't allowed to be encrypted.)

'That's us clear.'

Humphries and Martin had dealt with the problem on their own. They didn't much need the help of the Quick Reaction Force, which could, at least, escort them back to camp. What a feeling of relief. Now all we had to do was to wait for their safe return. Sure enough, within half an hour or so Colour Sergeant Humphries came back into camp still buzzing with adrenalin, as anyone would from such a major contact. Normally he was so cool that his heart rate seldom seemed to rise above thirty. But he was obviously still hyped when he sat down to debrief me.

'Right, what happened?' I began.

He said, 'They fired a burst over our heads and we gave them six or seven hundred rounds back. Then they did it again and we gave them another three or four hundred rounds back. Then it's all gone quiet.'

'What's your assessment?'

'We assess that we've neutralised them,' he replied. That line was delivered in a more understated way, typical of him.

'Do you assess that you've killed them?' I wanted to hear him say it.

'Yes.'

I wasn't sorry. One of those positions had killed Adem, the little boy.

I could have sought out Adem's family and told them in person that we were confident we'd got the people who'd murdered him. It didn't seem right somehow – it wasn't going to bring him back. It felt more respectful to leave them to their mourning. Besides, I was fairly sure word would reach them of what we'd done. If that gave them any comfort, I'd be happy but we hadn't taken out the Serbs simply to avenge Adem; we'd done it to try to protect his school friends from a similar fate. We'd needed to stamp our authority on the Serbs and, in a sense, we'd engineered that fire-fight to show we meant business.

The Serbs were soon claiming we'd only wounded two of their soldiers. At first they wouldn't admit to the truth, which was that five Serb soldiers had been killed. To acknowledge such losses immediately would have dented their pride so that revelation only came later, confirmed to me by two separate Serb sources. For now, all they were interested in was money. There was a clear-the-air meeting, once again at the Kopace wire factory, the Serbs local HQ. Once again, poor Selma received an ear-full of filth and threats from the Serb guards as we went in. She remained stony faced and stared straight ahead, not wanting to draw any more attention to herself.

Captain Kepic, who seemed to be developing a grudge

against us, coldly presented me with a bill for what we'd done. Our CO, Lieutenant-Colonel Jonathon Riley, joined me halfway through that meeting, while I was still examining the bill, for 20,000 Serbian dinars. My men hadn't just killed Serbs, for which there appeared to be no charge, if only because they weren't admitting to it yet; we'd also damaged some radio equipment and they were charging us for the hospital treatment their wounded men had required.

Kepic watched me study the bill and asked, 'Have you got any questions?'

I said, 'Yes. Are you going to refund me the money for the ammunition I've expended?'

Selma quickly hid a smirk as she translated.

'Steady on,' said Riley, who wasn't averse to making a controversial remark or two himself, though he clearly thought I'd gone too far. But I was making a point and didn't care if I was offending Kepic. If they were charging us damages for a fire-fight they'd made entirely necessary through the cold-blooded murder of a child, the good guys might as well put in a counter-claim. I wasn't going to let that pig take the moral high ground. And although I'm not sure any money changed hands in the end, one thing was certain: whoever had paid for our bullets in the first place could rest assured it had been money well spent.

Riley and I were going back to Gorazde in separate vehicles so Selma waited until he was out of earshot before she burst out laughing. 'A refund for the ammunition!' she repeated, as though it was the best thing she'd heard in ages. 'Major Richard, you are so funny!' She deserved a smile after the way the Serbs had treated her.

Sadly our sense of satisfaction was short-lived, as it always was in Gorazde. If only the boost we Brits felt after defending the school and those innocent children had been destined to last. We did follow up and tried to improve their lot in whatever way we could. Schools in Wales, home of our regiment, began to send out pencils and books for those kids. Although it was a fine gesture, such generosity was soon rendered unnecessary. Did we win the battle to protect the rights of those poor kids to enjoy their school and continue their education without being terrorised? Can't say we did. In a separate incident we neutralised more Serb marksmen while they casually tried to kill Muslim kids right in front of us. Those Serbs mistakenly assumed they were protected during their murderous games if they stood on 'their' side of the 3-kilometre exclusion zone around Gorazde. They were wrong. But the Serbs were never going to leave the Muslim children alone. And so, for the safety of the remaining children, that school had to close within a couple of months. It wasn't the kids who decided to stop going due to the danger; that call was taken out of their hands – and understandably so. This showed me that the Serbs were not only capable of any level of brutality but for any length of time. And Adem wasn't the last, or even the youngest, child to die and leave my memory scarred by the sheer absurdity of the situation in Gorazde that lethal summer. Indeed, the screaming of children became a familiar daily sound and one that would haunt me for some time to come.

What good could we do here? There had been a complete breakdown of what we liked to call normal European behaviour and it seemed beyond repair. Under normal circumstances, a diverse society finds a way to hold itself together to allow people of different ethnicity and religion to co-exist, whatever the underlying tensions. All that had imploded in Bosnia and the fragmentation brought with it a level of violence most of us struggled to comprehend, even as career soldiers. We had come in to safeguard the civil population in wartime. But we couldn't do it; not entirely. We never stopped trying and it's distressing when you don't succeed. We all felt the hurt of it and I don't see how anyone could have stayed in Gorazde for long without being emotionally scarred by it.

Unfortunately, the damage to B Company wasn't purely psychological. The idea that we could do this impossible job and all get home physically unscathed was equally unrealistic.

# CHAPTER TWO

# THE INCUBATOR

'**C**ontact... shooting... casualties... wait out...'

It was very garbled and difficult to hear. I didn't recognise the voice of the Fusilier on the radio and that was unusual because I knew all my guys extremely well. Had the traumatic impact of the event he was trying to report made him unrecognisable? He was shaken up and I was asking him to calm down and explain was happening.

'We've got three casualties and we're in the shit!'

That much was clear. What kind of casualties? Finally he managed to tell me that one of my men had been shot in the chest and another in the face. Some kind of ambush, I assumed. At any rate, it didn't sound good.

We'd started the day in good spirits, Jonathon Riley and I. The Commanding Officer was tall and thin, with a big nose and a sharp wit. He was fearless and he had a favourite saying: 'If I have any faults, which frankly I doubt, being wrong is not one of them.' He'd already decided what was right for us on this particular day. Riley was a very fit man, very active, and he liked to get out on the ground and visit his companies. So we were going out on a 35 to 40-kilometre foot patrol of Gorazde's East Bank, including a tough climb up Mala Biserna, an imposing mountain where we controlled all the key high ground overlooking Gorazde.

We'd start by going up to Check Point 1, through Observation Post 2, then out to the limit of the 3-kilometre zone and right the way round to bounce in at our other OPs too. This would be a good opportunity for Riley to see the troops and experience some of the issues we were reporting on a day-to-day basis.

We were joined by a member of the SAS. We had six SAS men based in the camp with us. Although they operated independently of the Royal Welch Fusiliers, we knew they'd be able to control air support superbly and guide planes onto targets if ever we were allowed that kind of help on operations. Otherwise, if the shit really hit the fan, they'd be the ones to bring in air to get us out of there. Officially, the SAS men were termed 'Joint Commissioned Officers' (JCOs) in Bosnia. It didn't matter what you called them; they were highly skilled in the art of talking to planes. The problem we had was that there were no planes for them to work with, no matter how many times we surveyed the skies and wished the air cover over from Sarajevo. So it wasn't entirely clear to me what these superb soldiers were supposed to be doing each day.

The SAS team commander was a rock-hard sergeant-major from the North Midlands called Wez Harris. Ronny Collins, from Essex, was his number two, then there was Archie, an amusing but aggressive Scot with long, curly black hair, and another cheeky Scot called Ed Grey, the baby of the four-man troop, who was very intelligent and mouthy with it. In addition to that troop, there was a two-man SAS Forward Air Control Party, featuring the irrepressible Billy Walters from Worcestershire and a short northern bloke called Mick Ramsden, who was very personable but less of an extrovert.

Wez Harris was the one who said he fancied the physical side of the 'tab' Riley and I had planned. Wez had joined the SAS from the Parachute Regiment. He was a big, muscular bloke who loved a bit of banter and always gave as good as he got. My own unflappable sergeant major, Mark Adams, MM, made up the party. Adams was a physically powerful specimen too – in fact, he looked a bit like Arnold Schwarzenegger. He'd seen plenty of action and he was confident and loyal. With Harris and Adams flanking us, Riley and I knew we were in good company.

The four of us set off at a sharp pace, as we had a lot of ground to cover in the daylight hours.

When Adams was out of earshot for a moment, Wez came up alongside me and said, 'Your sergeant major. How did he win his Military Medal?'

'He shot a couple of terrorists in Northern Ireland,' I explained.

'Fuck me,' said Wez. 'I shot two terrorists in Oman and all I got was, "Roger, out."'

The tab had been going well and we were fairly relaxed until about an hour into the patrol, when we received that garbled contact report.

'We need CASEVAC urgently. I can't move,' the mystery voice had added. 'Vicinity of OP2 Alpha.'

The wounds sounded serious and I set about getting an ambulance out to a rendezvous point at Cemetery Valley, which was close to OP2 Alpha, one of our observation posts. Cemetery Valley suddenly had an ominous ring to it and there was no time to waste. We needed to reach the scene even before the ambulance did, in order to secure the area. We couldn't all go, though, and Riley quite rightly decided to return to our camp in the town, to organise a helicopter to come in and airlift the casualties out of Gorazde. He headed back on foot to arrange for the anticipated helicopter evacuation to Tuzla. Safe passage for the chopper had to be brokered with both sides in the war, otherwise we'd have another tragedy on our hands.

The SAS team commander and I had a Land Rover brought out to us. The moment it arrived, we set off across the rough terrain of the East Bank's foothills to try to reach the point where the contact was happening. Wez Harris was exactly the right man to have with me. You just couldn't imagine him ever having lost a contact. He was hugely experienced; he'd fought in the Falklands as a young paratrooper in 2 Para and he'd been in the SAS for more than ten years. Wez was approachable and fun when nothing was happening but he was very, very professional when he switched into operational mode. Even as we were heading towards the contact, he was reminding himself and me of the priorities for casualty treatment, while running through checks on his weapons. As I was trying to work out what was happening, he had gone into an automaton drill of checks, which was absolutely brilliant because he made me go through them as well.

As we drove closer to the contact, we wondered how long the mystery man on the radio could hold out. It sounded as though he had been incapacitated too, so now there wasn't a single soldier still combat-effective from a four-man patrol. It would only be a matter of time before they were overrun and, with mercy in such short supply around Gorazde, you suspected they'd all be finished off by their attackers. Shit. What were they up against? The soldier on the radio was very, very excitable and it was difficult to get much sense out of him. Did he think he was surrounded?

'It's mines!' he revealed at last. 'We're in a minefield and we have gunshot wounds.' There was rising fear in his voice; he didn't seem to be able to make much sense of a chaotic situation.

Harris and I quickly decided what we were going to do when we reached what was left of the patrol. If they were still stuck in the minefield, we would prod our way in from OP2 Alpha, clear a lane and drag them out. Then I would assess the situation and make sure the security was good, so my role was going to be one of co-ordination and reporting. Meanwhile, Wez and Mark Adams would deal with the casualties.

The voice on the radio updated us once more. This time he sounded a little calmer. They were all out of the minefield and he was getting the casualties onto stretchers and down to the entrance to Cemetery Valley. How was he doing all that on his own? It sounded little short of miraculous, though we still didn't know how bad the injuries were. We'd soon find out because we were nearly there.

A small crowd of people had gathered at Cemetery Valley, probably attracted by the screams. We had to move the locals away but there were no security problems as far as I could see. In fact, the locals seemed to have helped the uninjured soldier get the wounded out of the minefield. At first I only saw two of them, lying in pain on stretchers, leaking blood. Then a third stretcher was brought up with the remaining casualty, carried at one end by the man who had been on the radio. Now I realised why I hadn't recognised his voice. Corporal Williams 49 (we used serial numbers to distinguish between popular Welsh names) had recently come in on a convoy escort from D Company. He'd been unable to get back out so he'd joined B Company. Calming down a little now that we were there by his side, Williams told me what had happened.

The patrol had moved out and the lead man, Fusilier Thompson 17, had trodden on a 'Gorazde mine'. These are improvised anti-personnel mines. They're wooden, so you wouldn't even find them if you went in with a metal detector. They have a bullet in them with a .22 percussion cap. As Thompson had trodden on it, he had fired the mine upwards and its bullet had passed through the base of his jaw and out of his cheekbone. The bullet hadn't gone through his foot because he had only trodden on the extremity of the box and it hadn't reached his brain either, so he was comparatively fortunate.

The second and third men in the patrol, believing Thompson had been shot in the face by enemy, broke left and right, following their normal drills to provide a fire base. As they did so, Corporal Jones 10 had trodden on another mine and its bullet had gone straight through his foot, opening the top of it up like a crown roast of lamb. He now lay in agony on a stretcher. The third man, who had broken right, was Fusilier Mee and he'd trodden on yet another mine. That bullet had not only gone through his foot but continued up into his chest, so he was in a bad way and his wounds were potentially life-threatening.

Harris was all over it like a rash. Superb, as you'd expect from the SAS. He prioritised the casualties in an instant. First had to be the chest wound, Fusilier Mee, and second was Corporal Jones. In no time at all, Wez had drips into both of them. Although Mee would need his intravenous drip, he couldn't have any morphine because it can be counter-productive when you've been hit in the chest. We didn't know the extent of his injuries, so Wez just got him bandaged up and dripped up, ready for evacuation. Jones received morphine as soon as Harris was done with Mee. He was out of it from the moment that morphine went into him.

Thompson was less urgent and Mark Adams was able to chat to him calmly while dressing his wounds. Although the bullet had gone through Thommo's face, he could still talk. He had an entry and exit wound and, as this was a head injury, he wasn't going to get any morphine. He was lucid and clear throughout, the least troubled of them all. Although that bullet had taken out a couple of teeth, it had gone through the fleshy part of his face and not done any structural damage to it, other than to make holes in it.

Wez, still in SAS medic mode, had all three casualties dealt with in the space of a few minutes. A four-man patrol had taken three casualties so, without the right help, there could have been a major problem extracting them. As it was, we were able to move the locals further away, get the ambulance in and have the casualties on board within fifteen minutes of arriving. First we evacuated them to the Norwegian medical station in our camp, where the team stabilised them. Then they were away to Tuzla on the chopper that Riley and Battalion HQ had organised.

I was relatively pleased with the way we'd handled the incident and got them out because everything had worked pretty smoothly. However, I was disappointed that the BiH hadn't told us in enough detail where all the mines were. It was a Muslim-laid minefield and we thought we knew that East Bank like the back of our hands; we clearly hadn't been told the full extent of the minefield. My men had pushed through an area they hadn't been in before, thinking it was free of any nasty surprises, and then it all had all gone bang.

I was depressed that three of my blokes had just been classified 'End of Tour'. They were on their way to Tuzla, which was great, but there was no way they were coming back, which wasn't great at all. I just hoped no one was going to lose a foot, or worse.

It was time to see Salko and demand an explanation. 'Why didn't you tell us about those mines?'

He shrugged his shoulders. 'We thought you knew about the mines.'

He was quite casual about it. He could almost have been saying, 'So what? Nobody died. This may be important to you but it's not to us.' This *was* important to me. I loved my soldiers and they were young guys. I was worried they wouldn't be able to serve in the army anymore.

The Muslims saw so much death on a day-to-day basis on the front line that this incident didn't even register. We weren't going to change the desensitised state of these men; we just had to make sure they put the whole area out of bounds until they had led me through that minefield. Then I could lead my commanders through it too and everybody could be clear what the safest route was. This, to their credit, they swiftly did.

Happily, the three wounded men of B Company would go on to make full recoveries. Unfortunately, however, the incident had a pronounced effect on those left behind. Already the guys were getting hyped up about going out on the ground because of the number of contacts we were running into. When you introduce anti-personnel mines into the equation, a more insidious threat, it becomes even more challenging psychologically. Not only have you got to look out for people trying to shoot and kill you; now you've got to watch where you put your feet as well. It's a really unnerving feeling; one you have to force out of your mind. If you're worrying that wherever you put your foot it might go bang, you won't go out; you won't do anything.

And yet it's impossible to force the fear out of your mind entirely. My men were only human, after all. Before patrols every day, I watched them go through the ritual of their preparations. Some would lace their boots, loosen them and then tighten them up again. It was their lucky routine, a bit like an international rugby player before a big match. But my men weren't hoping for a good game; they were hoping to come back with two feet. And they hadn't been blown up so far, so why change the routine? 'Don't change the ritual, whatever you do; make it the same as last time because last time you survived.' It was a stressful state of mind and the pressure was mounting. The powers that be were already wondering how much pressure we'd be able to take before our minds went bang too.

In the first week in May, I realised what the SAS team were up to. Just a comment here or a nod and a wink there, especially when they were around officers. Maybe Wez Harris hadn't decided to come out on patrol with us merely because he felt he could do with the exercise that day the mines had gone off. Riley had been there. I'd been there. Had the SAS Commander seen it as a good opportunity to get up close and personal with people they wanted to assess?

Typical SAS roles were to act as observers and liaison officers and use their specific skills and special equipment to talk to aircraft, as previously mentioned. So we knew what they usually did and it was quite normal for them to be deployed throughout any theatre of operations in this manner. In Gorazde, however, I'd started to realise that they might also have been charged with a mandate of monitoring commanders for their performance and mental state. It was widely acknowledged that soldiers in Gorazde were under extreme duress. Could we handle it?

I couldn't be sure of my theory but there might be an opportunity to ask the SAS directly. What was the worst that could happen? They'd deny it and change the subject. I'd built up a good relationship with the SAS lads, who seemed to appreciate my hosting skills at breakfast time. My portacabin was right next to one belonging to C Company's commander, Martin Leader. I'd persuaded the Pioneers, our own integral assault engineers, to build a roof to link the two portacabins and we put a burner in there. Sometimes I managed to get bread delivered from a local baker and we could toast it – a real luxury with food so scarce. One morning Wez Harris, the SAS Team Commander, had come round with his lads for some toast. We were talking about various things and then suddenly Wez pulled his trousers down and whipped out his suture kit.

'What are you doing?' I asked, slightly worried.

'Practising,' he replied.

And that's what he began to do, pinching his skin together as he put sutures into his own uninjured leg. He wiped away his blood as though it were an irritating inconvenience and showed no sign of pain.

'You can do that on an orange,' I suggested.

'Yeah, it's not the same.' He was blunt. Being a medic, he also knew.

Wez turned to one of his SAS mates, who understood his ways better. 'That's not bad, is it?' he said proudly, admiring his own handiwork. 'Billy, what do you think of that?'

'Second and third ones are shit,' was the response from Billy Walters. 'Let's have a go.'

I thought Wez might even oblige but, since there was no genuine wound, he didn't see why anyone else should practise on his body.

'No, fuck off.'

Wez and Billy loved arguing, even though they were both originally from the Parachute Regiment. Whereas Wez had served in 2 Para, Billy was from 1 Para, therefore they'd once been fierce rivals and sometimes acted as though they still were. It was amusing to listen to their banter and, while the mood was jovial, I asked the question that had been on my mind.

'Wez, is one of your roles to assess the combat effectiveness of the command here?'

'Yes,' he confirmed simply.

'Does that include me?'

'Yes, you're fine... for a Rupert.' All officers were necessary jerks; that was obviously his starting point.

'Fuck off,' I said, trying to make light of it, though he must have sensed some anxiety in me somewhere because he looked me straight in the eye.

'You've had the all-clear.'

'What about Riley?' I thought. Had he received the same thumbs-up? Riley had a lot of fine qualities but he was also outspoken and capable of ruffling a few feathers higher up the chain of command, especially if he felt he was under-resourced, as we were in Gorazde. Sometimes that candour could be a good thing but those above him didn't always see it that way. It seemed that Lieutenant-General Rupert Smith, the commander of UN forces in Sarajevo, wanted to be sure Riley was still a safe pair of hands and wasn't going to embarrass the hierarchy with any unforeseen outbursts if the shit really hit the fan. In fact, Smith clearly wanted to be convinced that all Riley's commanders were made of the right stuff and holding up adequately in the ludicrously termed 'Safe Area' of Gorazde.

So the secret of the Joint Commission Officers' added mission was out in the open. The SAS troop had probably decided that, if they were asked directly by people they'd cleared anyway, they were going to answer honestly. After a short silence, I made it clear that I didn't disagree with what they were doing, because it was obviously fair enough to assess the command in such a pressurised environment. But I also warned Wez I wasn't going to discuss Riley with him.

I had nothing but respect for Colonel Jon. He was, in many ways, the outstanding commander of his generation. If Wez had a report to make, he would send it up his own chain of command based on his direct observations. I didn't want any part of the way he formed that opinion; no way was I going to stab Riley in the back. I didn't feel any need to do that and, to be fair to the SAS, they didn't expect me to criticise my boss either.

That was just as well because I owed Riley. He had given me my command when, technically, I'd had no right to it at the time. I'd been in Northern Ireland as a surveillance officer responsible for the covert-overt interface between 3 Infantry Brigade and RUC Special Branch. That meant I was involved with the covert agencies, Special Branch and also with the overt 'green army'. After two years, I received the call from Jonathon Riley, who knew I'd been a Royal Welch Fusilier for ten years after leaving Sandhurst.

He asked me, 'How do you fancy coming back to become a company commander?'

'I can't command a company, I'm not a major,' I pointed out. I was a captain at the time and not due promotion for a couple of years.

'I'll get you that,' he assured me.

I had no idea how he would do that but I said, 'okay.'

Riley had rung me because one of his company commanders had suddenly said he was leaving the army. Colonel Jon was as good as his word. I was made an acting major, posted back to the Royal Welch – and found out we were off to Gorazde about three months before we went. I did my homework. I read books on the fall of Yugoslavia and Riley filled in his commanders on recent developments to make sure we were abreast of it all. Everything Riley did was an education for us; his intellect and experience were invaluable. The conflict fascinated me anyway, which was probably just as well because pretty soon we'd taste it first-hand. I was given B Company just as it was going on its final exercises. From the point of view of a professional challenge, I was delighted we were going to Bosnia; I wasn't apprehensive. As a professional army officer, I joined the army to practise my trade. Otherwise it's a bit like being an understudy actor while some other smart-arse always hogs the spotlight. Suddenly you get a chance to show what you can do. Of course, you ask yourself the usual questions: how am I going to respond to the pressure? How good am I under the spotlight?

The SAS had just told me I was still fit to fight and doing okay but it felt surreal to be judged on my performance and psychological suitability by an SAS man who was casually threading stitches through his uninjured leg. I sat there surveying the scene and suddenly burst out laughing.

'Well, fuck you,' I concluded with a grin. 'We're all mad here.'

Closer to the truth was that most of us were normal people trying to operate in a complete madhouse. And, if you didn't at least try to see the funny side of Gorazde sometimes, you probably really would go mad. Luckily, soldiers try to see humour in almost everything – not that our bosses back in Britain would have approved of all of it. Tough! It was hard for them to understand the sort of world they'd dumped us in. People back home meant well with what they said and did; but reality in Gorazde didn't often respect good intentions.

One day I got a call from Sarajevo. Some UN pen-pusher was on the line on behalf of the British top brass.

'Is Gorazde hospital on your river bank?'

'Yes it is.'

'Do you go there often?'

I usually went once or twice a week to see the Director of Medicine and check with Sophie, the beautiful Belgian doctor from Medecins Sans Frontieres, to see if everything was all right.

'Fairly often, why?'

'Lady Rose has been on. She wants an update on her incubator.'

'What?'

'Her incubator. She raised enough money for two – one for each side – and she sent one of them to Gorazde.

It was true. A few months earlier, General Sir Mike Rose's wife, Lady (Angela) Rose, had decided she'd do her supportive bit for Bosnia while he commanded UNPROFOR there. She knew she had to be impartial, so she'd raised enough money for two child-incubator units. One went into a Serb hospital in Kopace or Visegrad, and the other one came to Gorazde.

'She wants to know that it's being put to good use,' explained Sarajevo.

I had other priorities. Like trying to help my men avoid being killed in the daily contacts they were having with the Serbs. 'Why doesn't she just ring up the hospital?'

'Major Westley, the phone line's down. Besides, this is Lady Rose we're talking about.'

'I don't care if it's Lady Godiva,' I told him. What was I supposed to do? Drop everything and pander to her?

'No need for that,' said the pen-pusher, who clearly didn't understand the pressures of daily life in Gorazde. 'Just go down and check, will you? Come back and say the incubator is up and running. That's an order. From the top.'

Irritated, I brought forward my next meeting with the Director of Medicine at Gorazde hospital. He was a weasel of a man with a straggly beard, glasses held together with micropore tape and a stained white jacket with pen marks on the breast pocket. I began with the usual routine.

'What do you need?' I asked him.

'We need some more Lignocaine and we need some more morphine.'

'We can do that for you. What else?'

'Bandages.'

'We can get you some more bandages. And you can do something for me.'

'What's that?' He wasn't used to requests being made in the opposite direction and looked taken aback.

'Lady Rose donated an incubator to your hospital. She wants to know how useful it's proving to be. All you've got to do is tell me you're using it.'

'Oh, we're using it,' he assured me, looking more relieved.

'Can I see it?' This was the question he didn't seem to want to hear.

'No.'

'Why not?'

'It's in a sterile area.'

I wasn't buying that. 'Fuck off. This is Gorazde hospital. I'm cleaner than your hospital is. And I've just walked over hills.'

The weasel looked uncomfortable. 'This is a bit difficult.'

I smelled a rat and I was holding all the cards. 'Take me now. Or no drugs. Nothing.'

'I'll just ring ahead,' he said, trying to mask his desperation.

'No, don't ring ahead. Just take me.' I knew something was amiss and I wasn't going to let him off the hook.

The weasel looked as though his world was about to cave in. In Gorazde it usually did and he was in the right place to see the results. So why was this man practically shitting himself about an incubator? Had they broken it? He shrugged and started shambling off ahead of me.

We walked down a few corridors and there, in all its splendour, was Lady Rose's baby incubator. Full to the brim... of tobacco. Never mind the babies: they were using the incubator to dry out – but not de-moisturize – their precious tobacco, so they could roll cigarettes properly for the soldiers on the front line.

You didn't mess with people's tobacco in this part of the world. The biggest celebrity in Gorazde was a huge blond bloke called Cisco, who was supposed to be a revered folk singer but was, in fact, far more revered for his skills as a tobacco smuggler. The only thing the Muslim and Serb soldiers had in common, apart from their language, was their mutual love of tobacco. Sworn enemies did black-market deals for the stuff and there had recently been a multiple shooting, not connected to the war but because a black-market tobacco deal had gone wrong. Was I going to grab the incubator, empty out the precious contents and walk off in a rage? Not a chance. It would have brought the wrath of the Muslims down upon us at precisely the wrong time.

## THE INCUBATOR

I suspected we might have to ask those Muslim soldiers to help us very soon. If a bigger battle broke out between us the Serbs, our lives might just depend on how promptly the BiH responded. We wanted their support more than ever. Admittedly, cigarettes were not going to enhance their ability to run anywhere very quickly to come to our aid. But to mess with their incubator now was going to cause a world of bad feeling, just when I needed them onside. Lady Rose had given the Muslims an incubator. How they used it was up to them. I was not about to cause a diplomatic incident over this.

What did I do about my little discovery? I called the pen-pusher in the Sarajevo office and told him I had a message to pass on to Lady Rose back in Britain. 'Yes, ma'am, I have now seen the incubator for myself and it's in full use every single day. In fact, it's probably one of the more useful bits of kit in the hospital.'

She never was told the full truth. She'll know the truth now though!

Nothing in my education or training had taught me how to tell a Lady that her incubator was being used for tobacco instead of babies. Two years of studying English at Goldsmiths in London, funded by the army, had failed to furnish me with the right words. Sandhurst hadn't covered this eventuality in any of their manuals either. As with so much of what we experienced in Gorazde, I was unprepared for what I saw but did my best to make the right call under trying circumstances.

You couldn't really train for the assault on the senses some of my lads in B Company suffered either, as the ground softened in the early summer sun and gave up its dead. I had to plan and then supervise body exchanges – a necro-truce in a wider war. Those involved – those still alive, I mean – probably never forgot it.

At separate meetings with both sides, they had expressed the wish to get the bodies of their dead back across the confrontation line, to repatriate them. There were shenanigans from the start because the Serbs maintained that one Serb was worth six Muslims. If they were going to return 20 bodies to the Muslims, the Serbs wanted 120 of their own bodies back from Muslim-held ground. We stopped those games. There was a lot of shuttle diplomacy between the two and eventually we hit on the most equal and logical plan, whereby we would exchange twenty Serb bodies for twenty Muslim bodies on a given date at a given time.

Then another problem emerged. Both sides wanted my soldiers to dig the bodies up. I refused and insisted that was their responsibility; after all, they'd killed them. Both sides were warned to treat the bodies with respect too. Reluctantly they agreed, though the packaging of the bodies was done to different standards. The Serbs put the Muslims in body bags; the Muslims put the Serbs in coffins. This caused consternation among the Muslims, who said, 'We returned your soldiers to you respectfully in coffins; you just chucked ours in body bags. You showed ours no respect.' With tempers set to flare, we were always relieved when the body exchanges passed off peacefully, without fresh bodies being created for later exchange. That's where our job as go-betweens and delivery boys was useful, I suppose. And the necro-truce continued for a good few weeks.

Our UN trucks used to go to the pick-up point in a convoy. The Serbs or Muslims would have the exhumed bodies waiting, they would load them onto our trucks and we would take them simultaneously back across the confrontation line. That way there was no chance of either side reneging on the deal once they'd got theirs back. The bodies were off-loaded by each side but the transportation and its aftermath represented a horrible task for the lads.

Some of these bodies had been buried in the ground for years; the stench was indescribable for the poor drivers, who were given gas masks to wear and breathed through respirators. It didn't stop the smell. The drivers' cabins came back full of vomit from where the drivers had been forced to empty their respirators, because those had been full of vomit first. You needed a number of our guys to perform that transportation job, so some of my men didn't even get to travel in the cabin; they had to travel in the back with the cadavers.

The trucks were hosed down afterwards but they stank for days and even weeks of decomposing bodies, putrefying flesh and death. You would have thought there might come a point when a body stopped smelling, after a certain amount of time, but there wasn't any evidence of that. It was hideous. I only smelled the unloaded vehicles when they came back in. We did two or three body exchanges like that. It was one of those things you were expected to do, part of your role as a peacekeeper, albeit with a miniscule amount of extra pay for 'work of an unpleasant nature'. We debriefed our men afterwards. They said it was not a task they ever wanted to do again, though none of them ever said they'd refuse to do it. They saw the importance of this necro-truce because the exchanges were so important to both sides. I was proud of my men.

Beyond a debriefing at the end of each exchange, I didn't

think any of the lads needed counselling. Although the smell was atrocious, they didn't actually see the rotting bodies. Besides, even if any of them had been badly disturbed by the experience, there just wasn't time for counselling, as far as I could see. Shocking experiences in Gorazde came so thick and fast that you'd be trying to process one traumatic event internally when another landed at your door before you'd dealt properly with the first one. Best if we just got on with it for now and tried to make sense of things later, that was my attitude. But attitudes were changing and rightly so.

The Army was starting to come to terms with the fact that people suffered from stress in war zones, otherwise the SAS wouldn't have been tasked to assess how we were handling that stress. Not that those SAS blokes were in Gorazde to give anyone a cuddle if they burst into tears. Not really their scene. But in May we received a visit from a psychiatric nurse; a guy called Pete Roberts. He was an Army Medical Corps captain and he came in to talk to us about Post-Traumatic Stress Disorder and how to recognise it.

'I'd like to do a presentation to your whole company on this,' he told me.

I said, 'No, I'm not having that. If you tell my men what the symptoms are, when it gets tough, people will start emulating them. I don't want my blokes knowing what the signs of PTSD are. Speak to the commanders, so they can make the judgement on the men.'

Pete reluctantly accepted this and started his thirty-minute presentation. After a few minutes I'd heard enough. I said, 'Right, stop. You've convinced me. You were right and I was wrong. Sergeant-Major, get the whole company in here.'

## THE INCUBATOR

We persuaded Pete to start again and tell the entire company how to recognise PTSD in their mates. He explained that this was absolutely normal when you've seen something traumatic, and in Gorazde there was a very good chance we'd see or experience things that traumatised us, as we knew all too well. Whether you were expecting these events or not, they could still turn out to be even worse than you thought, he pointed out.

'These things will have an impact on you,' he warned. 'Maybe not now. Maybe not tomorrow. Maybe not for years. But it will show in the end.'

The brain absorbs stuff and tries to make sense of it. If it can't do that, you can have either a psychometric or a physical reaction. Sometimes the brain just locks bad stuff away so you don't have to deal with it for the time being. The danger is this: at some stage the brain will replay this traumatic experience to you without permission and then you will suddenly have to deal with it when you don't want to. You've put it all away in a box, fair enough; but, if you don't open that box some time voluntarily, you're going to be in big trouble later.

I realised I was a real box man – and that wasn't going to change easily, especially when I was there partly to be strong for the men. In fact, I felt happy that my brain was able to lock stuff away in a box; we sort of did it together on purpose, my brain and me. There was a necessary consciousness to the process in my case and I told Pete as much after the talk. He understood people like me too but he warned that the rules were no different for officers. Whether you wanted to put the trauma in a box or not at first, you still needed to replay it sooner rather than later and talk about it. And I began to realise that the brain is a tricky organ; you've got to treat it right. It's not like getting a dead leg or an uncomplicated bullet wound.

Pete's message to us all was simple: 'You've got to talk about it. That's your release-valve. The risk-management on trauma is really important. It's not a sign of weakness to say you've got a problem with something.'

It was easy for him to say that, not least because he was right, but putting it into practice wouldn't always be that straightforward. The Army was a pretty patriarchal society and the infantry was founded on machismo. You didn't go sick for anything unless you were practically at death's door, because it wasn't regarded as acceptable. To take time out for emotional issues was a complete no-no. But Pete Roberts already had us thinking and I was glad he'd given us the talk. As it turned out, we were going to be seeing a bit more of him that anyone had foreseen. He'd only come in for two days but the Serbs soon locked down all the routes in and out of the enclave. He couldn't get out. I think he ended up staying for about three months – which was great for us because, if anyone developed problems, we had him on hand – an expert to send our blokes to!

There was always going to be an emotional, perhaps even a psychological, price to pay when you had so much daily interaction with civilians who were caught up in a war and suffering so terribly. We didn't pay nearly so heavy a price as some of the poor children in the enclave. But, when you send peacekeepers to keep peace where there is no peace to keep, when you don't equip them properly and when you don't know how to get them out, they will start to feel it. It's a Raymond Blanc recipe for fucking hell; Dante but real.

## THE INCUBATOR

Having acknowledged all that, were we cracking up in Gorazde? No we weren't. While we were there, we could cope, largely because we had to in order to survive. The SAS and their masters needn't have worried. When they put all the commanders in BRITBAT 2 under the microscope in Gorazde, everyone received the SAS seal of approval – including Riley.

It was just as well we were up to the task. We were about to find ourselves in a fight for our lives – and for the lives of the tormented citizens of Gorazde.

# CHAPTER THREE

# THE BATTLE BEGINS

The tensions hadn't just been simmering for two months; they had already boiled over on several occasions. As far back as March, the month we first took over, some of A Company might have lost their lives. Lieutenant Hugh Nightingale, a likeable twenty-two-year-old from Sheffield, led his men to a place called Podcovacev Dol, not far outside Gorazde. They were trying to extend our influence outside the 3-kilometre exclusion zone, just as B Company was doing. We were all constantly looking to gather military information on Serb strength in various positions, as well as assess their immediate intentions, and Nightingale gave orders to occupy a disused and partly derelict chalet, 400 metres from a Serb position he could see. But the Serbs suddenly opened fire from numerous positions, seen and unseen, and did so with such intensity that before long the house started to disintegrate. Somehow, Hugh and his men kept their cool and used

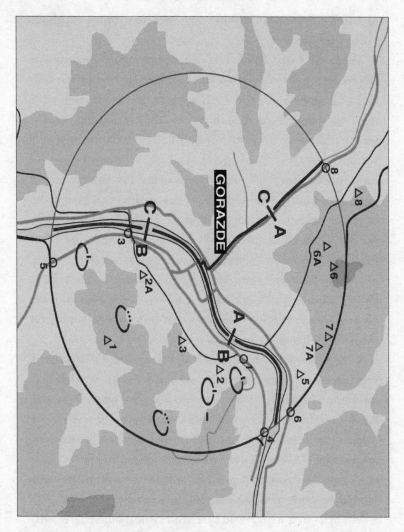

The Gorazde Force area of operations, showing the boundaries between A, B and C Companies. The triangles are our observation posts (OPs), the small circles our checkpoints. The elliptical 'goose eggs' represent Bosnian Serb Army strongpoints, where incursion inside the 3-kilometre exclusion zone had occurred (three dots = 50 men, one line = 120 men).

nightfall to manoeuvre their way back to Gorazde without serious casualties.

Then, in early May, Pete Humphries was escorting a UNHCR convoy to nearby Illovaca. Archie, one of the SAS men, had gone along for the ride, to familiarise himself with the kind of opposition the convoys usually came up against. He wasn't disappointed. Just after they had picked up a pregnant woman, who was in the latter stages of labour, the convoy came under heavy fire. Pete manoeuvred his Saxons into a protective position between the softer civilian trucks and the origin of the Serb barrage, so that the UNHCR people didn't get hit. Then Humphries coolly returned fire and controlled the battle, helped in no small measure by the fact that Archie, in typical SAS style, had jumped straight out of his vehicle and decided to attack the Serbs head on. He rained so much firepower onto the Serb positions that he virtually hammered them single-handedly.

With Archie safely back on board, Pete got the battle-scarred vehicles out of there, almost before the Serbs knew what had hit them. They headed for Gorazde hospital, where Pete and Archie began delivering the baby outside on a stretcher. I believe the little 'sprog' popped out before the doctors even reached them. What a way to be introduced to the world – practically dodging bullets while still in the womb! But this kind of welcome was not unusual in Gorazde.

'All in a day's work,' said Pete with typical understatement, after fighting a battle and bringing a new, innocent life into the relentless hell of Gorazde. I suspect he had been less comfortable delivering the baby than coping with the Serb ambush. But Humphries and the rest of B Company were going to be tested far more severely than that before the month was out.

General Rupert Smith, Commander of the UN forces in Sarajevo, had told General Ratko Mladic to remove all Serb heavy weapons from the exclusion zones around the so-called 'Safe Areas', the enclaves holding so much of the Muslim civilian population in eastern Bosnia. Either Mladic had deliberately ignored Smith or he had outright refused to comply; at any rate, the result was the same. On 25 May, NATO aircraft had attacked the Bosnian Serb military camp in their administrative capital at Pale, dropping bombs on an ammunition and logistics installation. We heard the rumble of the bombs and we could see the plumes of smoke rising, even from our distant vantage point. Our observation posts were on such high ground that you could see that far and anticipate the consequences.

We took in that scene, gulped and thought, 'These may be NATO bombs, not UN, but that's going to attract a response, isn't it?'

Riley read the situation the same way and rightly came to the decision that anyone who didn't need to be there – anyone who wasn't a fighting man or essential in some other way to the ground-holding task – should be taken up to a mountain retreat, out of harm's way. Brigadier Bahto, the local BiH commander, agreed to the relocation. Short, stocky and naturally aggressive, Bahto believed Riley when Colonel Jon told him he was moving people up the mountain to reduce the burden on the town and the risk of unnecessary casualties. What Bahto didn't realise was this: we were moving our non-essential people up to that particular wooded location not just because it was near the running water of a stream, but also because it was close to a plateau offering a potential helicopter landing site, from where they could be extracted if necessary. If things went badly wrong for the rest of us, and we all had to be flown out quickly, we would try to leg it up there and join them while the SAS called in enough aircraft to extract us.

Overnight, on 26 May, the SAS and our reconnaissance platoon prepared the non-essential group for the trek up into the hills, well out of the Serbian line of fire. One of the men being taken out of harm's way was our Padre, Tim Tucker. Gorazde had been his first assignment; they had sent a gentle college boy into the heart of darkness with no experience. Nice of them! Tucker looked about thirteen years of age and he was totally out of his depth, unprepared for practical military experience – the opposite of what we needed now. The SAS were told to make sure Padre Tucker completed the climb, one way or another. But the SAS were destined to get more than they had bargained for.

Before they left, I told their Team Commander, Wez Harris, 'Good luck with the vertical tab, mate. Rather you than me.' That was going to be a fearsome march and we both knew it. At least they were going to carry the bare minimum, water rations and ammunition only, though, in the Padre's case, a small Bible would have been acceptable.

Twenty hours later I was woken up by the scary sight of Wez staring down at me. He'd been up the mountain and back down again, and he was dripping with sweat.

'Your fucking Padre!' he said.

'What?'

'The Padre. He filled his bergen with books. The blokes

were tabbing it up the hill and all these books were soon "accidentally dropping out" of the Padre's bergen. This continued all the fucking way up. Even a Bible "fell out". And guess who had to pick all these books up, one by fucking one, and put them all in his own fucking bergen?'

I looked at Harris, trying not to smile, already knowing the answer.

'I felt like throttling him,' Wez added. 'I'd already told him exactly what he could and could not take. And a fucking library wasn't on the list of things he could take!'

Before I could offer any kind of apology, Wez was off again, presumably back up the mountain with food supplies, or off somewhere else to report the latest developments up his chain of command.

It would have been good to have the members of that SAS troop scattered among my men in our observation posts overlooking Gorazde, up on a particularly imposing and vital mountain called Mala Biserna. With tensions between us and the Serbs so high, those OPs were starting to look vulnerable. Strange as it may sound, though, fighting alongside my men wasn't the job of the SAS. Unless ordered to call in air, they were in Gorazde to assess the strategic situation, not get caught up in battles. So it was down to the men of B Company of the Royal Welch Fusiliers to try to hold the key East Bank positions on our own. And, on 28 May, I realised they were probably going to have to do just that.

It was just past midday and I'd organised what should have been a routine meeting with Captain Kepic. He couldn't come into the town because he was a Serb and the Muslims would have grabbed him, so I met him on the edge of the 3-kilometre exclusion zone at Checkpoint 4. Due to the deteriorating situation, I'd decided to leave Selma back in the town and use Kepic's interpreter. It wasn't ideal because his English wasn't as good as Selma's had become. But this was the safest thing for Selma and a very good decision as it turned out, because it was going to be no ordinary day, not even by the violent standards of Gorazde. Besides, Kepic's body language told me more than his words could. He was furtive; something wasn't right. He was sweating like a Royal Marine in a spelling test; he was acting like a man under pressure. You didn't need an interpreter – not even your favourite one – to understand which way the wind was blowing.

Kepic knew there was going to be bloodshed but he wanted to avoid that blood being British and UN if at all possible. It was almost as though he'd had a change of heart and suddenly felt sorry for us, though it was far more likely that he was aware of the potential backlash if the Bosnian Serbs had to kill us. At any rate, Kepic didn't want us to die needlessly; we weren't the real targets. His masters wanted to kill Muslims – civilians or soldiers, it didn't matter. The massacre could begin once the Serbs had taken our Observation Posts. Then they'd control the high ground above Gorazde, the approaches to the town, everything. Those they wished to obliterate would be trapped and the slaughter could start in earnest. So would we mind just stepping aside? It really wasn't our fight, after all. We were just peacekeepers and, if the Muslim army couldn't keep the Serbs at bay on their own, as far as Kepic was concerned, the Serbs had every right to do whatever they liked to Muslim civilians.

I'd read that, in Balkan-style conflicts, the majority of

casualties weren't sustained during the fighting between the two armies. The worst carnage occurred after one side lost its nerve and withdrew. The loser couldn't always take the civil population with it. So innocent people were left there, defenceless, and that was how the biggest atrocities happened. Rape, both female and male, was used as a psychological weapon, along with the mutilation of bodies. We already knew from our experiences around Gorazde that the Serbs wouldn't hesitate to hurt civilians. If we didn't provide a buffer zone and hold the vital ground on Mala Biserna – if we didn't stand firm against attack and help the town's defenders to hold their nerve – Gorazde might fall quite quickly. Then the killing would really begin – how many we didn't know.

The Serbs clearly thought they could talk us off the mountain, because they'd sent their liaison officer to do precisely that. He seemed to think it would be a straightforward task too. Kepic honestly believed he was reassuring me when he said, 'If we have to take your Observation Posts, you'll be fine, don't worry, you can come and live in my house in Rudo.'

But I wasn't based up in the OPs; I was based down in the camp in the centre of the town. He knew I didn't live in any of the Ops; he knew I simply visited them every day to see my guys out on the tripwire. So the inference I took from his words was this: if they take my OPs, they're going to take the town as well. He didn't say it but, then again, he didn't have to. If the OPs went, there was nothing to stop them rolling over the town. If they weren't going to do precisely that and take our camp in the process, why invite me to stay with him in his house in Rudo, over the border in Serbia?

What a shock Kepic was going to get. The Bosnian Serb

Army might have bigger and better weapons than us but we weren't going to go quietly. Already he could see how quickly this British UN officer was becoming agitated and that clearly hadn't been his intention at all, so he tried to reassure me yet again. 'Don't worry, if we have to come and take your Observation Posts, you and all your men will be well looked after, I give you my word.'

I fixed him with a stare and said, 'Don't come near my Observation Posts.'

The air was full of tension. I wanted to say more. I wanted to tell him exactly what I was thinking: 'Take our OPs? That would be a really unwise thing to try to do. You even think about taking Gorazde and you're going to get spanked. If you try to take my OPs to get to Gorazde, we'll resist you and hit you with everything we've got.' But there was no need; he already had the message. I'd only been in the meeting twenty minutes and they normally went on for about forty. I'd known Kepic for a number of months and it was fair to say we'd never been close but this was a new low point; the meeting really hadn't gone well, even by our fractured standards, and it was time to leave. There was nothing to be gained by staying a second longer. I'd made my point.

In truth, diplomatic relations had been deteriorating, as evidenced by all the skirmishes we'd been having. More and more meetings at a higher level had been postponed or cancelled by the Serbs, a process of separation, a withdrawal of consent. The Cessation of Hostilities Agreement, brokered by the former American President, Jimmy Carter, had run its course in April. Attacks on us had grown in frequency and intensity. We had also watched the locals in the town start to make preparations for something even worse than they were enduring already. With the increased shelling of the town, they had started to live in their basements. Windows in the top of those basements, designed to let in at least a sliver of light, were boarded up. We saw people carrying tins of food downstairs. It was quite clear they knew something worse was coming and the threat wasn't going to go away any time soon. Quite how their new subterranean existence would save them if the town was taken, however, remained very much open to question. With our OPs in Serb hands, they'd be free to shell the town to near-oblivion from close range and then follow up in person to deliver murder and mayhem street by street. Hiding in your basement wasn't going to save you from what the Bosnian Serb Army had in mind for you. They had brought in just the men for the sadistic task in hand too.

The Serbs rotated their troops every ten or twelve days. The sort of people we'd seen before were often scruffy, middle-aged soldiers who looked out of shape and past their prime. Then, on 24 May and 25 May, we had started to see different guys bolstering their various positions. Some of them were big, hairy, scary blokes who were apparently descended from a group of Partisans who had opposed the Allies during the Second World War. They looked much more combat-hardened than the previous troops. An even more sinister-looking group had arrived too, wearing balaclavas. Young, fit and hardened, they had a cold confidence about them. It was quite a combination, these malevolent groups with their contrasting appearances. And it wasn't just the men who had changed. Their load-carrying equipment was much more professional; everything about the new Serb soldiers looked more professional. They were ready for business and it wasn't hard to guess what their specific business was. I called them 'The Ethnic Cleansing Brigade'.

How would my younger lads in the OPs react to an attack from a hard-core enemy like this? I knew from my first time under fire that there was no way of telling how you'd perform until it happened. At least my men had a fair idea of what was coming; it hadn't been like that for me. Aged twenty, I'd gone to see my father for a two-week break in Oman, to try to play my part in mending what was a fractured relationship. He was working hard and couldn't spend very much time with me but he did organise flights in Jaguar and Hunter aircraft, which was a fantastic surprise. He also arranged for me to hang out with the Sultan's Special Forces and train with them. As it turned out, I did a bit more than train. I went on border patrols near the Yemen with them. We had a couple of contacts with smugglers and other 'Adoo' – Omani Arabic for enemy. The first time I came under fire was near a border town called Habrut. The bullets were flying all around us. The ones that came close made that distinctive sound like a hornet's buzz. Then you heard a thump nearby. Bullets landing a bit further away made a crack. I've heard people say a bullet has flown so close to them that they could feel the air splitting. I'm not saying that's wrong because a bullet does take air with it but you have to be bloody close for that. A few metres were quite close enough for me.

For a moment, under fire in Oman I'd thought, 'What's happening?' You could say I froze for a second. A big burly ex-SAS man had to punch me to get me going. He was a contract officer; a man who'd left the British Army's Special Forces and been contracted by the Sultan. That thump did the trick because I was soon firing at the enemy and putting bullets in the right area too, though the exchanges were so long-range that it was hard to tell if I'd killed anyone. They'd been trying to kill me, so I didn't have a problem with the thought that I might have done the same to some of them. The main thing for me was that I came out of it in one piece and was able to draw my own conclusions. 'Could have done better, could have done worse,' I decided, 'but I want to be tested like that again. I'm never going back to Goldsmiths.'

Instead of returning to college life in the English capital after a fortnight as planned, I stayed in Oman for four months. Of course, I didn't tell my mother about the contacts I'd had with the 'Adoo' when I phoned home. If she'd had so much as a suspicion that I'd been involved in genuine fire-fights in the desert, she'd have had kittens! But when I did get back to the UK I said goodbye to the laid-back student lifestyle once and for all. Sandhurst was calling and when I began there, they even treated me with a bit of respect, because they'd heard I'd seen some action.

So that's what the first time had been like for me. I hoped the younger men in my OPs above Gorazde would do even better than I did in Oman because, if I wasn't mistaken, the time was fast approaching when they'd have to face the 'Ethnic Cleansing Brigade'. And, by the look of those death squads, there wouldn't be time for even a moment's hesitation when the fighting started. Was this really going to happen, or was I reading too much into the signs? No, the Serbs were getting ready to overrun us, I was sure of it. I'd seen it in Kepic's piggy little eyes and in the sweat oozing from his fatty skin.

By 1.15pm, not long after I'd left the meeting with Kepic, I'd already ordered my OPs to reinforce as best they could and warned them what I thought was coming. I was still walking back towards my vehicle on foot with my escort when I received a message on my company radio. It was from Colour Sergeant Pete Humphries up in OP1.

'There's some unusual activity going on up here,' he said. 'There are combat indicators.'

OP1 was the most exposed of our positions, to the front of the ridge due to the re-entrants. It was a key vantage point because you could see all the low-level approaches from three different directions. If OP1 hadn't been situated so far out on a limb, we'd have had no early warning of approaching Serbs. All the other OPs were set back slightly, along a rough line. From his forward vantage point, Humphries must have been able to see the Serb positions slightly further round the mountain, about five or six hundred metres away from him. His men must have been peering over their sandbags up there as well, to see what was going on.

The Serbs weren't being subtle. They were smashing windows in the little huts around which they'd set up their own positions and they were bringing up medical supplies and stretcher-bearer parties. No point in doing that unless you're about to launch an offensive operation.

'Stand to!' I ordered.

My men were alert and ready to follow what we'd rehearsed. They were prepared to fight if necessary but their kit was also ready to go, in case they had to move.

With the situation so tense, there was no time to waste. I started to run back towards my vehicle at Checkpoint 1, still about eight hundred metres away. My job was going to be to keep an eye on the big picture for B Company. As soon as I reached my vehicle, I could hear the chatter on the battalion radio net. I actually had two nets: the company radio, which went forward to my platoons and was my means of telling them what to do, and the battalion radio, which also had the other companies, A and C, on it. On the latter I heard reports from Phil Jones and A Company, telling us that a Ukrainian OP and checkpoint, along with a Ukrainian vehicle, had all been surrounded. The British on that side of the river were soon in a similar predicament and trying to negotiate. But, within seconds, it became clear to me that the Serbs were starting to take British hostages as well – Hugh Nightingale among them – at some of the OPs on the West Bank. There was nothing I could do for Phil Jones. Like me, he'd been in many contacts; he was a big boy and he could look after his own blokes. I had to worry about mine.

It was time to turn my attention to the rest of those from B Company, who were higher up on the East Bank and most vulnerable in their groups of eight at OP2, OP3 and Checkpoint 3. Each of them started to report in.

'We can see movement.'

I gave the call sign to speak to all of them at once: 'Charlie Charlie 1... Stand to... Stand by.'

They already knew the rules of engagement: they could fire warning shots if they felt threatened and they could return fire directly if fired upon. No doubt they'd already guessed they'd soon be pulling the trigger.

OP3 was the most important Observation Post. Whoever held it had strategic control of the high ground overlooking the town. OP3 was commanded by Captain Tom Murphy. He was twenty eight years old, fair-haired and wiry, with piercing blue eyes. Tom was tough, bright and brave – a real soldier's officer. The men could relate to him because he'd done a couple of years as a private himself, then gone to Sandhurst and earned a commission. He wasn't a Royal Welch Fusilier – he was a Royal Fusilier, which isn't the same thing. But he was attached to my company and the blokes had welcomed him, not least because he always had a witty answer for the wise-cracking Welshmen. Tom was a great guy. Some officers are more comfortable in the company of officers. Tom was just comfortable with everyone. He earned further respect because he was one of the fittest in the company and planned to go on SAS selection when he got back... if we got back. Tom was in OP3 by chance on 28 May, as part of a rotation, and we'd need all his physical and mental toughness now.

With him was Corporal Dave Vaatstra. Short and stocky, Dave had joined B Company as another of our attached people, coming to us from the Milan (anti-tank) Platoon, along with Pete Humphries. Vaatstra would have been more senior had he not demonstrated a propensity for fighting civilians in the pubs and clubs of garrison towns as a younger man. He'd mellowed a little since then and, when he wasn't taking photographs around the camp in Gorazde, he spent his down time soaking up the early-summer rays. He'd never lost his natural aggression, though, and recently Dave had rigged up the tripod for the machine guns, as if sensing what might be just around the corner. If he still liked the idea of a fight deep down, perhaps it was just as well, because he was going to get one. Not that the odds would be in his favour.

# THE BATTLE BEGINS

To say we were outnumbered would be an understatement. We had a total of about forty men in the checkpoints and OPs; then there was my group, which was my immediate Tactical Headquarters, plus the men we had in the Quick Reaction Force. So, in total, there were still only about fifty-five of us on the East bank as the battle loomed. We'd be up against five or six hundred Serbs on our bank if they all came for us – roughly a battalion. There were always about a hundred and twenty Serbs in one hamlet, a hundred more in another position, a further hundred and twenty in another. Then there were two more groups of fifty in other places and plenty more dotted around in smaller groups of twenty or so. We had to hope they wouldn't band together in a perfectly co-ordinated attack, otherwise we might be overwhelmed quite quickly. And, if the Serbs decided they needed further support, they could call on the rest of their forces back on the extremities of the 3-kilometre exclusion zone: those ran into many more hundreds, perhaps even thousands. We didn't want to think about that. It was time to hold our nerve and make a stand.

We waited for the fighting to begin on our bank. Your heart is thumping in the silence but, even with the adrenalin pumping, you have to stay calm. Fortunately, the Serbs didn't keep us waiting for long. As soon as Pete Humphries felt compelled to fire a couple of warning shots over the heads of some Serbs who were breaking the rules by advancing on OP1, all hell broke loose and it sounded as though the skies were splitting above us. The Serbs unleashed Russian-made 12.7mm DShK heavy machine guns, PKK light machine guns and Kalashnikovs. These combined to create a fearsome horizontal rain and they hadn't even begun to use their 155mm artillery and 82mm mortars yet. Should they really want to turn up the pain, they also had anti-aircraft guns – one called a Praga, another called a CIZ. If they depressed those far enough into the ground-roll, their 30–35mm explosive rounds would be absolutely devastating. It was a terrifying prospect.

What could we reply with in B Company? We probably had about eight of the battalion's twenty-five general purpose machine guns (GPMGs), which fired 7.62mm rounds. We all had SA80 rifles, which was at least something. I also had a pistol and a number of grenades, which we'd previously taken from the Serbs. Although a grenade is not a peacekeeping weapon, we had them just in case. What we didn't possess in our limited arsenal were any mortars or Milan (anti-tank) weapons, as we hadn't been allowed to bring in any heavy weapons. We'd smuggled in a couple of 50-cal (0.50 inch) machine guns but they were back in town for the last-ditch defence of the camp. And, although the Battalion had snipers scattered around the various companies with some Barratt 50-cal sniper rifles, they weren't with us on the East Bank that day. Besides, as UN soldiers, the sniper boys weren't expected to kill people; they were supposed to use their Barratts for disrupting mines and unexploded ordnance. All in all, it wasn't an encouraging picture; we were going to be outgunned just as heavily as we were outnumbered. No matter, we started to use what we could.

Tom Murphy uttered the words, 'Charlie Charlie 1, this is OP3: contact, wait out!'

Vaatstra was the man who began B Company's return of fire with his machine gun. In that moment, Kepic and the Serbs knew I hadn't been bluffing an hour or two earlier. I'd told Kepic not to come near our OPs; his bosses had ignored me and now they knew the consequences. But, with their overwhelming superiority, the Serbs could only have seen our efforts as some kind of token resistance. We were going to need some help as quickly as possible if we were to keep them at bay.

I was already on the battalion net. 'Tell 801 Brigade to get up here.'

The Muslims' 801 Brigade had specific responsibility for the East Bank. So they were aligned with my mission to stop the Serbs from taking total strategic control of the mountain. It had been agreed with my friend Salko Osmanspahic that the BiH would swing into action as quickly as possible should we need them. But, even as the sound of the fire-fight bounced down from the hills and clattered around the town like an alarm bell, there was still official protocol to be observed. That's why 801 Brigade and the Royal Welch Fusiliers both had liaison officers in BiH headquarters, and I had a liaison officer with 801 Brigade. It seemed that fresh representations might still have to be made to the most powerful people before we saw some action from the Muslims. Was this really what it was going to take to persuade them to help save their own town?

I was still on the battalion and company nets, pleased to be feeling focused and relatively calm, yet desperately waiting to hear something encouraging from static headquarters in the town. In the meantime, I repeated my urgent request.

'Get the Muslim forces up here now. We need 801 Brigade up here. The Serbs are attacking. Tell them to get up here.'

Somewhere in a soulless building in Gorazde, our liaison

officers would be showing their passes and undergoing the routine searches, all the time trying to get through to the right people to tell them, 'The Serbs are attacking.' Surely the Muslims knew already? Couldn't they hear the gunfire yet? But we wanted to tell them directly, 'Get up here now,' to avoid any breakdown in communication, which was always possible in a crisis.

It was time for me to leave Checkpoint 1. I climbed into my vehicle and, along with the Quick Reaction Force, we drove along the bank of the River Drina and turned left up into Cemetery Valley. The focal point, as bleak and beautiful as ever, seemed fitting. There was every chance fresh bodies would be made ready for that cemetery before the day was out.

Above the river, a few hundred metres from the bottom of the valley, I saw Riley locked in conversation with Rhiad Rasic, the Mayor of Gorazde. They seemed to be trying to assess the situation and it was clearly going to be a conversation worth hearing. So I jumped out of my vehicle and sent Glyn Llewellyn, who was a confident platoon commander of mine, further up the slope with the Saxons. These armoured personnel carriers had machine guns mounted on their turrets, which meant that Glyn could provide fire support for our boys higher up the mountain.

Riley tried to bring me up to speed. 'Are you aware of what's happening on the West Bank?'

'I've heard on the radio they're taking hostages and there's some fighting.'

'That's correct,' confirmed Riley. Was he going to try to send me across the river?

'My place now is up there with B Company,' I insisted quickly, not wanting to be diverted anywhere else.

Riley agreed. 'Yes, I'll give you whatever I can. I'm going to get back on to Sarajevo and try to get some air up here.'

Surely now they'd finally give us close air support and hit these bastards hard around Gorazde, just as they should have done months ago? We'd been in plenty of contacts but this was fast turning into a significant tactical battle. If the UN really cared about its own soldiers and cared about the fate of Gorazde, this was the time to show it.

Riley left me with one parting comment. 'I don't want you taken.'

What do you say to that? I had no intention of being taken and the time for talking was over.

I started running up Cemetery Valley to join my vehicle and Glyn Llewellyn. By now I was getting contact reports from all the OPs and I warned them on the company net, 'The Muslims will be coming up on the pre-agreed routes to the rear. Be on the lookout for them.'

The last thing I wanted was for my boys to mistake the Muslims for Serbs and shoot them as they were coming up to help. It's often hard to tell one army from another and, although the latest Serbs looked more distinctive than the last bunch, there was no telling what might happen in the heat of battle. We'd agreed with the Muslims that, if the Serbs were attacking from their usual positions on the slopes, BiH would scale the reverse side of the mountain to reach our ridge, thus avoiding enemy fire as much as possible. Therefore, my OPs would each need somebody watching to the rear, ready to receive 801 Brigade. Once they arrived, it would be a case of pointing and using sign language, whatever it took to communicate with them, because there would be no interpreters up there.

One problem with all this planning remained glaringly obvious and deeply worrying: there was still no sign of the Muslims. And I didn't know how long the OPs could survive the onslaught above us. Lose OP3 and we couldn't protect the town and stop a massacre, if that's what the Serbs had in mind.

How could we best help Murphy, Vaatstra and the others to stay in the fight above us? Should I try to get my team up onto the high ground behind OP3? By the time I did that, it might be too late and then I'd have wasted whatever I could bring to this delicate balance. Carrying fifty or sixty pounds of ammunition each, it would take me and my team at least fifteen minutes of hard running to get up to that high ground. Meanwhile, the Serbs might rush OP3 in those same fifteen minutes and take it. I had to make some kind of impact now, so I decided it was better for me to provide covering fire to delay the Serbs and hope the Muslims could still scramble up quickly enough to make a difference. It was a calculated gamble with no 801 Brigade in sight, but surely they had to be coming?

'Where the hell are you, Salko?'

At that point, the Serbs increased their firepower. The crump of mortar and the scream of artillery filled the air as shells poured down all over the East Bank. Added to the substantial smaller arms fire, it sounded as though hundreds more men were now fighting us. The Serbs were lobbing shells towards our position and onto the edge of the town beyond us. Most worryingly of all, the mortar rounds were starting to land closer and closer to the Observation Posts above us. The blokes in OP3 were already up against it and we had to help them more from where we were in Cemetery Valley. We were trying to provide covering fire and we started to have some success. From inside his Saxon, our machine-gunner was firing upwards onto the ridge and, so far, he'd been able to traverse effectively from one target to another. We could see Serbs trying to move past OP2 and get further along the ridge-line towards OP3. But there were more Serbs appearing from the other direction too, closing in from the opposite end of the ridge in a pincer movement. Everything we could do to direct fire onto the Serbs and stop their movement would be vital now because it might buy OP3 a little more time. Hold up the advance on both sides, hit one group of Serbs, traverse, hit the other advancing group and then traverse back again. We were delaying the Serbs nicely. Then, at about 14:30 hours, we encountered a problem with the Saxon.

We shouldn't have been surprised, because the Saxon APC was little more than one big design fault at the best of times. What the army had done in their wisdom was to take a troop carrier used in Northern Ireland and bolt a turret on the top of it, with a machine gun mounted on that. Apart from the fact that the turret made the entire vehicle incredibly unstable, there were other design issues, such as the 'bins' – the racks or rails – they'd positioned around the turret. We'd thrown our bergens in there as we were supposed to but, on this day of all days, the straps from one soldier's bergen had become trapped in the turret ring, which usually allowed the thing to rotate. Suddenly, the machine-gunner couldn't do his job properly – he couldn't traverse from one target to another and back – and, as soon as the Serbs realised that, they'd become much bolder again. We had to free up the turret ring before they realised.

Glyn Llewellyn climbed up onto the roof to try to fix the problem. I was standing next to the vehicles, doing my best to direct the battle, while Glyn was perched on the roof of his vehicle, frantically trying to rip the bergen away. He seemed to be blissfully unaware that rounds were pinging off the vehicle, inches away from his wiry frame. He was so focused because he knew that, if he didn't get this machine gun back into action, we were fucked. But I could see he was about to get himself killed and that wasn't any good either.

I shouted, 'Get off the fucking roof, Glyn!'

There were three reasons for issuing that order. First, he was one of my officers, second, he was a friend, and third, he was the son of the Colonel of the Regiment, Major-General Morgan Llewellyn. I didn't want the Colonel of the Regiment's son killed on my watch. I'd met the Colonel many times, including before we'd left for this tour. He was nicknamed 'Colonel Fury' for the way he'd handled the army leadership and politicians during a firemen's strike back in the 1970s. He'd never told me to 'look after my boy' or anything like that; he was much too professional and, besides, as a platoon commander, Glyn would be expected to be able to look after himself. But now Glyn was in mortal danger, he clearly wasn't thinking of his own safety and his death was not something I wanted to have on my CV or my conscience. Was it the pressure of his father being the head man? Did he feel the need to impress at all costs? He'd never tried to make play of his father's status; he'd always been his own man. During down time he was a dyslexic poet and rather a good one; he was a unique character in his own right, not the sort who seemed driven by the feeling that he had something extra to prove. So I didn't think the family connection was pushing him into desperate heroism. But, whatever was happening, his life was now very much on the line and he was about to get his ginger nut shot off.

'Glyn! Listen to me! Get off the roof!'

I was in danger too. The hornet-buzz of those bullets told me they were close; the rounds were flying all around us. Most of the stuff coming at us was medium machine gun, 7.62mm. You hear a very distinctive noise from that weapon – a steady thump – and those rounds ruin you if they hit you. We were taking a big chance by staying as exposed as we were, especially Glyn. And that's why I just couldn't believe he was still up there. Either he was so brave that he was consciously ignoring the hail of bullets and trying to shut out the danger, or he just didn't get it.

I shouted at him one more time. 'Glyn, get off the fucking vehicle!'

But he was still so focused, because he realised the importance of what he was doing. If we didn't get that machine gun into action, we'd be non-effective. He cracked on until, finally, he managed to pull the trapped bergen strap out of the turret ring. In that instant, the gun was back in action. He'd done it! At last, Glyn finally obeyed my order and got off the vehicle.

Freeing up the turret didn't solve everything, of course. We still didn't have enough men. We didn't have enough ammunition either. This could never be anything more than a holding battle. Hold the high ground. Make a stand. We'd always be playing for time until the Muslims got their act together but there was still no sign of 801 Brigade. Where were they? How many times did I have to send in the call to arms? They must have received the message; how they responded was out of my control for now. We had to have faith in Salko and his men; we had to believe they were coming otherwise the risks we were all taking would count for nothing in the end.

Although B Company was giving a bloody good account of itself, that didn't mean the Serbs wouldn't be able to take all our OPs eventually; sooner rather than later if we didn't get the right support. The lads were coming under increasing pressure and there were decisions to be made. The first one concerned OP1, stuck out on a limb and by now under the fiercest pressure from the Serbs. The crisis came to a head for them at about 15:00 hours.

I was talking to Sergeant Pete Humphries when he said, 'I can't hold on much longer here. I'm very exposed.'

I trusted Pete and his judgement implicitly; he was a wise old head and I appreciated just how vulnerable his position was.

'Move now!' I told him. It wasn't worth losing him. Pete and his boys deserved a chance to stay in the fight some other way, instead of being surrounded and killed or captured where they were. We tried to offer Pete and his boys covering fire as best we could from our vehicles. We could keep a few Serb heads down but, without hearing more from Pete, we didn't know how else we could help him.

'Move now!' I repeated.

No response. That really worried me. No 'Roger, out.'

Nothing. I wasn't just frustrated; I was going mental. I wanted to talk to him. I was very confident in his ability but part of me assumed something had gone badly wrong. In that moment, I realised the Serbs had taken OP1. Did that mean Pete Humphries and all his men were dead? My heart sank. Had Pete obeyed my order to move in time? Could he? There must have been a close-quarters battle around OP1. The result was obvious, whatever the casualties: we were no longer in possession of the Observation Post.

Next I received a worrying report from down by the river, where Sergeant Adrian Kent was commanding eight men at Checkpoint 1. 'Shady' Kent was a battalion rugby player, a junior leader and one of the sharpest soldiers I'd met. Glyn Llewellyn was his Platoon Commander and there was a fierce, unspoken sense of competition between them, perhaps even a tussle to decide which man was the true leader. Shady was happily married to Rachel, who used to babysit for one of the company commanders. Kent was a hard, uncompromising soldier and, crucially, he was very, very calm in a crisis. Sergeant-Major Adams had often said, 'The thing about Sergeant Kent is that I always think he's one step ahead of me.' He'd need that kind of foresight now.

The Serbs, in a small convoy including armoured vehicles, were moving slowly down the riverside road towards him. 'Shady' had two Saxons right next to the Drina and I thought it best to pull him back a couple of hundred metres to the next bend in the road. He'd have a bit more protection there and it would buy us a bit of time. This was an indication of just how finely poised the battle was; I'd already resorted to trying to trade space for a bit of time above and below me.

Shady Kent was still on the radio as his Saxons began to move and then he told me they had a problem. One of the two Saxons had driven too close to the river bank, which had given way. The Saxon had rolled down into the river. Knowing the Drina was the fastest-flowing river in Europe, I could only hope it wasn't deep enough in that spot to sweep the Saxon away. Mercifully, Shady was soon able to tell me there'd been no loss of life. There wasn't going to be time to drag the damaged Saxon out of the river though. So I told Kent to take the men from that Saxon, some of whom were injured, put them into his own vehicle and get the hell out of there. Would he have time to do that before the Serbs came round the corner and captured or killed them all? Shady had his orders; it was up to him now.

We'd suffered a reverse on the mountain, we had a serious problem by the river and there was a very real possibility we were going to lose the entire battle. If they maintained this sort of momentum, the Serbs might roll us right up along the ridge-line and the battle would be over almost as quickly as it had started. This was the genuine worry as I tried to stay calm and assessed the situation. At least they didn't yet have the Observation Post they wanted most, OP3 on Mala Biserna. As things stood, they still didn't control the mountain; they couldn't use OP3 to bring fire down on the town and dominate all its approaches. We couldn't let them take OP3 because, if they did, the consequences were scarcely imaginable. With the right heavy weaponry in place, the Serbs could obliterate Gorazde at will from there; or they could simply provide covering fire if their comrades wanted to attack the town from the north or south or both. For now we were denying them because Captain Tom Murphy was hanging on for dear life up there. Thanks to Murphy, Dave Vaatstra and the rest of the men, we still had hope that we could achieve our objective. Tom, however, was sounding significantly tenser every time he talked to me on the net. I could tell he was under terrible pressure.

The Serbs were still coming along the ridge at him from both directions. They were also trying to come round and up the front of his position. We were pinning down some of them from Cemetery Valley but there was only so much we could do against a determined enemy from where we were. Tom and his blokes were really stepping up though. They were knocking the Serbs down whenever they got close. Though I couldn't see the bullets hit home from my position, I could hear the fire and knew they were inflicting casualties. While Tom and Vaatstra could still fight, I knew they'd continue to do so unless told otherwise.

Back down at the river, Shady Kent was showing remarkable composure as the Serbs closed in. Very calmly, and under fire, he had managed to cross-deck everything, including the weapons, from the stranded Saxon to the healthy one. Only then did he follow orders to get out of there. Crucially, Kent was able to confirm to me that he and his men had all avoided being taken hostage and they hadn't left anything behind, except the skeleton of the damaged Saxon in the shallows of the river. What a brilliant piece of work!

Events were unfolding at pace and I got on the radio to Riley, to tell him what was happening at the various points of contact. He told me to prepare to withdraw all my OPs but to defend ourselves if attacked. We were already doing that. By then, Riley was back at the camp with Nick Lock, the Operations Officer, so I was the man on the spot and he wanted my assessment.

'We can hold this for now,' I told him, 'but we can't hold it indefinitely. Can you confirm that you've got a message through to the Muslims? We need them up here now! There must be at least two thousand armed BiH in 801 and they can still help us if they hurry.'

'They're on their way,' Lock replied.

But how quickly could they get where we needed them to be? I couldn't even see them. We didn't have much time. Where was my friend Salko? I'd lost contact with OP1 and Humphries could be dead for all I knew. We still held OP2 and OP3 but the latter was in big trouble and could fall at any time. Shit. I was starting to flap a bit inside. If it got any worse than this, we'd lose the battle. And since the Muslims were going to be late arriving, we needed some help from our own side immediately. It was just past 15.00 hours.

'We need some Blue Sword over here right now,' I said, using the familiar code name for either UN aircraft or UN-controlled aircraft.

Silence. I repeated the plea. 'Requesting Blue Sword urgently.'

'Roger, trying to get Blue Sword released from Sarajevo,' was the reply.

So where the hell was it? Riley and Lock must have been trying for an hour already. Wasn't anyone at the UN in a position to authorise air? Was the head office in New York pretending to be closed again?

I imagined Wez Harris, Billy Walters, Ronnie Collins and

the rest of the SAS boys holed up somewhere, trying to get authority for NATO air. They'd be able to guide in the air support with superb precision, if only they were allowed to do so. Then reality hit home. Nobody was going to give them the authority either. We were in deep trouble and we knew it.

# CHAPTER FOUR

# HOLDING ON

'Be aware. The BiH are moving up behind you onto the high ground.'

At last! It was Nick Lock, from Battalion Headquarters in Gorazde, giving me the good news. I walked about fifty metres round a bend to a spot where I might be able to see 801 Brigade climbing the reverse slope. Yes! The first groups of thirty or forty, slowly making their way up Biserna towards the high ground. Mentally, I was willing them to get a move on but they were struggling. Come on, Salko! Even though it was steep and it was harsh, I still couldn't quite understand it. They had shown me how quickly they could get up there in the past. I'd asked them to take me on a route through the minefields and they'd sent me up with three or four of their guides. They were like mountain goats that day. Admittedly, they hadn't been carrying bergens but they were so wiry, fit and fast that they'd been up there in fifteen minutes flat – and it's a big old feature. Now they seemed to be taking an age on the same slope. Soon their progress was even harder to monitor because I lost sight of them completely. Where the hell were they?

They must have taken cover. I could see smoke coming from a big house called 'Scabs', which was next to OP2 on an adjacent ridge-line. It was gunfire. That didn't look good for OP2. And the reason Salko Osmanspahic and his men were taking so long on the lower slopes was because they were taking a lot of fire as they tried to climb towards the high ground. The Serbs behind OP2 had spotted the BiH and they were letting them have it, yet the Muslims were determined to carry on with their ascent. To my relief, I saw they were on the move again.

Salko was made of the right stuff. He'd trained at the JNA (the Jugoslav National Academy for NCOs). That made him just as well trained as the men he was fighting against – in fact, identically so. Salko was confident and measured in everything he did. He wasn't scared of risking his good looks in this fight or any other. He was top notch and he needed his leadership qualities now more than ever, to take his men through this hail of fire.

They weren't short of motivation, of course. The men of 801 Brigade were just as keen to reach the ridge as we were for them to help us. They knew this wasn't our town, so they must have been wondering how long we were going to hold. They had no way of knowing whether we were going to put up a determined resistance or not. Did they trust us to save them? Probably not, so they had to take control of this crisis. It was their town and their people who were going to be obliterated if we lost this battle. For that reason, the Muslims were now pouring out of the town and round the base of the mountain to scale the reverse slope and reach OP3. They understood the strategic importance of OP3 as much as we did and they were prepared to die trying to reach it if they had to. Sadly, that's what appeared to be happening.

There was a big burst of Serb fire and again I lost sight of the large, leading group of Muslims. This time there was no sign of movement afterwards. Shit! Had Salko and his followers all been killed or wounded? Surely they couldn't all have been hit by that burst? There had been so many of them. Now there was nothing. Just heavy rain coming down in sheets, pissing all over us. More time was passing; more time for the Serbs to complete their assault. This was looking bad. Then I caught sight of Salko's men again. They were moving! They must have gone to ground to plot the next stage of the climb. They were trying to make a covered approach where possible and you couldn't blame them for that. They reached some trees and used the natural cover to climb faster. They were already higher than me but, as they came out of the trees, they faced another hail of bullets from above. The Muslims were now bravely fighting uphill to stop the Serbs from advancing along the ridge from OP1 to OP3. The latest arrivals were taking a lot of casualties and you had to admire their courage. However, the fact remained that they still weren't where they needed to be to make a genuine difference to the balance of the battle.

Until 801 Brigade climbed higher, my men would have no real help up there. Some were in more trouble than I realised. At 15:45, Corporal Dave Parry realised he was in a battle he couldn't win at OP2. I'd known Dave Parry since 1985, when he was one of my youngest soldiers in the first platoon I'd commanded. With dark, cropped hair and sharp blue eyes, Dave was well educated and the son of a Welsh vicar. Yet, despite his undoubted intellect, Parry had always been in trouble as a young soldier. These days Dave was a junior leader, devoted to his wife Carol, and his life was more stable. Until now. Unfortunately, Dave was suddenly in more strife at OP2 than he had ever known as a youngster.

The house we called 'Scabs', so close to his position, had been full of Serb soldiers since the start of the action. In the last few moments, they had poured out of the house and started to attack OP2. Dave and his boys had fired off a few rounds and hoped to keep them at bay. Then the Serbs brought up anti-tank weapons and Parry knew the game was up.

He came on the net and told me, 'Zero Alpha – I'm surrounded. I've got a hundred enemy around me with rocket-propelled grenades and worse.'

'Is there any opportunity to cut a deal with them and move back?' I asked optimistically.

'Absolutely not,' he said, as though there were more chance of General Mladic becoming a vicar like his dad.

'All right. Keep them talking.' Any kind of dialogue was better than none; it might save them from the worst of Serbian brutality.

Parry knew the writing was on the wall. 'We're going no-where,' he said. 'Roger, out.' That, to me, meant he was no longer viable and all I could do was echo his last words.

'Roger, out.' Speak to you later... thinking I wouldn't.

Shit. Poor bloke. Dave Parry, a first-class soldier, always

proud of the latest kit he'd bought himself, a man who'd turned his life around and took his job seriously. And now it looked over for him. This was definitely a low point. Apart from any personal feelings, I'd lost OP2 as well. I couldn't talk to Dave – he was clearly no longer in the battle and I knew all eight men had been captured. I had no choice but to divorce myself from the personal side and look at the wider picture.

It was quite clear that, if they'd just wanted hostages, the Serbs would have been content with the hostages they'd just taken at OP2, along with the bigger batch they'd grabbed on the West Bank. They could have stopped their onslaught right away. They didn't. What they actually wanted was the OPs themselves on the East Bank, every single one of them – especially OP3. It was frustrating not to be able see everything from where I was. I could see the entire reverse of the slope but what I couldn't see was the other side of the mountain and the slope the Serbs had been climbing. Luckily, once they became a threat up on the ridge, they came into view. And, crucially, it was evident to me that the Serbs weren't making any significant progress where it mattered anymore. The main attack on OP3 was now coming from the direction of the captured OP2. But the Serbs were also still trying to get round the other way to complete their pincer movement. What we had in our favour was that the ridge-line was narrow – only about thirty metres across – so were able to pin people down there and stop them. Pretty soon we had them bottle-necked. We kept hitting them and we imposed more and more casualties until it looked as though there were scores of Serb bodies piling up on the ridge. They were reinforcing failure, the idiots. They weren't changing tactics to try to get round the back. If the Serbs tried to come down off the ridge and get in behind our boys, they might run straight into a minefield, and they knew it, so they preferred to take their chances on the ridge. But what was happening to them there was just as deadly.

'You just keep doing what you're doing, stupid bastards,' I said to myself. 'Like this, we're still in the game.'

From inside our vehicle, one of Glyn Llewellyn's men was still doing a great job on the gun. He was controlling and directing his fire, not blazing away in huge bursts. The accuracy of his shorter bursts was lethal. From our position, we managed to take down about three groups of ten Serbs as they went across the top of the ridge. They'd been trying to get round from the direction of OP1 but Glyn's gunner was onto them in a flash. He wasn't just causing casualties; he was forcing those still in one piece to keep their heads down. Crucially, we were slowing the Serbs down for long enough to give ourselves a chance of success.

As company commander, it was more important for me to maintain an overview than to kill Serbs personally. My rifle was meant to be for self-defence. My role was to make sure other people were doing the right thing and to make tough decisions for them when necessary. But, in this situation, I wasn't going to pass up on an opportunity to help protect my men directly, not if I saw a target. And I did. I spotted Serbs on the ridge and knew I had an opportunity. By the time I moved into a firing position they were 250 to 300 metres away and running towards OP3. I took aim with my rifle and pulled the trigger several times. A couple of people went down. They 'went firm', as we said in the army – they'd been stopped in their tracks. I got some more rounds off, right into their position. They didn't move again. Was there any way to verify that I'd killed them? No. But they didn't reappear and I'm prepared to assume that I did kill them.

Salko's men weren't very far from completing their climb up the back of the Serb position to join Tom Murphy at OP3. My first concern was to let Tom know what was happening. Otherwise there was going to be a very unfortunate fire-fight and Tom's blokes were going to shoot the wrong guys. But Tom had other worries. As soon as one group of Serbs went down, they seemed to be replaced by others and now they found fresh momentum. Tom started to sound so frantic that I began to think the Muslims were going to arrive on the scene too late. The Serbs had taken some heavy losses and they wanted something tangible to show for all those casualties. They were pressing on recklessly. Tom was getting more and more hyped and he was already naturally as hyperactive as they come. He always had to be doing something, even during calmer moments, and, if there was nothing to do, he would practise conjuring tricks with handkerchiefs. How he must have wished he could do a disappearing act now, because he was under massive pressure.

In what seemed to be a final push, the Serbs were coming at him from both ends of the ridge. It was quite a long ridge, thankfully, and there were long hooks to get round on either side. Corporal David Vaatstra had an extended range on his machine gun, still perched on his tripod in OP3. He was hammering them left, right and centre. The bodies were still piling up and Serb progress stalled every so often. But then they came at him yet again and it required almost continuous fire to keep them at bay.

## HOLDING ON

Tom Murphy got on the radio and told me, 'I can't hold out much longer here. We're going to run out of ammunition.'

'No, you've got to hold,' I insisted. OP3 was how we were going to prevent a massacre here. No more innocent people murdered. Not if we could help it. And if that meant Tom had to risk his life, so be it.

'I need to move.' Tom's survival instinct was kicking in. He was thinking of his men up there too.

'No. I'm up here with you,' I said, trying to reassure him. Even though we were some way below, I was close enough to see with my own eyes that he still had a chance. 'I can see the right-hand end of your position. You've got to hold.'

I stayed as calm and focused as I could, all the time hoping he'd do the same. He certainly wasn't panicking. What he'd told me was an objective assessment as he saw the situation. He wasn't screaming, 'We're all going to die, we've got to get out of here!' It really was a question of him warning me that the situation was becoming critical for them.

'We're running out of ammunition,' he repeated. It was a warning about what might happen very soon but, for now, I was adamant he had to stay. I knew he was still on his game up there. And, if he did finally run out of ammunition, he had rehearsed his escape with his men time and again. He knew what to do. Just hang in there a little longer, Tom.

At that precise moment, a voice burst in on my company radio net – the one I was using to keep Tom in the game. It was Riley or Lock, both of whom should have been using the battalion net.

'Withdraw all your OPs now,' the voice said.

'Get off my net! I'm trying to control this.'

The words had left my mouth before I could edit them but they needed to be said. Yes, it was a clear case of adrenalin-fuelled insubordination. I didn't care because the situation was more important than any backlash that might come my way later on. Besides, I knew Riley would get it; I was the man on the ground.

Withdraw all your OPs? It was a lovely thing to say – he just wanted to get everybody safely back – but it couldn't happen, and not just because two of the relevant three OPs had been taken already. I wasn't going to withdraw my remaining OP, not yet. There was too much at stake. Battalion HQ was trying to make this decision from over the river in the town. They were completely unsighted in terms of what was happening where we were. It was absolute bollocks and not very helpful. If we moved now, without the Muslims on the high ground, it would give the Serbs vital minutes to take the position we'd worked so hard to save. OP3 was the one they couldn't have.

So Riley and poor Nick Lock had felt the sharp edge of my tongue. They shouldn't have been on my net anyway but, then again, I probably wasn't answering the battalion net so they saw it as their only means to deliver the order I couldn't obey.

'Get off my fucking net!'

Silence. I heard nothing back at all in response to that little suggestion. They'd obviously decided to respect my request, though the air probably turned blue at their end too in the aftermath of my outburst. I didn't give a shit. I only had time to focus on the priority. Tom Murphy was in trouble and I wasn't even sure how much of OP3 was left. It must have been taking a hell of a structural battering. Tom had already told us he couldn't hold out. Where was the close air support? Fucking

Blue Sword! What was the point in the code name? Battalion Headquarters must have got through to Sarajevo several times by now, trying to get some UN air assets sent over our way. They clearly weren't coming. So we were willing the Muslims to scramble up the last part of that slope and get onto the ridge to save the day. They were still hindered by the fire they were taking from the vicinity of OP2. Could they make it up the final hundred metres or so, before this all went tits up?

Tom Murphy came back on the company net. 'I've got a couple of guys hit but they're okay.'

Fuck. What did that mean? Flesh wounds? Stunned and knocked back on their arses and then back up on their feet again, because the bullets had been stopped by their body armour? I hadn't a bloody clue but I knew they weren't dead or dying and that was good enough for me.

'Hold, Tom!'

It's a hard thing to say to someone you know well. Especially when he's just told you the Serbs have found their range. Murphy, Vaastra and the boys had managed to dodge most of the horizontal shower of Serb bullets. But it would only take one piece of bad luck, a well-aimed mortar or sniper's head shot and their brave stand at OP3 would be over, just when the cavalry were in sight. My men were living on the edge; they'd faced wave after wave of Serbs all afternoon. Heavily outnumbered, with no hope of turning back the tide on their own, they'd resisted grimly. But perhaps the tide was about to turn anyway.

'OP3, this is Zero Alpha. Be aware you have BiH forces within fifty metres of your position.' That was me telling Tom, 'Salko's nearly with you, mate.'

'Roger that,' said Tom. You could hear the relief in his voice. He was allowing himself to think he might just be able to pull this one off – and so was I. As the Muslims drew closer and closer, you could almost sense his excitement on the radio. You could hear him thinking, 'They're nearly here.'

I knew what he wanted to do because it was what I would have wanted to do in his boots – get the fuck out of there as quickly as possible. He'd been fighting relentlessly; he'd done his bit and more. But I needed Tom to grab Salko Osmanspahic, or the first Muslim commander he saw, and point out where the enemy were.

I told Tom, 'Make sure you give them a proper handover. I say again, make sure you give them a proper handover.'

Now the Muslims were within metres of OP3 on the precious high ground. I couldn't see everything from where I was, so I had to trust Murphy and asked him, 'Can you confirm that you have BiH in your position?'

That's when I heard the magic words from Tom. 'They're here. Handing over.'

'Move now!' I ordered. No command had ever given me such relief.

'Moving now, out,' he confirmed.

Murphy had held the vital ground. Vaatstra was the first man to fire and last man out when they withdrew off the position. He had fought tooth and nail. Now it was the turn of the BiH, who were straight into a fire-fight with the Serbs. Salko's men had OP3, that was the big difference, and they soon seized the upper hand. There was to be no massacre in Gorazde, not if we could help it. Selma and thousands like her would be able to breathe just a little more easily after our stand. But could Murphy, Vaatstra and the rest of the men of OP3 extract themselves safely, with the bullets still flying? A withdrawal in contact is one of the most complicated things you can do. You can't just turn and run because you'll probably be shot in the back. You've got to fire and move, using a series of report lines, so that you delay the enemy's advance. You have to cover each other and do it in stages. But once Tom had got his men over the ridge, there was nothing very complicated about what happened next.

We provided covering fire as Tom's guys slid down the back of the mountain in the mud. The rain that had begun to fall earlier was their friend now, aiding their speedy extraction as we kept the Serbs busy from below. The heroes of OP3 slithered all the way down on their arses, holding their rifles and bergens in front of them. I saw them flying down towards me like kids on toboggans and it was an exhilarating moment. As they came closer, that's when I knew for sure that none of Tom's guys had been wounded earlier. They might have been knocked on their arses but they were clearly okay if they were able to whizz back down to me like this.

I checked everybody through.

'Have you got all your blokes Tom?'

He confirmed my headcount. Brilliant! There was a feeling of euphoria; they'd all made it down in one piece. Cemetery Valley wasn't going to claim any of Tom's crew. In fact, I still hoped all of B Company could somehow escape this crisis with their lives.

The men at Checkpoint 3 hadn't had it as bad as those in OP3. They'd been able to hold their position under less pressure and they, too, were still in one piece when they confirmed that the Muslims had reached them. They were able to drive along to join us in Cemetery Valley before they were seriously threatened. And that meant we could load Tom Murphy and his men into their Saxons for their journey back to the camp.

My relief at watching some of my men driving away towards a safer place was tempered by the fact that I still hadn't seen or heard from Pete Humphries or his blokes. I feared the worst. Something must have happened, otherwise we would have heard from them by now.

Then Humphries appeared right in front of me, shrugged his shoulders and gave me a philosophical shake of the head as he joined my group as an additional reserve. Incredible! Cool as a cucumber. I hadn't heard from him for ages and reckoned I deserved more of an explanation than a shrug. Pete Humphries told me what had happened. He hadn't talked to me on the net because he'd been in overload. He'd been fighting his battle, trying to get his blokes out. The group he led were trying to fight their way back through Serb positions on foot because the Bosnian Serb Army had got in behind him. At the same time, he'd had me shouting in his ear. What had he done? Something had to give, so he'd taken his headphones off to shut me up. Then he and his men had fought their way successfully through two Serb positions, while branches were blasted off trees and, in some cases, entire trees were knocked down around them by the weight of fire. As he was moving back, Pete spotted a Serb ambush position before they spotted him. So he took his guys down a dip and round to the left and crept up behind the Serbs. It would have been the easiest thing in the world for him to kill them all. He didn't.

Instead of shooting them, he jabbed his weapon into the back of the first bloke's head and forced him to drop his weapon. The rest followed suit. Humphries collected up all the Serb weapons and threw them into a ravine. Then he told their former owners to get up and fuck off. Remarkably, he did much the same to another two positions and didn't kill anyone on his way out. The man's judgement was outstanding. Everyone around him was trying to kill him and yet he still had the presence of mind to draw the distinction between when he needed to kill someone – as when his boys had been defending OP1 – and when he was able to spare people. That had to have been a good thing. Then he realised he was leading his men into a minefield – not such a good thing. And this was a close neighbour of the minefield that had blown bits off three of our soldiers a few weeks earlier. It was too late to turn around so Pete told his men to wait while he picked his way through the minefield, trusting his feet to fate. Nothing went bang this time. No bullets shot up into his body. So Humphries told his men to follow in his precise footsteps and they came through in one piece.

Meanwhile, the other half of Pete's group, under Corporal Jones 73, had used their vehicle to smash through a Serb barrier and they all linked up to reach us unscathed. It almost sounded too good to be true but that's the way it happened. To say I was impressed with all of them is an understatement. They could have one immediate reward. I told Pete, 'Right, take my vehicles.' We loaded Humphries and his men into our Saxons and got them out of there before their luck could change. I could still see Serbs on the far side of Cemetery Valley but they seemed to have their hands full fighting the Muslims.

# OPERATION INSANITY

As Pete and his men sped away, another wave of relief swept over me and I had to remind myself this wasn't over.

For a start, the ride back to camp wasn't going to be straightforward for anyone. The vehicles had to cross the River Drina by bridge to reach 1RWF Camp – our base in town. The bridge was regularly being shot at by a Serb with a 50-calibre machine gun – a huge weapon. Just as well the Saxons were armour-plated because some poor driver was going to have to come back the same way and pick up my little group, which had been reduced from about fifteen men, including Humphries and his boys, back to a mere handful. Everyone was heading back to camp except us, so it was only natural we felt vulnerable for a while and yet our senses were heightened and we remained ready for anything. Even so, it was one of the longest half-hours of my life, isolated in Cemetery Valley, until the reassuring, rumbling sound of a Saxon engine came back into earshot. Sure enough, Pete had sent back the vehicle that had taken him to camp. We were clambering inside almost as soon as we saw it.

One last burst of machine-gun fire tried and failed to take us out on the bridge. I'm proud to say we were the last back into the camp from the East Bank. But there was no time to give anyone a pat on the back because the wider picture was chaotic. A Company had been doing more or less the same as us, pulling their OPs back as the Muslims came forward to replace them on the other side of the river. However, including Dave Parry's group, a total of thirty three British hostages had been taken.

Amazingly, I was able to have a conversation with Parry that same evening, even while he was in captivity. He'd hidden a radio inside his smock and, when he had an opportunity, he covertly told me what was happening. The prisoners were still in the basement of the big house next to OP2. That night his OP team were led away by the Serbs and were shot at by Muslims for over a kilometre as they crawled through the night. All the time, Dave kept in contact with me by radio, at great risk to himself, because they were still very much prisoners.

Finally, Parry said, 'We're moving again now. Be out of range soon. I'll see you on the other side, boss.'

That remark brought the biggest lump to my throat. He'd always had a sense of humour but what did that mean? I was choked up; it was a really emotional moment. I'd known this kid since he was a sixteen-year-old soldier and he was one of my favourites. I just thought, 'Oh, fuck.'

See you on the other side. He probably meant when it was all over, rather than, 'see you in the afterlife.' Even so, that remark carried a haunting finality.

# CHAPTER FIVE

# AFTERMATH

**A** pair of grey socks, still worn by their owner. Nothing unusual, yet destined to stick in the memory. The other fourteen feet protruding from a makeshift cover were still inside the boots they had worn in battle. Seven bodies, feet untouched. And then the other guy, whose boots must have been something special and now had new owners.

Had we killed these men? They were certainly Bosnian Serbs. Were they gunned down by B Company during that last stand two days earlier? It was hard to tell because the Muslims, who were digging graves for the dead when they weren't digging trenches to keep themselves alive, had done their share of killing too over the previous thirty-six hours.

It was dawn on 30 May 1995 and my friend Salko Osmanspahic had invited me to inspect the new BiH positions on Samari ridge and Mala Biserna, complete with a trench system designed to ensure the Serbs would never take that precious high ground overlooking Gorazde.

The Serbs were still launching sporadic attacks in the hope that they could regain the initiative. Although it wasn't working so far, this was a time for caution and stealthy movement, for using the early-morning mist as cover, for whispers rather than shouts. That's why it was a little unfortunate that Salko had been temporarily deafened the previous day by a tank shell that had landed barely ten metres from him. It could easily have killed him instead of rearranging his eardrums. No wonder he'd appeared slightly shaken up as we'd prepared for our pre-dawn climb.

We'd trekked through the town towards Bridge Bravo – our name for Gorazde's central bridge – and been relieved to see the low mist hanging over the Drina to shield our movement from any prying Serb eyes. It felt unusually secure to be shrouded in this way, as Salko set a brisk pace, the simple action of marching towards his men visibly settling him. Not wanting to subject Selma to the front line, I'd brought Mark, the SAS interpreter, with me.

Fairly soon we were clambering up the south-western edge of the Samari Ridge towards Gornje Kollievka, a collection of houses that had previously been deserted, situated just short of what was once OP1. A day in the bunkers had taken its toll and I was soon breathing hard as we climbed rapidly onto the ridgeline, still protected by that merciful mist. And that was just as well because Salko seemed determined to speak loudly to me, as if taken in by the deceptive sense of peace around us. Perhaps I was imagining it but it seemed as though his words were booming all over the hillsides, inviting any Serb with a grievance to air it with a bullet. I grunted responses to Salko, partly to save energy and partly in an attempt to deter him from speaking at all.

'Shut up, Salko!' I didn't say it but I thought it.

We soon had two problems. Rays of sunlight started to creep through the morning mist; once our natural cover had been burned away, we'd be exposed to the Serbs. Still, there was nothing we could do to give the thinning mist a longer life. What we could control was the way we spoke; we could do it quietly. But Salko still wasn't keen to take a hint because he probably thought he already was speaking quietly.

Over the first crest, we met a group of tired-looking BiH soldiers – youngsters mostly. They were frantically digging and I marvelled at the pace at which they shifted the hard-baked earth.

'Trenches?' I asked.

'Graves!' was Salko's alarmingly loud response.

No Cemetery Valley for these corpses.

We pushed on and I saw a row of Serb bodies, partially covered in UN sandbags, which had been cut open to create tarpaulins. I counted seven pairs of boots and one pair of socks. Must have been a good pair of boots, no doubt about it. Round a corner another row of Serb cadavers lay in a large rectangular grave. An Imam stood over the bodies and conducted a brief ceremony, which seemed respectful, even though these men had died fighting for the destruction of Gorazde as a Muslim enclave. A group of BiH soldiers waited patiently, ready to fill in the makeshift grave. Doubtless there would be a call for body exchanges in due course but, for the moment, it was important that these corpses were buried, in order to avoid disease and to allow the BiH soldiers to focus on the defence of the town.

After another fifteen minutes' climb, we reached the front line of BiH trenches. Off to my right were a couple of Serb ponchos, probably abandoned by their owners when Humphries and his men had surprised them so suddenly a couple of days earlier. 'They were the lucky ones,' I thought, still proud of the restraint Humphries had shown in the midst of the wider bloodshed.

As we continued upwards, I was impressed by the defensive positions Salko's men had created. There must have been a couple of hundred men up there overnight, wielding picks and shovels. Deep, well-constructed defences ran along the ridge-line and were surprisingly extensive. He asked, with pride, what I thought of it all. I told him he'd done a good job but that he needed to add some geographical depth to his defensive line in case of a flanking attack by the Serbs. Some more overhead protection would be useful against airburst munitions, I added. For a moment he looked as though he were about to castigate me. Then he smiled, inclined his head and said, 'Sure, good idea.'

All around the position, tired soldiers dug, smoked or brewed tea. It's the same the world over for any infantryman. Fight, dig, smoke, brew. I felt an empathy with these soldiers. They had experienced the buzz of incoming fire, the crump of mortars and the scream of artillery. They had held their collective nerve, they had stood firm and now they were burying the dead.

We hunkered down in Salko's command post as a stream

of stretcher-bearers marched past. Another ten dead; more burials.

'You've been busy here,' Salko said. 'There are more on Biserna,' he added. 'Many more killed by your soldiers. We found them as we came up the hills.'

Salko wasn't gloating. In life, these men had been hell-bent on the destruction of his town yet, in death, it seemed that his enemy became human beings again for Salko, and he took no more pleasure from the loss of life than I did. For Osmanspahic, there were still plenty more living Serbs to hate, such as those now bombarding Gorazde with shells from afar.

It was numbing to see the bodies on the hills and you had to remind yourself how very necessary these killings had been at the time. We also felt duty-bound to put some kind of number on this latest loss of life, especially after seeing more Serb corpses lined up for burial near our former OP3, others still piled in a contorted heap where they had fallen, no more than fifty metres from Murphy and Vaatstra's position. That showed how dangerously close the Serbs had come to achieving their objective.

Salko and I estimated that, between my B Company and his 801 Brigade, we'd killed around two hundred Bosnian Serbs on the ridges and crests in the previous two days, most of them falling on the first afternoon of fighting; the crucial one – the stand we'd that been involved in. I figured that my men of B Company must have been responsible for between 70 and 120 of the dead on 28 May. Though this clearly wasn't what peacekeepers were supposed to do, there was still a pervading sense that it had been the right thing to do under the desperate circumstances inflicted upon us by the Serbs. They had misjudged us. And on a personal level, perhaps Captain Kepic had misjudged me and my warning to him. For whatever reason, I heard later that Kepic had cracked up in shock at the Serb casualties. Apparently, he had been close enough to the action to witness the deaths of some of those Serbs personally. They clearly meant more to him than the deaths of Muslim children. Perhaps he blamed himself for failing to remove the British from the high ground through diplomacy. Maybe, in his own twisted mind, he still thought he held the moral high ground and couldn't cope with what he saw as the injustice of it all. Quite honestly, I was beyond caring how Kepic felt because I felt he'd brought his misery upon himself.

What mattered to me was the fact that the Serbs were no longer in a position to start a massacre in the town at close quarters. If those two hundred Serb deaths were the price that had to be paid, so be it. Unfortunately, their former masters had already decided that they would not take this tactical defeat lying down and had started to shell Gorazde from afar instead. And as the barrage intensified, it was already painfully apparent that our UN 'peacekeeping' mission was in disarray. We had no choice but to shelter in underground bunkers to survive the aerial onslaught, just as the rest of the town had been driven into a subterranean world, at least by day.

Each evening I went to see Salko in the basement of the town's biggest bank, where other local dignitaries gathered too. Naturally, I also saw Selma in the basement of that bank every evening too, since her job was to translate when I had meetings with Salko and Major Hrapo, the BiH's Divisional Liaison Officer. The SAS had joined us down there, using the bank as their temporary headquarters. It was as good a place as any to collect information from local officials, assess the situation and send their findings up their own chain of command. Sometimes little snippets of news filtered back to us from Britain too. We knew the hostage crisis would attract the close attention of the biggest players back in the UK. We knew the Prime Minister, John Major would be working hard to resolve it. The fact that the Serbs had paraded some of the British hostages on TV, and made it clear that our captured men were to be used as human shields against possible retaliation from the air, had only inflamed the situation.

In response, Major let it be known that he was prepared to send an Air Mobile Brigade, two artillery batteries and an armoured engineer squadron to Bosnia like some kind of cavalry coming to our rescue. However, quite how they'd be able to help us without making the crisis even messier, or, indeed, whether they would be able to reach us at all, once the logistical realities and risks were properly examined, remained to be seen. Neither did Major seem to know whether such a show of muscle would ultimately be designed to reinforce our defences and help the British to stay in Gorazde, or help us to escape from the enclave and get home to safety.

Later on Tuesday, 30 May – the same day Salko had taken me up to see the new trenches and fresh graves – Major used a London press conference to outline what he had done so far to ensure that Dave Parry and the other captured British UN soldiers didn't become casualties too.

'As Prime Minister,' he acknowledged, 'I sent our troops to Bosnia and I intend to do everything in my power to ensure that our soldiers are released from their present captivity... We have sent a letter to Mr Karadzic, the leader of the Bosnian

Serbs, that we shall hold him and General Mladic personally responsible for the safety of British troops in Bosnian Serb hands... This new development, this taking hostage of peacekeepers, is an outrage, condemned by the whole international community, and rightly so. But not only is it an outrage, it is a self-defeating folly... So let me say quite clearly to the Bosnian Serbs, this sort of action is the path to total international isolation and permanent pariah status.'

A reporter from the *Sun* newspaper apparently asked Major, 'How did you feel last night when you saw the footage of the British soldiers who were being paraded on Serbian television? Did you not think it smacked very much of during the Gulf War when Saddam Hussein did the same thing?'

The Prime Minister replied, 'I think how I felt was expressed very clearly by the message that has been sent to Mr Karadzic and General Mladic; they will be in no doubt about how I felt about it.'

John Major trying to act hard, but that wasn't necessarily going to put the fear of God into a ruthless man like Mladic, the Butcher of Bosnia. Even so, Major had some big hitters to call upon, at least one of whom had the ear of the Serbs. Boris Yeltsin was the eccentric, hard-drinking Russian president – perhaps the one man who might have been able to make an ally see sense if he found a sober moment between bottles of vodka. Otherwise the Serbs probably knew they could expect less friendly overtures from the rest of the world's most powerful men.

Major revealed how active he had been behind the scenes, as he explored ways to solve the crisis. 'In the present circumstances we now have to think coolly and with a clear head about the way forward. In the past few days I have been in close contact with Chancellor Kohl, President Yeltsin, President Chirac, President Clinton and Prime Minister Chretien [of Canada].'

Despite attracting the focus of the world's leaders, however, there seemed no obvious solution. All options were being considered yet none had been chosen. Where Major sounded clearer was when he talked about what the British troops had achieved in Bosnia and, quite chillingly, what might unfold if we left prematurely.

The Prime Minister reminded his audience:

It is very easy to forget in present circumstances precisely what our troops have achieved. They have stopped the fighting from spreading more widely throughout the Balkans... they have delivered literally thousands of tons of food and medicines to people who would otherwise surely have died... These are achievements that our troops can rightly be proud of and they are not to be lightly discarded... I don't think the British people would wish lightly that British troops should turn their back on Bosnia and open up the dangers of what might then happen in the enclaves and don't be in any doubt about what might happen if United Nations Protection Forces came out... The Serbs would certainly be able to take the enclaves and I don't know whether you or anyone else can tell me quite how many people would be killed... Once we move away, the danger of a full-scale attack on the enclaves is clearly there. If there was a full-scale attack on the enclaves, you would see bloodshed on a scale we have not previously seen. I believe we have both a strategic interest in preventing a wider Balkan War and I think we have a humanitarian obligation to try and prevent that sort of bloodshed and it is for those reasons that the United Nations Protection Forces are there as a whole. I believe it was right to send them, I believe it has been right to keep them there, I believe it is right that they are there now and I believe it is right to keep them there for as long as they can remain there without unacceptable risks to the lives of British and other United Nations soldiers.

Either the risks we'd faced just two days before he spoke (and would continue to face almost every day) were acceptable, or he just didn't know how close we'd come to having people killed. Maybe he did have some knowledge of what had taken place and had concluded, as I had forty eight hours earlier, that those risks were worthwhile, at least on a short-term basis, if they meant saving a town from a massacre. Whatever perspective the Prime Minister had, he wasn't the only national figurehead back home to take a keen interest in our predicament.

As our Colonel-in-Chief, Her Majesty the Queen was never going to ignore us in our hour of need. On 1 June the Queen visited Haverfordwest, home of the Royal Welch Fusiliers. If this visit hadn't already been planned, it probably would have been put together anyway, in response to the hostage taking and attacks. The idea was to see how our families were bearing up, particularly those of the men who had been taken hostage by the Serbs.

I'd already been able to call my wife Jane, who was still pregnant with our second child, to insist that all was well. What I didn't know was the extent to which the hostage crisis had been all over news bulletins back home. Even as I tried to reassure her that we were in no danger, she was apparently thinking, 'Liar, it's terrible. I've seen the news and you're all going to die.' She was well practised at making light of the numerous problems she experienced back home. In fact, she didn't like to bother me with her own issues very much at all because she knew how much pressure I'd be under on operations. Jane wasn't the type to make matters worse by openly expressing concern for my safety either because she knew it wasn't going to help. But she would have had to be an extraordinary actress to erase all trace of anxiety from her voice, knowing what she knew this time. How could any of the families ignore our plight?

Although it might have been a trifle pessimistic to conclude we were all going to die, there was genuine cause for concern. And it would do the families good to know that the Queen was not only thinking about them but prepared to be with them in person in their hour of need. She arrived at the Regiment's Families' Centre on the Trafalgar Road estate in Haverfordwest just before 3pm, wearing a striking red coat, red broad-brimmed hat and black gloves. Reporters described the cheers of about three hundred residents who had gathered to greet her, waving Union Flags and Welsh Dragons all around her. Inside the Families' Centre, the Queen was warmly welcomed by some of the soldiers' wives and children, while about twenty more youngsters watched from the crèche.

Although Jane couldn't be there, because in the middle of

all this she was overseeing our house move due to our growing family, we'd both had the honour of meeting the Queen before. That meant we both knew what a positive effect she'd have on the soldiers' wives. We knew how effortlessly she would make each and every person she met feel special, their worries understood. The first time I'd witnessed this phenomenon had been in my very first week with the Battalion, at Battlebury Barracks in Warminster in 1984. What a start! I was a brand-new second lieutenant and my uniform and blues cap had only arrived from Meyer & Mortimer, our regimental tailors, the day before the Queen's visit. When she arrived on the parade square, I was watching from the stands. She commanded so much loyalty and respect that there was a real buzz when she stepped into the square. Afterwards, we were in the Officers' Mess and arranged very neatly in small groups. She worked each group with such ease. When she came to our group, I was introduced and she spent about three minutes asking me how long I'd been in the Battalion and how I was settling in. The Queen had this incredible ability to be serious but also to show a sense of humour wherever she could. She would ask a sensible question then raise an eyebrow or come up with a witty rejoinder. It was really impressive and I couldn't wait to ring my parents to tell them I'd actually spoken one-on-one with the monarch.

I was fortunate enough to have a second chance a few years later, as the regiment celebrated its tercentenary at Powys Castle. I'd been on a course and the commandant there had tried to block my release for the celebrations. I sought advice from the Colonel of my regiment, Major-General Morgan Llewellyn – Glyn's father.

He said, 'Go and stand outside the commandant's door in ten minutes and I'm sure this will be resolved.'

Sure enough, the red-faced commandant was soon opening his door with a smile.

'Richard! Come in! There seems to have been a dreadful mix-up! Of course you must go. And enjoy it!'

Good men, those Llewellyns! The tercentenary celebrations were full of pageantry and we enjoyed a spectacular lunch, after which we were organised into small groups. The Queen breezed from one little gathering to another and Jane and I were lucky enough to have a few words with her. Jane marvelled at the Queen's ability to make everyone feel special without asking any person the same question. It's either a huge natural talent or the result of great training.

The visit to Haverfordwest was a very different occasion, of course, because some of the people she was there to comfort must have been worried out of their minds. Yet there can be little doubt that her natural warmth and her personal touch still shone through.

The Queen was led into a side room at the Regiment's Families' Centre for a private meeting with our soldiers' loved ones, including five wives of men spending their fifth day in captivity in Bosnia. The meeting was held in private at the wives' request, although six of their children were also present and the mood was informal. First she chatted to the wives in a group and then she did so individually. A Palace Spokesman explained later, 'The Queen was keen to find out how they were and what news they had received. She realises what a worrying time it is for them.'

Back out in the main play area, the Queen took time to

chat with Dave Vaatstra's wife, Glenys, who was asked about life on the estate. 'She wanted to know what it's like to be a soldier's wife,' Mrs Vaatstra told reporters afterwards. 'I told her there was a tremendously good camaraderie among the families.' Even now, it is strange to think that just seventy two hours after Vaatstra was involved in the ugliest fight of his life, his wife was chatting to the Queen back home, with the two events inextricably linked. To say it had been an unforgettable week for the Vaatstras was something of an understatement.

Apparently, HM was given another poignant reminder of the situation in Bosnia when she saw stacks of refugee clothing and equipment, collected by the soldiers' wives and the people of Haverfordwest. There was a map of the former Yugoslavia pinned to a notice board and surrounded by photographs of serving soldiers and pictures sent by Bosnian children in gratitude for earlier supplies collected in Pembrokeshire. Perhaps some of poor Adem's friends were among those who had sent pictures, because that school in Vitkovice had been the focal point for a lot of our attention.

Back outside, the Queen was cheered all over again, those Union flags and Welsh Dragons fluttering afresh as she paused to speak to one or two lucky members of the crowd before getting into her Rolls Royce to leave for the next part of her schedule.

The Royal Welch Fusiliers' Colonel of the Regiment, Major-General Morgan Llewellyn, summed up the effect of her visit and the widespread appreciation everyone felt over her personal concern for our plight. 'The visit by the Queen, the Regiment's Colonel-in-Chief, has done a lot for morale,' Glyn's father said. And once 'Colonel Fury' found out that his son had dodged countless bullets to keep our battle going in Cemetery Valley a few days' earlier, his morale would doubtless soar higher still.

The Queen hadn't stopped thinking about the Royal Welch Fusiliers after she left Haverfordwest either. She was keen to pass on her impressions of the day to those of us trapped in Bosnia, to make us all feel better. We had no idea what was coming as we neared the end of a routine meeting in our makeshift home. Our base in Gorazde was made up of a bus depot at A Company's end of the camp and a sports complex at our end. Those of us in the O-group (orders group) were gathered in an old shelter in the bus depot, sitting on a mixture of coach seats, ripped out of the decrepit hulks of old buses, and wooden benches. As first-line commanders, we were receiving our daily Ops Update. There were the usual contributions from A, B, and C Companies, Recce Platoon and the JCOs (SAS). Then we endured various pieces of administrative piffle from the Adjutant and the Quartermaster.

'Any questions or redirects?' asked Riley towards the end. 'No? Okay... I have here a telegram from the Colonel-in-Chief. It says, "I visited your Regiment's families today in Haverfordwest. Despite the grave situation which you are facing, I found them in good heart and supporting each other in the finest tradition of the Regiment. You can be proud of them, as I am proud of you. I send my warm good wishes to you all."'

No one wanted to follow that. We just nodded sagely, acknowledging the fact that the Queen had done the right thing by us and our families, expressing in our own understated way how much we all appreciated it. Words weren't necessary because knowing looks did the trick in the silence. Even the constant Serb barrage seemed to have paused out of respect. It was a magical moment but no one wanted to show too much emotion because we had to get on with the business in hand. We all had to head back to brief our own O-groups. As I left those dirty old seats with a fresh sense of pride, I looked forward to briefing my lads on the Queen's telegram. I knew how much it would mean to them.

B Company's platoon commanders, sergeant-major and quartermaster sergeant had all been called to my Saxon vehicle for the daily update brief. We varied the time for this get-together; we didn't want to set patterns in case we were being observed. Rigid routines meant that something very nasty could be planned by the wrong people and some of our key groups might just get wiped out all at once. So we stayed on our toes and kept things flexible, and this particular evening was no exception. I started with an intelligence and operational report, so they could understand the wider political and strategic moves that were being mounted. When you've had your face down in shelling for most of the week, information is scarce, so that didn't take very long. Then I drilled down into the tasks for the men for the next day and the following seventy two hours. The advice of CSM Adams was invaluable, as we sought to ensure these jobs were not seen as 'time-fillers', but something worthwhile instead. People wanted to hear any news we might have on the hostages. There wasn't much at this stage but they were still 'missing, presumed alive'. It was our job to stay positive in any references to them, just as they would be trying to stay positive wherever they were being held. Then, to finish on a high, I relayed the message from the

Queen. It was well received; you could tell by the nods and pursed lips that everyone agreed she had done a good thing.

'Make sure everyone knows that she's thinking of us,' I said in conclusion.

A little later, Riley shared with me something the Queen had told the wives she had seen in Haverfordwest.

'The Serbs would never dare harm my Royal Welch Fusiliers.'

That's what the monarch had said and we smiled at that. She was undoubtedly referring to the plight of the hostages. She might not have known how hard the Serbs had already tried to harm her Royal Welch Fusiliers on the high ground above Gorazde but they had failed, so it didn't matter, and the Queen's positivity was much appreciated. Perhaps she was right and Mladic would realise what a terrible backlash would be unleashed against him if the hostages were killed.

The Prime Minister should have been more fully briefed on every aspect of our situation. Yet his over-optimistic advisors appeared to have prevented him from realising that we were, for the moment at least, powerless to do any more good in or around Gorazde. John Major had been asked an awkward question back at that press conference on 30 May: 'Does the fact that you want to concentrate UN troops in a more defensible space in Bosnia mean that we are no longer able to protect some of the outlying Safe Areas?'

Major had replied, 'I don't necessarily know that that is the case. Certainly we are going to have to bring some of the more exposed UNMOs [United Nations Military Observers] closer in, I think that is self-evident, that has clearly been learned. Beyond that, on this occasion, I don't wish to say any more about the concentration of troops; we are still discussing that with the Commanders on the ground and with our Allies.'

We were certainly no longer able to protect the 'Safe Area' of Gorazde, though, luckily, the BiH had taken over what was left of our Observation Posts before the Serbs could establish decisive control. The more exposed UNMOs hadn't just been brought closer in already; they were hunkering down in bunkers to avoid the barrage of long-range shells now raining down on the town from Serb positions many miles away. It was Serb revenge for defeat in our recent battle; understandable, perhaps, but still tough to endure – especially since we didn't know when the bombardment would end or, indeed, what might bring about that end. Neither was it clear to us how any proposed reinforcements were going to get through to Gorazde in order to share our hell with us, since they'd either have to go through or over the Serbs in order to do so, risking many casualties in the process. And what was the point in them coming if none of us could get out again?

When it came to discussing the situation with commanders on the ground, however, Major soon proved to be as good as his word. On 2 June, to his own astonishment, Riley spent twenty five minutes on the phone with the British Prime Minister, who still didn't seem to have a full understanding of the gravity of our situation. It wasn't standard practice for a Prime Minister to make a call to a commander of Riley's rank, a mere lieutenant-colonel. Convention would normally have demanded that John Major spoke to a general, such as Rupert Smith in Sarajevo, because he was more senior and more likely to have the bigger picture. But John Major clearly felt that the senior officers in Sarajevo weren't at the sharp end of the crisis. What worried him most was our fate in Gorazde and he may well have been receiving mixed messages about how much danger we were facing.

So it was to Gorazde that his call was placed, though there were moments during that phone conversation when Major might have regretted his decision. Riley, remember, wasn't the kind of man to beat around the bush. If he felt something needed to be said, he would say it, whatever the consequences. As he admitted later, he quickly realised he had to be true to himself and his men. 'Either I can behave like a typical army officer, or I can tell him the truth.' So Riley was in the mood for some straight talking as the Prime Minister began their little chat.

'Do you think the Serbs intend to take Gorazde?'

This is understood to have been one of Major's key questions. He must have known the answer already, judging by his comments back in that press conference of 30 May, yet he wanted confirmation from the man on the ground.

'Of course the Serbs intend to take Gorazde!' replied Riley, perhaps irritated to hear that the Prime Minister appeared to be unaware that B Company had just been involved in a fight for our lives to prevent precisely such a scenario from unfolding.

While Riley didn't criticise the PM directly, he did let Major know, in no uncertain terms, that we had effectively been given 'mission impossible' without the resources to achieve our brief. The planners had failed, in his view, to take into account one key fact.

'Your advisors are bloody fools if they think it's a good idea to have peacekeepers in a place where there is no peace to be kept.'

## AFTERMATH

That is how Riley later relayed his remarks to me, once the Prime Minister was off the line. Whether he really used the expression 'bloody fools' I don't know, though I can well believe it. All Colonel Jon's frustrations had tumbled out, born of the fearsome weight of responsibility on his shoulders as he tried to protect his men in an increasingly perilous environment. The fact that we'd been able to do some good in Gorazde was not, in our view, down to careful planning back in Britain. A price had already been paid and all hell had now been unleashed upon us.

Riley left the Prime Minister in no doubt about how grave our situation was. 'Thirty three of my men have been taken hostage. One hundred more are in a hide. There are shells falling all around. No one can get to us. We can't get to anybody. But every man here knows his duty and, by heavens, they will do it.'

Major assured Riley that everything possible was being done behind the scenes to ensure that the hostages would be released. That was all very well but into what kind of hopeless siege would they be released if, indeed, they were freed? And, although Riley had assured the Prime Minister that his men would do their duty – meaning that we would not simply surrender to our fate – it was a complete mystery to all of us, and perhaps even to the Prime Minister, what our duty would now be, other than to maintain some kind of basic order among ourselves.

By the time Riley had finished with him, the Prime Minister might well have been relieved to get off the phone. Perhaps he wasn't used to being spoken to with quite such passionate honesty. And, although John Major probably had no deliberate intention of getting Riley into trouble, it seems that the PM did make some kind of comment to Colonel Jon's superiors about the frank nature of the discussion and Riley's clear sense of frustration.

One of the most senior Army officers in the UK seemed dismayed that Riley had apparently spoken out of turn. 'He should stop thinking and get back in his trench,' this officer is understood to have said. Another top officer allegedly went even further and said, 'Riley should get back in his trench and die.'

Riley was soon called and given a personal dressing down. 'Stop thinking and do your job,' he was ordered.

'What job?' was apparently the essence of my CO's reply.

And Riley had a point; with no peace to be kept, we didn't seem to have a role to play in all this chaos any more. What part of our mission was now really tenable? Observe and report. No more than that.

But Riley's superiors had apparently launched into him with such force that it left our commander, normally so full of confidence, visibly disillusioned.

When I next saw him, in his bunker, he appeared very withdrawn and downhearted.

'You need a pretty dark humour to be where I am at the moment,' he admitted.

It's a lonely place, the top. Riley may not have been at the very top of the British hierarchy in Bosnia but he was certainly at the top of our tree in Gorazde. He felt let down by his superiors in the British military and I could sense the disappointment, the pressure and the strain he was feeling. It was time to build back up a man who had commanded us well under the most difficult of circumstances, often feeling he had no one to turn to, because in Gorazde the buck stopped with him.

'We need your experience, we need you back in the game and I'm right behind you all the way,' I said.

It was true. We needed Jonathon Riley back at his feisty best and we wouldn't settle for anything less. I told him repeatedly that he had our total support and we required him to step up once more. Perhaps Colonel Jon needed to hear something along those lines, because his strength soon returned. And who wouldn't have allowed Riley a moment or two of self-doubt when at least one of the senior SAS men was experiencing it too?

The SAS are used to doing short-term jobs. A month away, back to base, onto something else. They weren't so happy about being stuck in Gorazde, having to operate out of the basement of a bank in a town centre at night. Being cooped up in bunkers and basements, their roles not much more clearly defined than ours – it just wasn't their style. And then there was the constant barrage, the fact that the Serbs seemed to be softening up Gorazde by pounding us incessantly with something between 300 and 600 shells daily, perhaps before they attacked once more. It looked pretty hopeless and the SAS are nothing if not realists.

The next day we were outside again briefly for a conference next to Riley's Saxon, when it was disrupted by the scream of low-flying shells overhead. Most people took cover. Wez Harris, the SAS Team Commander and I ended up on some steps, flanked by low concrete walls, which at least offered some kind of limited protection.

'I've never been through anything like this before, being shelled twenty four/seven,' I confided to Wez.

'Don't look at me,' he said. 'I haven't either.' He had a worried look on his face.

'Are you all right?' I asked him.

'Been better,' he admitted.

'Hang on,' I reminded him. 'You're a sergeant major in the SAS; you're the hardest fucker on earth!'

Wez just shrugged his shoulders. He wasn't enjoying the shelling very much either. He was a big family man with a wife and two daughters, all of whom he adored. Even SAS soldiers were human. I looked him in the eye and asked him straight.

'What do you think is going to happen to us?'

'Honestly? I think we're going to get our arses kicked.'

It wasn't exactly what I'd wanted to hear. The SAS were supposed to save our arses if the shit hit the fan and now it seemed they were no longer confident they could do so. You couldn't blame Wez, of course. What could four SAS blokes do anyway? What could any of us do now? Harris didn't seem to think we were going to get out alive, if I understood him correctly. Perhaps Colonel Batalin, the Ukrainian UN Commander, had been right when he had told us the day we arrived, 'You're all going to die.'

These moments were a real low point for all of us. Despite the Queen's best efforts a day or two earlier, morale was starting to wobble.

# CHAPTER SIX

# TIMING

**Y**ou could try your hardest to secure the freedom of a few hundred hostages and, at the same time, you might unwittingly condemn thousands to death not far down the line. That's how complicated it was for the UN in Bosnia, as those with the most power decided how best to use it and made some catastrophic errors along the way.

It was still 3 June when the first of over 300 UN soldiers of various nationalities were released. They had been suffering for days in captivity, not knowing if NATO or UN air strikes would hit the Serbian installations where some of them were chained up as human shields. Although our men weren't among the released hostages, the breakthrough had to be a good sign for Dave Parry and the other Royal Welch Fusiliers. Were there strings attached? History is still trying to judge.

The Serbs' gesture apparently created enough good faith for General Bernard Janvier, head of the UN in Bosnia, to meet General Ratko Mladic face to face on 4 June. This was not something Riley's boss, General Rupert Smith, regarded as appropriate – not while British hostages were still being held in captivity. Some felt the meeting was tantamount to bargaining with terrorists and others have since argued that the long-term consequence of Janvier's policy of appeasement was, for many in the enclaves, fatal.

The fact remained that Janvier was above Smith in the UN chain of command and had already told the British general to stop requesting UN air support. Therefore, Smith's reservations about Janvier's decision to deal with Mladic in person, even if expressed openly, were always likely to be ignored. The Frenchman, who had far less faith in aggressive peacekeeping than Smith, was uncomfortable with the notion that the UN should take a hard-line stand against any side in the Bosnian War, let alone back up its position with the threat of air strikes. The British had a record of military success in the Falklands and the First Gulf War, where they felt tyrants had been put back in their place on both occasions through the use of military force. Janvier, whose French military career had been less action-packed, believed that talking was the solution to all Bosnia's problems. Most remarkably, he seemed to think there must be a warm and cuddly inner Mladic, just waiting to escape through that atrocious veneer. All Mladic needed, according to Janvier, was a little encouragement to show his true humanity. The question is this: what sort of encouragement did Janvier give Mladic in that meeting and others?

Janvier has repeatedly denied that he promised Mladic he would prevent any more NATO air strikes against the Serbs as long as the hostages were released. Whatever the truth, there can be little doubt that Mladic left that meeting on 4 June confident that Janvier's goodwill represented something useful in real terms. Mladic seems to have decided that the release of more hostages would, indeed, protect him from the threat of UN air power and NATO air strikes too. Worse still, for the security of the enclaves, was another apparent Mladic conclusion: that, if he rode out the brief storm of international outrage against his hostage-taking, he could soon use the key lesson he had learned from his piece of brinkmanship; that the UN had no teeth or genuine determination to stop him. In any crisis, Mladic appears to have sensed that Janvier's priority was for Western UN soldiers to be protected.

On 7 June a second batch of hostages were released and scores of French UN soldiers, who seemed to personify Janvier's chief concern, were now free from danger. There was still no sign of Dave Parry or any of our boys but we had more hope; enough to start bringing a bit of humour back into our situation and theirs. Where there was humour, a bright corporal called 'Scouse' Hughes was usually to be found. In fact, where there was no reasonable basis for humour at all, Scouse Hughes was still to be found. Hughes wasn't actually a Scouser, though his Deeside accent was close enough to give him the nickname. A big lad with fair hair and a front tooth missing, he had once appeared on parade back home with cuts and bruises all over his face. When I'd asked him what had happened, he'd said, 'Well, sir, I was in this nightclub and there were these two bouncers who thought they were hard... and they were.' Scouse was a very good footballer and a decent back-row rugby forward but, in this harsh environment in Gorazde, there were no ball games. You had to find your own amusement.

Scouse and I both liked Steve Coogan's comic creation, the painfully clumsy and insensitive interviewer Alan Partridge. One of the 'interviews' Partridge had done was with a guy who'd been held hostage in Lebanon for years and just been released. Hostages, you might have thought, would have become such a sensitive subject in Gorazde that they'd represent a comedy no-go area for us. Not so; in fact, quite the reverse. Our way of dealing with the uncertainty surrounding Parry and the others was for Scouse and me to re-enact the Partridge hostage sketch as best we could remember it. (Apologies to Coogan if we got this wrong but it was the best we could come up with at the time.)

The sketch starts off with a typically ham-fisted introduction. 'It's dark. I'm chained to a radiator. And I haven't spoken to a soul for years. Well, I have, of course, I'm Alan Partridge, but my next guest spent two years like that in Beirut. Here he is: still suffering from Post Traumatic Stress Disorder, would you please welcome...'

The guest comes on looking uncomfortable, sits down and Partridge says, 'Tell me about the funny times.'

'Alan... I don't recall any funny times.' It's an honest reply.

'Okay, well, some lighter moments,' says Alan encouragingly. Silence. 'Think about it, think about it,' urges Alan, becoming slightly impatient.

'Alan, I was chained to a radiator, I didn't see anyone, I thought I was going to be executed at any moment. There wasn't much levity.'

Partridge isn't satisfied with this, thinks he can avoid being picked up by the microphones if he whispers, and confides to the interviewee, 'Look, I'm just trying to lighten it up a bit... you're coming across as a bit of a sour puss...'

Scouse Hughes and I were screaming with laughter, quoting this to each other spontaneously. Tasteless, given what was happening to Dave Parry? Certainly. But it was our way of dealing with the tension. If you didn't retain your ability to have a laugh, you might really crack up.

Finally, in mid-June, we heard the news we'd been hoping for: Dave Parry and the other hostages were freed. The relief I felt on their behalf was indescribable. 'See you on the other side,' Parry had said. Now he was out and safely on the other side. 'The Serbs would never dare harm my Welch Fusiliers,' the Queen had told the hostages' families. Broadly speaking, she had been right again.

We could assume that John Major had been working away behind the scenes, just as he had promised Riley he would. The formation of the Rapid Reaction Force – the one Major had touched upon in that 30 May press conference – may have been a factor in Mladic's decision to relent. 'Release the hostages or get your arse kicked one way or another, Uncle Ratko.' That was the gist of Major's message. Mladic saw enough sense to comply, not least because the UN soldiers never had been his primary target. It was the Muslims he wished to massacre and, having probed the resolve of the West through his hostage-taking, Mladic probably felt he had learned all he needed to know about what the UN would or wouldn't allow NATO to do in order to prevent a massacre in one of the enclaves.

The possible long-term repercussions didn't necessarily register with Dave Parry and the other released hostages or, indeed, any of us. Their ordeal was over – that's what mattered in the short term. The immediate political crisis regarding Bosnia was over too, though Major still had another crisis to deal with back in London. A little domestic rebellion that same month was headed off at the pass: Major simply reinforced his own position, for the moment at least, by resigning. That way he could be voted back in as leader of the Conservatives instantly, which automatically allowed him to remain as Prime Minister. So Major had a new mandate of sorts and the release of the hostages probably only bolstered his credibility. Despite his improved standing back home, however, Major couldn't inspire any wider agreement on UN or NATO-led aggression against Mladic; not of the kind that might prevent a potential massacre in one of the enclaves, a tragedy he had foreseen in his public remarks of 30 May. Whatever tough line Major might have wanted to take, the general mood seemed to be to wait for the time being and see how events unfolded in Bosnia for the rest of the summer. That didn't help us much but at least the nightmare was over for some.

Once freed, Dave Parry and the other hostages were moved to the relative safety of Bugojno, except for any injured, who were repatriated. They certainly weren't going to be sent back into the hell we were still stuck in, though, typically, Dave did his very best to rejoin us. He had several requests denied, before he finally had to accept that his Bosnian War was effectively over.

I could stop worrying about him and his mates now and concentrate instead on worrying about those of us who were still in danger. 'See you on the other side, Dave.' We were now in almost as much shit as he'd been in when he was captured so

I couldn't be entirely confident that I could fulfil my side of the bargain. It would depend on a number of factors outside my control. What Parry had shown was that you could conduct yourself in an exemplary manner even when it might seem easier to take a back seat.

In time it would emerge that Dave Parry had been particularly heroic in captivity; he had refused to let the Serbs give his men direct orders and he had taken a physical beating for that insistence, yet he had inspired his group to remain composed, even when they were chained to radiators as human shields at various installations. The same went for Lieutenant Hugh Nightingale, the twenty-two-year-old from Sheffield who had shown such courage under fire three months earlier. Nightingale revealed that, as a senior hostage, he had had been subjected to the psychological torture of a mock execution. Even as he realised that no bullet had entered him when the trigger had been pulled, his torment wasn't over. He firmly believed all the British hostages would be executed in the fullness of time. Nightingale hadn't let that fear show during his horrendous period in captivity – not even during his darkest hours – and he, too, had led his men well.

Dave Parry and Hugh Nightingale were destined to be awarded the Military Cross for their leadership in what must have been a terribly strained situation for all concerned. Thoroughly deserved by all accounts and much appreciated by their men. I can't speak for Hugh because I didn't know him so well but I'm pretty sure Dave Parry refused to give an interview to Alan Partridge, despite rumours of repeated requests.

The horrors of war were still all around us and I could see the fear in Selma's eyes. We were in the basement of the bank, where we still met most evenings so that she could translate for me. Selma often took the opportunity to tell me about the civilian casualties she'd heard about, the inevitable consequence of the constant Serb shelling. This time, however, the Serbs had done something that shook her to the core.

'My friend, Adiata, the other interpreter,' she began. 'Adiata was crossing the central bridge in town and they fired at her with a machine gun.'

My heart sank. Adiata was dark, very attractive and very tactile. She could not chat without reinforcing her words by holding your arm or touching you. She had a collection of fleeces, given to her by admiring soldiers. Had the Serbs destroyed her now too? Was she dead? Somehow the Serbs still had a heavy machine gun aimed at that bridge. The rounds would have ripped her apart.

'Those bastards,' Selma said. 'Can you believe it, Major Richard? They just missed her but they tried to kill her. Adiata!'

I felt relief and anger. We already knew the Serbs habitually targeted defenceless women and children. But when the woman who'd had a lucky escape was someone you knew personally, it provided a further reminder of the dangers the civilians faced daily within the town itself.

'When is all this going to stop?' Selma asked me.

I felt helpless because I couldn't offer her the kind of answer she wanted. We both knew the Muslims had the upper hand locally. The BiH was taking Serb positions outside the town one by one; they were still winning the battle for Gorazde, though they hadn't mopped up entirely, as Adiata knew all too well. When would it end? We weren't sure if it would ever end. But the Serbs clearly weren't going to take Gorazde any time soon and that was the only crumb of comfort I could give Selma.

Then the wind began to change.

Perhaps the Serbs started to accept that, for the moment at least, there were softer targets to attack elsewhere. Slowly, almost imperceptibly at first, the intensity of the shelling in Gorazde began to subside. Furthermore, some diplomatic headway was being made behind the scenes, at least where the supply routes to Gorazde were concerned. General Janvier met General Mladic again on 20 June and somehow persuaded him to allow a route to be opened up for much-needed humanitarian aid to reach our besieged 'Safe Area'. Once again, precisely what Janvier offered in return is still open to question. Did Janvier promise to make every personal effort to ensure that the Bosnian Serb Army was not subjected to NATO air strikes? It is difficult to see what other assurance Mladic could have been given in return for his co-operation, though Janvier always denied that any deal had been struck. And Mladic was cunning so he might just have gone out of his way to give the world the impression that he had a heart... a fortnight before he did the most heartless thing Europe had seen since the Second World War.

For us, the Serbs' switch of focus meant some breathing space. By 25 June, after almost a month of constant shelling, the bombardment had subsided sufficiently for us to emerge from the bunkers for longer spells and assess the situation around Gorazde properly. As we'd expected, we found that Salko's Muslims were still in control of the key areas we'd vacated on the high ground so our last stand appeared to have had a lasting effect. Though still vulnerable to sporadic shelling in the town, we decided that the very worst of this particular crisis was over so we brought our non-essential men back down the mountain.

Padre Tim Tucker soon announced that normal services would be resumed, starting with a full service on the first Sunday after our little reunion.

'I hope I can count on the support of B Company,' Padre Tucker urged me.

'Don't look at me, Padre. I don't believe in God, as I've told you before, but I'll put it round to the blokes and see if they'd like to come.'

'I'm sure they will. They always do,' he said with surprising confidence.

'Do they?' I asked, somewhat taken aback.

'Oh yes, B Company are always there. It's never too late for you to join your men, Major Westley, never too late,' he chirped as he moved on in triumph.

Why were the men of B Company always there? They'd never shown Padre Tucker much respect before. Right from the start of the tour he seemed to have been a figure of fun. If you'd been stuck in one of our Observation Posts on those bleak, 3,000-foot mountains during the early weeks, time had passed particularly slowly. So little usually happened on those limestone ridges back then that the boys had constantly been looking for something to laugh at. One day I'd been on patrol and gone up to OP3, where 'Scouse' Hughes was holding the fort. I'd been sitting in the OP when I heard Scouse on the radio.

'All stations, OP3: sighting, over.'

My ears pricked up because he must have seen something suspicious. 'Hunchback on the Samari Ridge, over.'

Hunchback? What was he talking about? I'd looked across and, sure enough, I'd seen a hunchback on the horizon. Then there'd been a response on the radio: 'OP2: eyes on the hunchback... Moving from Green 1 through Green 2 towards Green 3. Over.'

Scouse had started howling with laughter. The Serbs and Muslims listened to our radio chatter every day. Were they now following the progress of the 'hunchback' too? Then someone from the Operations Room down in town demanded that everyone grow up.

'All stations, stop messing around on the net.'

'Roger, roger,' came the reply from Scouse. 'By the way, sir, can you see the hunchback from there too?'

Except that it wasn't a hunchback. It was our Padre, unintentionally doing an impression of a hunchback. To be fair to Tucker, he was trying to do the right thing by going on a patrol to get round and see the lads up there. He'd also put his bergen on his back, which was, of course, the right place for a rucksack, but then he'd put his waterproof jacket on over the top of his bergen. Who in their right mind would even attempt to do that? The blokes couldn't believe it.

And now, months later, I couldn't believe that my men were flocking to this same Padre for spiritual comfort. Had the horrors of Gorazde tamed them all? I was determined to get to the bottom of this surprising attendance and asked Sergeant-Major Adams about it.

'Do we have a lot of God-botherers in the Company?'

'No, sir.' He looked as surprised as I was.

'What the fuck are they up to? Why are my boys going to church services?'

'I'll find out on Sunday, sir.'

Sure enough, Adams reported back the following Sunday to confirm that the men of B Company had, indeed, been at the service in large numbers. But, unusually for the CSM, he hadn't yet been able to get to the bottom of the mystery. So I asked Scouse Hughes what it was all about.

'Corporal Hughes!'

'Sir?'

'You. Church. Explain.'

'Ehm, I never miss a service when they're on, sir.'

Indeed, I'd been told that Scouse had even read the lesson that Sunday, starting with the memorable words, 'The lesson is taken from the Book of John, Chapter Twelve, verses twenty to twenty-eight, from the Bible the Padre chucked away on the march up the hill...'

'Hughes, I know you,' I said. 'You're an irreverent bastard. Why are you at these services?'

'Oh, I'm very religious deep down, sir.'

'No you're not. Explain.'

And finally he confessed. 'It's the wine, sir.'

They were pretty much all there for the wine. I didn't have the heart to tell Padre Tucker.

Not that it was necessarily a bad idea to say a few prayers if you had any religious belief in you at all. One Serb shell could still finish you, even though things had started to improve. Though the bulk of the shelling had stopped, we were still careful about the way we moved about the camp.

Meanwhile, our movements outside the camp became even more problematic. We became aware that the Bosnian Muslims were starting to increase pressure on us in the town. They seemed to have forgotten that we'd fought and held the hills for them. They'd forgotten that we'd got convoys through and we'd been feeding them. They were strutting around like the daddies now and they started to put checkpoints on the roads all around us, restricting our freedom of movement as the main UN force in the area. It was a daft thing to do but, in the Balkans, you were nobody unless you had a checkpoint. It's visible, it's demonstrable, it says, 'I control this road.' That didn't mean we had to respect their claims. Every time I reached one of their checkpoints, I used my Saxon to drive straight through their barriers and sandbags, to show they had no right whatsoever to take away anyone's freedom of movement.

I fell out with Bahto, Salko's superior, over that.

At first Bahto tried to reassure me. 'We're just protecting you.'

'You've no right,' I replied.

'Yes, we have,' he warned. 'And next time one of your vehicles destroys one of my checkpoints, I'll fire an RPG at it.'

Although bullets couldn't penetrate an armoured personnel carrier, rocket-propelled grenades (RPGs) could do serious damage to the Saxon and the people inside if they struck the right place.

'You fire an RPG at one of my vehicles and I'll tell the world.'

Bahto balked at my warning. That was the ultimate sanction. If the world heard that the Muslims were attacking and killing UN soldiers, they would lose sympathy instantly. 'You're no longer the good guys.' That would be the world's verdict. Bahto's men never did carry out his threat to fire an RPG at one of my Saxons. Instead they started positioning mortars around our base and firing out at the Serbs, which was almost as bad. At best it could be described as using us as a shield from retaliatory Serb fire. If you're a cynic, at worst you'd suggest that the Muslims were hoping the Serbs might lose patience, chuck a round or two back and kill a UN peacekeeper in the process. In political terms, that would represent a double plus for the Muslims because the Serbs would have been shown to be directly targeting the UN again.

By 1 July I'd been sleeping in my Saxon for more than a month because of the threat of incoming artillery. There wasn't enough room for everyone to have a bed in the bunkers; the Saxon at least gave me some protection against shrapnel and also contained the communications kit, so I could talk to key people at any time. My usual driver, Fusilier Grimshaw, my other driver, 'Scud' Jones, my second-in-command, Captain Ian Lawrence and I, we all called the Saxon home. At about one o'clock on this particular afternoon, while Grimmy and the lads were playing cards, I left them to it, spotting the chance to go back to my portacabin and grab a couple of hours' shut-eye on a proper bed. Some precious time to stretch out and kip! Who could resist? I went back to the portacabin, lay down on my bed and nodded off. It seemed as though no time had passed at all when something woke me up again. I checked my watch and saw an hour had passed.

A little nagging voice told me, 'Go and do some stuff.'

It was guilt, probably. I'd been lying on my bed when I

should really have been in the Saxon. There was no getting away from the nagging voice.

'Enough. Get back to the Saxon Command Post to see what's happening. You know damn well that's where you should be anyway.'

I was only twenty yards away from the Saxon so there was just time to see if Martin Leader, the C Company commander, was up and about in the next portacabin, or whether he was already off doing something useful, as I should have been. There was no real reason for dropping in to see Martin next door, except that he was such a brilliant bloke. He never dressed up his words but he was sharp and intuitive, good to talk to. He was also rugby mad, to the extent that his army career had almost taken a back seat while played the game at a good level as a flanker. Having been in an England Under-16 regional training camp as a sixteen-year-old, I was still quite passionate about rugby myself. We had plenty in common and I fancied a chat. You don't think deeply about everything you do. So I just went to find him next door.

BANG!

A shattering noise assaulted my senses. I thought we were being shot at because, after the bang, it sounded as though bullets were hitting the frame of the next portacabin – mine! I dropped to the floor and crawled out of Martin's little dwelling. Right outside the portacabin were some concrete steps, which had been part of an old five-a-side football stadium in more peaceful days. Remaining on all fours, I negotiated those steps and shouted to Ian Lawrence to open the back of our Saxon. I broke into a little sprint, still keeping low, and climbed into the back of the Saxon. After reporting the attack on the radio,

I went back out and realised it had gone strangely quiet. Had everyone come through unscathed? It was too much to hope for because I soon heard there was a casualty – one of the SAS guys, Billy Walters, who had been in the portacabin two down from mine.

When I saw him, Billy moved his arm sharply, shook his head, looked at his elbow and said, 'I think I just got fragged.'

It was a light-hearted remark; although he had taken a piece of shrapnel in the elbow, this was nothing to an SAS soldier. So, when he realised a few minutes later that his 'wound' was going to be reported as an official injury in the medical record, he was mortified.

'It's a fucking scratch. Don't you fucking dare record it!' This was the angriest I'd seen him.

The doctors bravely wrote the wound into the medical record, regardless of his protests.

'Too bad, Billy. You're in the 'sick note' book!'

No one said that to Billy more than once because he was SAS and the look he gave you wasn't pretty.

Some of my regular soldiers had been wounded too – Smiley, Powell, Nash, Daniels and Brown. They were also very lucky because, even though several had sustained shrapnel injuries to their faces, none had been blinded or even had significant eye injuries. Fusilier Smiley had a face like a blistered piss-pot anyway, to be fair to him, so he wasn't worried. Lance-Corporal Powell was a classic shock case; his swarthy complexion lost all colour and his lips went purple.

Scouse Hughes was enthused by this sight and said to his blokes, 'Classic! Gather round, men. THIS is what shock looks like. Look and remember. This is free training.' It sounded funny, though, in reality, nothing about this shell had been amusing.

I was soon back on the radio to give the Serb and Muslim liaison people the same basic message. 'You've just hit the UN camp. If you do it again, we're reporting it as a direct targeting of the camp.' Both sides denied all knowledge of it, of course, and continued to do so, though, in my view, both were to blame, either directly or indirectly. The Serbs had almost certainly fired the shell, though perhaps without any deliberate intent to kill UN men this time around. It was more likely they had wanted to send a message to the Muslims, who had been setting up artillery positions right next our camp, effectively trying to use us as human shields.

'If you think you can get away with using the UN as a shield, have some of this.' That was the gist of it from the Serb point of view.

The Muslims may or may not have thought the Serbs would retaliate; I'm not sure they cared. I sincerely hoped that my friend Salko had not been involved in the decision to fire out from so close to our camp. I'd still like to think he wasn't. My life would have been over had I slept a little longer, and other British lives in the camp could have been taken too.

It wasn't until about an hour after the incident that I returned to my portacabin and saw that it had been shredded by a direct hit, right above where I'd been seconds earlier. Just that little nagging thought had saved my life; that little voice telling me to get back on duty. Had fatigue prevailed – had another little voice told me I could get away with a few minutes more sleep, stretched out so comfortably on my bed – that would have spelled the end. Our first death in Gorazde. Me. Fuck!

Apart from feeling intensely annoyed and concerned for the injured, for some reason I didn't feel shaken up by my near miss. Sometimes delayed shock can set in after all the fuss has died down. That didn't happen in my case. Who knows why but I just thought, 'Bloody hell, that was lucky!' And it was true. I had been lucky, no doubt about it.

This time I was almost more annoyed with the Muslims than with the Serbs who had fired the shell. I don't think Selma felt too proud of her side on this occasion either, not while she had to translate some of the tension-filled exchanges I had with the BiH. We had long discussions on the Muslims firing mortars out from near our perimeter and the possible consequences of that provocation for me and my men. Eventually, thanks to a persistent mixture of bullying, cajoling and encouragement, the BiH moved their mortars.

It might have been a coincidence but Selma came into camp a few days later and told me, 'You provide the ingredients and I will cook you pizza!' My healthy relationship with the local baker – plus some cheese and tinned tomatoes that had arrived when the supply route had opened – made this dream reality. It isn't possible to describe what pizza tastes like to men who have been slowly starved for months. As usual, Selma was a little marvel.

But was it wise to stick this out for much longer? The Serbs were still in a position to shell us at will and it only seemed a matter of time before our luck ran out and we took some serious casualties. If our mission was no longer viable, there might come a moment when we had to take advantage of a lull in the fighting in order to exfiltrate – even without the blessing of the Serbs or Muslims. In that scenario, the risk of capture would be high, particularly in Serb-held territory. We weren't at the stage whereby we had to seriously consider this option yet but I shared my thoughts with some of the SAS lads anyway, including Ed Grey, the younger and cheekier of the two Scots.

'Escape and Evade,' I began. 'What do you reckon? If we were captured by the Serbs while trying to get out of here and later saw a way to break free, could it ever be an option?'

'Could be,' Ed replied. 'What kind of scenario do you foresee?'

'We'd have to be sure we were no longer doing any good here. But, if we ever find ourselves trapped here under those circumstances and the food's running out again... and we decide to try to get through the confrontation lines while we've still got the strength... and then, if we get caught in Serb-held territory... I'd be thinking 'Escape and Evade' if the opportunity arose.'

'Aye,' said Ed, his face lighting up. 'Capture doesn't necessarily have to be the end of the matter, that's for sure.'

The very next day, Ed presented me with a gift. It was an immaculate map, drawn onto a piece of cloth – the sort that could be stitched into the inside of your tunic. There was the River Drina, the towns along its banks and those to be found further afield, along with all the topography of the region. There were all the important hilltops, even navigational tips you could take from the stars, usually so visible in the Bosnian night sky. You couldn't assume you'd always have a compass in an emergency but there were always natural navigational aids to help you on your way. This was a wonderfully considerate thing for Ed to have done. And, for all I knew, it might even prove to be a lifesaver one day soon.

'Escape and Evade. Just in case, mate,' Ed said with a wink as I thanked him. Then he was off on his way.

Would it come to this? Would we have to try to lead our men out of this hell, slipping away one night, perhaps from a start-point up in the mountain hideaway? Would we have to split into small groups to try to evade the Serbs on our way out? How long would it be before they hunted us down and threw us into one of their infamous camps? I stitched the escape map into my smock that very night, putting together the makings of a plan I hoped I'd never have to use.

It was a strange existence, that midsummer of 1995, because one moment you could come within a whisker of losing your life, the next you were back to playing the waiting game, not knowing how this nervous limbo would end for us. You'd feel worried and then, even worse, you'd feel bored out of your mind. Each man had his own way of dealing with it and a sense of humour undoubtedly helped. That sense of humour could be warped by the environment. With all the tension we felt, little things began to make us laugh almost hysterically, triggers that probably wouldn't even have raised a smile in the normal world.

One day I saw Scouse Hughes sitting on the back of his vehicle and rocking with laughter. 'What's he up to there?' I thought. 'Has he cracked up or something?' Another soldier walked past, they exchanged a couple of words, Scouse Hughes let him pass, and then he began rocking with laughter all over again. Even more curiously, he was writing something down in a little notebook. I was intrigued, so I went over.

'Scouse!'

'Hello, Sir.'

'What's so funny?'

'Oh, fucking brilliant morning, sir.'

'Why's that? Been laughing at Alan Partridge again?'

'No, sir.'

'What then?'

'I've just been conducting a bit of market research.'

'You? A corporal from Rhyl, stuck in Gorazde, and you're conducting market research?'

'Yes, sir. I've just asked thirty two people the same question.'

'What question?'

'What's happening, mate?'

'That's the question?'

'Yes. "What's happening, mate?" That's the question.'

'And?'

'And in thirty out of thirty two cases, I've had the same response.'

'What response?'

'Fuck all, mate.'

We looked at each other and, within seconds, I was almost wetting myself laughing as well. That's how bored we'd become. It was like something out of 'Waiting for Godot', that existential play by Samuel Beckett. Due to the tension, we could laugh for any little reason – and it was infectious.

'Try it,' Scouse said. 'Go on, try it, sir.'

When I'd composed myself for long enough to keep a straight face as one of my men walked past, I did exactly as Scouse had suggested.

'What's going on?' I asked the unsuspecting soldier.

'Fuck all, sir,' he replied.

We split our sides again for no good reason but I had to get a grip when I saw Sergeant-Major Adams looking over, like a stern teacher who had caught two naughty schoolboys up to no good. It was time to turn back into a major in the British army, instead of Scouse Hughes's sidekick. Looking back, this episode suggests that we were nearing the limits of our endurance. But, believe me, at the time, it really did the men no harm to know that you could share a joke with them now and again, because there was enough sadness all around us to last anyone a lifetime.

I still have a photograph of the next tragic incident; the picture was taken by one of the SAS men, Ronnie Collins. It shows me and Martin Leader wearing broad smiles, blissfully unaware that a baby has just been murdered behind us. The picture isn't as horrific as it sounds but the event is. The photo is taken on a glorious summer's day. All had been relatively quiet; Martin and I had been for a run on a circuit we'd created around the camp.

I said, 'Right, I'm going to get some sun now, just chill out before we have to wash and change back into uniform.'

'Good idea,' said Martin.

We were chatting away and stood up to have our photo taken by Ronnie. At that point, there was a 'whoosh' over the top of us but we barely blinked. We knew it was a shell but so many had been flying around us during the previous month that we realised when we were under direct threat or not.

'That's not even close,' I thought.

Martin had clearly come to the same instant conclusion

*Above*: Why we fought: me with some Gorazde kids I hoped to protect.

*Below*: Neutralising child-killers: seen from one of our OPs, the two Serbs on the left, standing just outside the 3-kilometre exclusion zone, thought they could murder children and get away with it. They were wrong. Moments later, the OP commander ordered the GPMG's gunner to open fire on them, killing them both.

*Left*: Inspiration: our interpreter, the diminutive but brave Selma, between Sergeant-Major Mark Adams (right) and me.

*Below*: Gorazde and the River Drina from the East Bank: a beautiful and dangerous place.

*Above left*: Life and soul: Scouse Hughes poses with a member of the Ukrainian contingent. He and his opposite number have swapped weapons for the photo.

*Above right*: Balaclava-bully: a member of the Serbs' 'Ethnic Cleansing Brigade'.

*Left*: General Ratko Mladic. The photo is creased at top right where the Butcher of Bosnia had signed it for Riley.

*Above*: Royal Welch Fusiliers on foot patrol: the shell- and bullet-scarred town was safer than the OPs and minefields.

*Below left*: Battered! OP3 – the vital ground. How did my fighting men survive?

"I DON'T CARE IF IT DOES REMIND YOU OF THE ALAMO, FUSILIER JONES AND THAT DAVY CROCKET WORE ONE — GET THE BLOODY THING OFF!"

*Holland Roberts.*
*June, 1995.*

*Above*: Close call! Where the shell entered my quarters.

*Below left*: Our situation in Gorazde was likened to the Alamo by cartoonists. Felt like it too! *(Cartoon by and © Tom Holland Roberts)*

*Right*: Martin Leader, the C Company commander, and I pose – unaware of the tragedy unfolding behind us.

*Left*: Gorazde ablaze: the constant Serb shelling took its toll on buildings and inhabitants alike.

*Above*: Future lifeline? An SAS team tests ground-to-air comms from the stadium steps.

*Below*: Lieutenant-General Rupert Smith (right), commander of UNPROFOR (UN Protection Force), with Lieutenant-Colonel Jonathon Riley, commanding officer, Gorazde Force, outside Battalion HQ.

*Above*: Her Majesty the Queen, our Colonel-in-Chief, inspecting her Fusiliers. Riley (centre) and I accompany her.

*Below*: 'We didn't think you'd get out of there.' Her Majesty empathised with our situation throughout.

because we were still posing happily for the camera as the shell flew in and landed a good distance behind us. In that instant, Ronnie took the picture.

'Did you get the shell landing in the background?' I asked him. A stray shell for a bit of dramatic effect; that would only enhance the photograph and remind us what we'd been through when the time came to look back on this strange and dangerous time. Sure enough, the photograph shows the smoke rising as we wear our fixed grins regardless.

Just seconds after that shell landed, a terrible wailing started. It wiped those smiles off our faces.

'Oh my God.' Martin and I shared a look that said it all. Though the woman didn't sound injured herself, someone had been, judging by her reaction.

The awful sound of the wailing impacted on Martin immediately. He was quite junior to be commanding a Company, which is why he'd been given the smallest in the regiment. He also had such a caring nature. That's probably why his face drained so completely of colour. It was a horrible realisation for both of us, to know that someone's life had probably been ruined while we'd been showing the SAS Second-in-Command how unflappable we were. Martin and I put our uniforms back on as quickly as we could and hurried over to the Ops Room.

'Did you get that?' I asked.

'Yeah, just trying to find out what's happened.'

A few minutes later, the operations people gave me the answer. 'We're getting reports from the Mayor's office that a child's been killed.'

Later that week, I had a meeting with the Brigade

Commander, Salko Osmanspahic. As usual, Selma was at my side to do the translating.

'Sorry to hear about the child; the one killed the other day,' I said.

'Yes, absolute tragedy,' Salko replied. And for him to say that, in a place like Gorazde, meant there was something more to this. Then he told me. 'The woman in question lost her husband last year and this was her one and only child.'

Had that husband been one of Salko's soldiers? I guessed that he probably had, though there seemed no point asking. That man was gone and now so was his child. Salko hadn't finished.

'The baby was in its crib and it was a direct hit.'

Not just a child – a baby; one who had barely, if ever, seen its father and had now followed him into the unknown. Salko continued his grim tale.

'It was a tank or artillery shell and it went straight through the wall, straight into the kid's bedroom. The mother was on the other side of the house; she was unscathed. When she reached her child's room, she found the place in bits and the little one... dead.'

'Please don't say any more, Salko. Just leave it at that.' I didn't say this, I only thought it but, mercifully, he offered no more details. Selma was a tough little thing but you could tell she had heard enough too.

Just as with young Adem's senseless murder, you felt a mixture of anger and helplessness. What could we do, Martin and I, except put another piece of unspeakable nastiness away in that psychological box we all had handy by now? The rest of the lads had been through enough by then, so this was not a story I felt tempted to share with them. Why burden my men with more sadness? And yet we knew the underlying danger, Martin and I: that you still had to open that box at some stage in the future and piece the incident back together, you had to remember how you'd felt about it too.

To this day, I still feel bad about that horrible moment in time, captured on camera, and a helpless sadness lingers within me. The murder of a baby – while we smile in the foreground. How can you find words to convey your feelings about something like that? And yet it wasn't our fault. This was down to Mladic and his Ethnic Cleansing Brigade, who still hadn't been dealt with by the world's most powerful people. We were just witnessing the consequences. Ronnie later gave me a copy of the photograph, though we didn't talk about the context again. I never threw that picture away, just as I knew I couldn't erase from my mind the tragedy it captured so superficially.

As we drove away from our meeting with Salko, Selma sat stony faced before breaking the silence. 'How many more innocent people have to die in this war, Major Richard? Why does it seem like more civilians are dying than soldiers?'

It seemed that way because it was true. As for how many more innocents would die, I just didn't have an answer. Sometimes it felt like you were doing your very best and yet that just wasn't good enough for the level of violence we'd been told to deal with in this place. In Gorazde, despite our best efforts, the kids weren't safe at school and they weren't safe at home either.

# OPERATION INSANITY

What sort of fear were they living with? How could we even start to understand it? It's bad enough to see anyone living in fear, yet somehow it's even worse when it's children. We probably all remember the most scared we ever were as kids. When I was seven, for example, my mother put me on a plane from Cyprus to London and I flew unaccompanied. I was met at the other end by an RAF guardian and put on a train to Worcester in the West Midlands, where I'd be going to school. It all started to go wrong on the train, when I had a sudden craving for one of those delicious apple-and-blackberry pies they used to sell. I started walking through the carriages towards the buffet car, got as far as the baggage compartment, opened the door and that's when I saw him – Dracula.

I can still see Dracula to this day, standing there, big and tall, his white face more terrifying than his tail coat and top hat. I froze for a moment and looked up at him... and he looked menacingly back down at me. Determined to reach that apple-and-blackberry pie, I risked his fangs and carried on. As I edged past Dracula in that baggage compartment, I saw his coffin next to him. Or was there another vampire in there? I thought, 'Oh my word, if that coffin opens while I'm going past it, I'm just going to run like hell!' Looking back, the man must have been an undertaker bringing someone home to be buried but that's not how it looked to me. All I saw was the big white face of Dracula and the coffin. I found the courage to carry on though and that delicious pie was my reward. I ate it in the buffet car, in case Dracula sank his fangs into me on the way back through. For a seven-year-old, that walk back to my seat was the toughest I'd ever endured. But

I made it through the nightmare of the baggage compartment and, after sitting down, I said to myself, 'I'm not going to be afraid of anything now, ever again.' It was a real seminal moment for me.

The difference was that I'd only overcome an imagined danger. For the children of Gorazde, the danger was all too real and they lived in a state of fear almost constantly, either subconsciously or otherwise, while at the same time trying to live life as normally as possible. Sometimes a Gorazde child might try to face down his fear, as I'd done on that train. But, if they did, it often ended badly for them because the true horror of their situation caught up with them. That's what had happened to Adem, the boy on the bike. He'd tried to ride back from school instead of taking the school bus. That small piece of defiance had cost him his life.

Mercifully, the baby that had just been killed had probably been too young to understand true fear. That wasn't much comfort for anyone who heard the story, though, because that baby had been blown to pieces anyway. Older children would soon hear about it and wonder when a random shell might land on them too. Without firm intervention from the UN or NATO, only the Serbs would decide when the torment of Gorazde's children would come to an end. And the Serbs we'd met were not merciful people.

When Mladic did relent somewhat around Gorazde, it wasn't out of the kindness of his heart; rather so that he could create fresh atrocity elsewhere. We were about to find out whether the head of the United Nations in Bosnia, General Bernard Janvier, had achieved the UN's overall objective with his attempts to appease General Ratko Mladic over the previous month. The dreadful answer was almost beyond comprehension.

# CHAPTER SEVEN

# SREBRENICA

**B**lue lips. That's what I most remember about him. He had blue lips because he was almost walking dead. He probably wouldn't have survived many more hours up there. But now he had found us and we had found him. It was 18 July and we'd received news of a worrying development from Gorazde's Mayor, Rijad Rasic. He'd said that 'survivors from Srebrenica' were reported to be on their way.

Before long, I'd heard from the ever-reliable Selma too. She wasn't just my favourite interpreter by then, we'd formed a strong bond. She was my 'interrupter', as we joked, but she was also a friend because, when you're working under the sort of pressures we faced every day, you become close. You're working in an environment where you're drawn together by the horror of it all.

This was to be the day we heard of horror on a new scale.

Close to atrocity: Srebrenica – scene of the worst massacre in Europe since the Second World War – lay little more than 60 miles north-east of Gorazde. Zepa was also the scene of much bloodshed. Only Gorazde was never taken by the Serbs.

She'd said that what the Mayor had foreseen was now happening. 'I'm hearing from the townsfolk that there are people coming in. They're approaching from the north-east, Major Richard, over the hills.'

'Where exactly, Selma?'

'Along the Samari Ridge.'

We drove straight up there. She still hated travelling in the Land Rover. As usual, she suffered from travel sickness and there were no pills available to help her with it. Of course, it didn't diminish her determination to do her job. It never had. We reached the ridge and saw a bearded man, shambling in alone. We drove as far towards him as we could and then got out and walked along the track he was trying to follow. That was the only way to intercept him because he was in a world of his own. As we drew nearer, he seemed to notice the blue beret on my head and recognise it. There may even have been a trace of disdain for it. But he tolerated the approach of the blue beret now. What else was there? What strength did he have left? He was practically on his knees and we were probably the first human beings he'd seen since leaving his home.

The man looked completely finished. There was no visible sense of relief when he saw us; he was almost beyond positive feeling. His route in over the Samari Ridge meant he'd probably come past Zepa. He must have assumed, correctly as it turned out, that Zepa was too close to Srebrenica for comfort and the same would happen there straight afterwards. He'd made the decision to steer clear and walk as far away as he could. Unfortunately, that decision, although the correct one, had also nearly killed him.

This poor man was blundering around, eyes all over the place, in total shock, exhausted by the trek over the hills and the mental stress that goes with picking your way through mines, because there were an awful lot of mines out there. Had he known he was going through potentially mined areas? He probably guessed but what else could he do? His deadpan face was grey and the colour of his lips said more than any words they could shape to describe his condition.

When he could form words, he wasn't concerned about the state he was in though. He talked of others, and the first words he spoke, I'd never forget.

'They're all dead. They've gone. They're dead.'

He must have been walking for days and, even though the Bosnians were hardy people, he barely had the energy to speak. We sat him down and I looked at this man and wondered if he would survive; he seemed to be lost somewhere between life and death. The first thing we did was to get some water down him in small sips. We also gave him a couple of biscuits. He started to shake. That's classic shock. Then he mumbled a few more words.

'I've come from Srebrenica and they're all gone.'

'Who's all gone?' asked Selma, remaining totally objective. She stood there and translated the words coming from this gaunt, bearded man like the little professional she was. But these were her people and what she must have felt as she tried to make sense of this was anyone's guess.

'All the men. Murdered.'

When the words were translated back to me, I could hardly take in what he was saying either. Was this an exaggeration born of delirium? Perhaps the man saw a confusion bordering on disbelief in our eyes.

'They're all dead, I tell you.'

What the fuck had happened? I didn't realise it at the time but I was probably one of the first Westerners to hear a survivor speak of the worst European massacre since the Second World War.

For me, personally, the start of an atrocity that became infamous throughout the world had been marked by a dose of typically crude SAS humour. A week earlier, on 11 July 1995, we'd been on a patrol, partly to see what was left of our Observation Posts. We'd been walking about five hours and we'd just got up on to the high ground above Gorazde again. Wherever they went, the SAS had to have their means for calling in air. If that meant carrying heavy radio equipment up mountains in addition to all their other kit, so be it. Although the SAS boys were super-fit, the Royal Welch had been tabbing up and down Mala Biserna for months too, and we'd been as fit as butchers' dogs before the shelling. We were all a bit rusty after being stuck in bunkers and confined to our camp for so long but one man was bound to feel it more than the others that day – SAS radio man Billy Walters. If you're carrying a radio at 3,000 feet above sea level and that radio weighs a ton, then you're being led up and down these hills after a month of static festering underground, it all takes a bit of getting used to again.

So I'd said gleefully, 'Does anyone want a rest?'

'Fuck off,' came the reply from Billy, one of the most colourful SAS characters. Affectionately known as 'Pig Man',

Billy was an exceptional runner, despite his stocky build. But he was the one carrying the radio and, therefore, somewhat uncharacteristically, he was also the one most feeling the physical demands of the tab. Pig Man realised he'd been rumbled and didn't like it.

'Who do you think you are, the Grand Old Duke of fucking York?' Billy asked.

'Eh?'

'The number of fucking hills you've marched us up and down. Come on then, let's have a brew and a fag.'

We stopped and got the flasks out for a cup of tea. We could carry on working because we could look out at all the surrounding terrain from our position up there.

Pig Man looked at the radio and said, 'I've carried the fucking thing all the way up here. Might as well have a listen.'

What followed was a mixture of good fortune and good drills. Whenever you can, you have the radio on. Billy was due to make a call and say, 'This is where I am.' It just so happened that five or ten minutes later, while we were enjoying a brew and a cigarette, we heard something unusual:

'Bravo Fortune 4-2 Alpha.'

That was the call sign of John Callow, from the SAS platoon over in Srebrenica.

Pig Man was just about to get on the radio and say 'Bravo Fortune 42 Alpha, this is Bravo Fortune 4-2 Delta, how's it going?'

Then John said, 'All stations, this is Bravo Fortune 4-2-Alpha. Any aircraft up for trade?'

Why was John calling for any available air support? 'This sounds interesting,' I thought.

'This is Nasty1-1,' a young woman's voice said in a sexy Dutch accent.

Pig Man turned the sound up and said, 'Listen to this!'

'Nasty 1-1, this is Bravo Fortune 42-Alpha, please turn onto Vector 147.'

John Callow was calling her in to the initiation point, the IP. From what we could gather, he wanted her to take out a T64 – a Serb tank.

Then she said, 'This is Nasty1-1, I'm coming in hot.'

That was too much for Pig Man, who wanted to give me the radio. 'Hold that, boss. I'm going for a wank,' he said.

But there was nothing funny about John Callow's situation on the ground outside Srebrenica. He was in a forward position in a trench, on the outskirts of the town – which was where the Dutch UN boys should have been, in my opinion. They should have had OPs out there in order to delay anything hostile, just as we'd had in Gorazde.

John went off the radio for a few minutes because the very tank that Nasty1-1 was about to plink had fired a high-explosive tank shell straight at his bunker. His mates had to dig him out. He was completely covered in earth, apparently. He was also deaf and in a hell of a state for a minute or two. But he was SAS so he recovered more quickly than any ordinary person would, then he got back on the radio and started calling for more air. We knew there must be some sort of concerted attack going on because he was calling in fast air and we were listening to it on the TACSAT.

SAS HQ came on and managed to speak to him. They asked who was involved in the contact with the Serbs. John said, 'It's just us.' That meant the Joint Commissioned Officers (SAS),

John's immediate group, not Dutch UNPROFOR on the ground. Nobody else seemed to be taking part in the battle, even though John confirmed, 'I'm on a hillside calling in air because the enclave is being attacked.'

We stayed there and listened to the whole contact, at least when I wasn't getting on the net back to Riley to give him an early heads up. I told Colonel Jon, 'Look, you should be aware there's something happening in Srebrenica. The TAC-P (Tactical Air Control Party, in this case the SAS) are requesting all and immediate air over to Srebrenica. We heard them trying to bring in Dutch fighter planes to halt a Serb attack on the enclave. Picked it all up on the JCOs' radio and one of their guys is right there.'

John didn't give us any indication of what was happening in the town, only on the outskirts, and, eventually, he had to get out to avoid being taken hostage. The SAS were extracted by helicopter later and John won a Military Cross. Of course, just because we'd heard a contact unfolding didn't mean there were lots of people being massacred. We knew there'd been a significant skirmish, we knew the Dutch peacekeepers weren't doing much about it, with the brave exception of Nasty1-1, but we didn't know whether the Dutch were going to be able to negotiate for the safety of the Muslims there, or what the UN and NATO intended to do about it. From where I was, we could only report what we'd heard up the chain of command and try to get air cover over Srebrenica to take a further look. It was down to our superiors in Sarajevo to organise the appropriate response as quickly as possible.

Some serious alarm bells should already have been ringing among those privy to the bigger picture regarding Srebrenica though. On 8 July the Serbs had taken over a UN observation post. On 9 July thirty Dutch-Bat soldiers had been taken hostage. On 10 July, at 6.30pm, Ratko Mladic had arrived on the hillside outside Srebrenica. We'd heard reports from the Dutch on the satellite communications system, almost suggesting that resistance to the Serbs was futile because 'their Commander himself, General Mladic is here.' Would he dare to commit an atrocity right under the noses of the UN?

I'd already formed an opinion of Mladic, without ever meeting him. Here was a man who'd commanded an army with some success over the previous couple of years but he'd stop at nothing to achieve his aims. You followed the accounts of his various battles and their aftermath and a picture emerged of utter ruthlessness along former Soviet lines. 'We've just got to win this and we don't care how.' That was his attitude. The whole idea of minimising civilian casualties by isolating your military enemy from the civil population was an irrelevance to him. 'Just shell the place.' That was his way of doing it. So, although you could see that professionally he'd achieved plenty, the civilian casualties were appalling. Both sides in this war pursued a policy of ethnic cleansing, of course; it wasn't just Mladic. But I'd seen for myself the sort of casual killing Mladic inspired and it turned my stomach. How could you respect a man like that? But the more pressing question for the Dutch was this: how could you stop him?

Realising, belatedly, that a clear threat to the enclave did exist, the Dutch UN Commander, Colonel Thom Karremans, requested air support on that same evening of 10 July. At 9.40pm, his UN superior, General Janvier, agreed to that air support in principle. But then ridiculous red tape made a desperate situation even worse. On 11 July Colonel Karremans was told his request for air support had been submitted on the wrong form and that he must submit it on the correct form. Infuriated, he had no choice but to comply. Once that was done, Nasty1-1 was clear to 'come in hot' – and we'd heard the results on the radio. Officially, it was reported that, on 11 July, at 2.40pm, two Dutch F16 fighters dropped two bombs on Serb positions. One of those was Nasty1-1.

That same evening, at 11.30pm, Karremans met Mladic for crisis talks. Mladic warned the UN officer that it was unwise to attempt air strikes on Serb positions while he had total power over the peacekeepers he had captured. And it wasn't just the hostages who were in danger. Mladic issued a thinly veiled threat to all UN forces in Bosnia by saying, 'The future of your people is in your hands, and not just in this area.'

By then, the local Muslim men could have been in little doubt that their lives were severely threatened. Around fifteen thousand of them left the enclave immediately and embarked on a perilous journey towards the nearest Muslim territory at Tuzla. However, many thousands more remained. On 12 July Mladic walked through the enclave at Srebrenica, handing out treats and assuring refugees that all would be well: 'Don't be afraid,' he said, like some merciful conqueror. 'No matter whether you're old or young, you'll get transport. Women and children first.'

Mladic had moved some buses into Srebrenica and was separating the men from the women by playing the role of a chivalrous gentleman. The women must have had a good idea of what was going to happen, though, because they were crying. At best, they must have thought their husbands and elder sons were destined for the Omaska concentration camp – the one eventually exposed to the world by infamous television images of starving, emaciated men peering through barbed wire. At worst, however, the male population of Srebrenica was going to be executed. The Serbs didn't bother with the concentration camp on this occasion. The massacre unfolded in all its horror over the next ten days. The murders began immediately.

For me, the immediate impact of the first days of the massacre arrived in the shape of this solitary, shambling man, who stumbled around up on the hills before telling Selma and me, 'They're all dead. They've all gone.' We wrapped him in a blanket, took him down into the town and got some sweet tea into him in the UN Military Observers building. We thought he'd feel a bit more secure there and, if he felt it was safe, he'd start talking.

'What is your name?'

'Ahmad Pleh.'

'Address?' He gave us an address in Srebrenica.

'How did you get here?'

'I walked.'

'But how did you survive?'

'I hid. I hid under a car. And then, when I had a chance, I ran into the bushes and hid again for about five or six hours, and then, when it got dark, I started to move. I had to walk through areas I knew were mined. I did it in the dark.'

'Weren't you scared?'

'Yes, I was terrified. But I had to keep walking. And I got through. I kept moving. Finally, I saw something which told me I was close to Gorazde. Then you found me.'

'You walked all this way?'

'I am a farmer.'

That explained it a little. He'd always been a tough, outdoors type. Yet even he had been reduced to almost nothing. He'd also been lucky with the time of year if, indeed, the word lucky could be fairly applied to him at all. Ahmad probably wouldn't have made it through at any other time of year; the combination of a harsh Bosnian winter, for example, and having to walk at altitude would have finished him. As it was, he would need urgent medical assistance following this, the briefest of interviews.

All sorts of thoughts were flashing through my mind. 'If what he says is true, this has changed the game, in my mind. We've found out something important here. But we can't question him any further, not now. We've got to get him some UNHCR medical help as soon as possible.'

UNHCR were the lead UN agency for this sort of situation, so it was time to hand him over. The UNHCR facility was closer to the hospital than our medical facility. We couldn't detain him for any longer than it took us to establish his identity and address anyway. So pretty soon Selma and I were left to reflect on what we'd heard. Could it be true, what Mr Pleh was saying? We had to be careful. This was one individual, claiming to have come from Srebrenica, but we didn't have the full picture. We had a single source and we had to try to verify his account. You couldn't take everything at face value; even so, Mr Ahmad Pleh seemed credible. And, although we still weren't sure what was unfolding in Srebrenica, we'd already come to the early conclusion that something sinister had happened.

## SREBRENICA

I reported Mr Pleh's account to our Military Information (Intelligence) people immediately and I'm confident his claims went all the way up the chain of command to UNHQ in Sarajevo. From where we were, there wasn't much more we could do. The UN in Sarajevo had the wider picture of events in Srebrenica and they commanded both Srebrenica and Zepa directly. They had the authority to get airborne reconnaissance and satellite imagery over the relevant areas. We did not. They had radio-intercept capability, to listen in on the Serbs. We did not. They had direct communications with the Dutch and Ukrainian peacekeepers in Srebrenica. We did not. For all these reasons, they had a far greater chance of verifying the story than we did. They also had access to the Bosnian Serb High Command and Diplomatic staff, so that the alleged perpetrators could be confronted and an explanation demanded. Protests or ultimatums could then be made to the Serbs at the highest level. And, if immediate military action was to be authorised to stop these massacres from continuing, it had to go through Sarajevo.

Swift action by the UN was required, yet it wasn't to be forthcoming. The horrible fact of the matter is that, when Ahmad told us his story and said, 'They're all dead,' it wasn't true, strictly speaking. For Mr Pleh, it was true, for it was clear enough to him that all the men he'd been with were dead. If he hadn't seen them die with his own eyes, which was entirely possible, he must have heard the gunfire from their execution nearby. So he had reason to give us the impression that the atrocity was over. Tragically, however, the ten-day massacre hadn't run its full, bloody course at that stage. The murders were set to continue for another four days, until 22 July.

I couldn't have known this from where I was. Up to that point, an hour or two after this Srebrenica farmer had come over the hill, Selma and I had heard only this single, sketchy account of an alleged atrocity – and poor Pleh had been almost delirious as he had spoken his ominous words. We believed him though. And because we believed him, there was much to take in, particularly for poor Selma on a purely emotional level. That poor young woman. It was shocking enough for me to hear the account; what must it have been like for her, when the slaughtered were practically her neighbours? She had been so professional and focused all day and that was typical Selma: she was a tough cookie. But this horrific news from Srebrenica was too much, even for her. She went home in silence. That night, she told me later, she cried her eyes out. The next day, Selma was back in touch with me and business-like once more.

'Others have come in,' she revealed.

Selma had spoken to more survivors, who had circled round and come in from the other end of town. She'd since been walking near the town centre and seen them, so she'd taken the opportunity to ask where they'd come from. They'd said, 'We've come from Srebrenica.'

'What else did they say?' I asked her.

'It's what the farmer told us the other day, but maybe worse. The men... and the older boys... they have all been killed.'

Boys too? Other accounts reached us, sent on by the Muslim authorities in the town. And then the United Nations High Commission for Refugees told us that even more displaced people were coming in from the southern end of Gorazde, so we sent another vehicle down there, with

Allan Finn, the Military Information Officer. They picked up one man and one woman, who gave a fresh account of how the Serbs had taken all the men and bigger boys away... and they feared the worst.

The words of Captain Kepic invaded my mind once more. 'How old was this "child"? Ten? In six years' time he would have been carrying a Kalashnikov and I wouldn't have expected any mercy from him.' Children weren't children if there was a foreseeable time when they would no longer be children. That was how the Bosnian Serbs viewed Muslim children. If you'd reached your teenage years at Srebrenica, you were in trouble. At fifteen or sixteen, you'd probably be treated like a man and suffer the same fate as an adult too.

I've asked myself what else I could have done, as one of the first Western Europeans to hear about Srebrenica, knowing what we know now. But even that question comes with the benefit of hindsight. We were fixed in Gorazde and we just didn't believe we could influence Srebrenica because it was for Sarajevo to deal with. We could only report what we believed had happened. If you were going to contemplate leaking something to the media, in order try to exert extra pressure for swift UN or NATO action, you had to be sure of your facts. We were not sure of the scale of the atrocity, and the evidence was, so far, anecdotal. Besides, we'd had a moratorium placed upon us with regard to speaking to the media. The UN and our own Ministry of Defence were constantly concerned that information might be leaked to the media while uncorroborated. That could provoke NATO or the US into action that was not impartial. In this case, of course, it would have been exactly the right way to go and perhaps the Americans had been right all along to want to show less patience than many of the other major players. But, as far as we were concerned at the time, just smashing everything up wasn't the answer either because you had to consider how this mess might be resolved eventually for a lasting peace. You had to be armed with total certainty about the scale of this atrocity before you reacted. We weren't.

That didn't stop us trying to find out what the ground truth was, both locally and regionally. But, until the full picture emerged, we were very nervous about anyone having a knee-jerk reaction to the Srebrenica stories. Was there really only one set of bad guys – the Bosnian Serbs, as seemed to be the case, broadly speaking – around Gorazde at the time? We didn't have a clear enough picture of the other enclaves and whether anything had prompted the Serb aggression there. Remember, the Serbs, Croatians and Muslims had all been guilty of atrocities in the wider war in Bosnia. Was it right for the Western world to come down hard one side only, or should we try to remain objective, whatever our gut feeling was telling us once more? Locally, around Gorazde, we hadn't entirely given up hope of resuming an impartial peacekeeping role, strange as that might sound. So we tried to adopt a measured approach to what we heard by word of mouth from the Srebrenica survivors, for the moment at least.

By the time we found out for sure what had happened in the other enclaves, it was too late. And it is easy to forget that the scale of the massacre was unprecedented since the Second World War. Sure, we were all too familiar with the dreadful threat of mass-slaughter; for months we had feared a massacre in Gorazde and fought to prevent one. But did we really believe that thousands upon thousands of people would be murdered in any ethnic cleansing operation locally? Or did we assume somewhere deep down that the murder of hundreds would be sufficient to create the panic that would see an area like Gorazde 'cleansed' to Serb satisfaction? It is difficult to speak of subconscious calculations and conclusions, to talk of the numbers of lives we thought would be lost if we failed. We had realised that many innocent people would die if we didn't try to save Gorazde; that thought in itself had been enough to persuade us to put our lives on the line. But did that really help us to get our heads around events in Srebrenica, as explained to us by the refugees who had escaped, in terms of the sheer scale of the alleged executions there? I'm not convinced it did. So all we felt we could do at the time of Srebrenica was to pass the information we were receiving up our chain of command for assessment by those with a wider perspective. What else could we reasonably have been expected to do?

As soon as we'd passed on what we'd heard to our Military Information people (we couldn't use the word 'Intelligence' while we were UN peacekeepers), they started trying to work out what the population of Srebrenica was. That in itself was difficult because the creation of these enclaves had prompted such a population shift. UNHCR figures were available but might not be accurate. We knew little of the true population, and the problem with multi-national operations is that units from different countries seldom pass information sideways. Dutch Bat and UKRcoy (the Ukrainians) reported up to UNHQ along national lines and probably came up with estimates of their own. We Brits thought there might be a minimum of five thousand males trapped in Gorazde and a maximum of ten, so we were there or thereabouts. We were trying to get some satellite imagery sent across from Sarajevo. Could the UN get some new air imagery from the Srebrenica area?

The situation was still very confused. There was by now, however, a clear message coming from those who were arriving in Gorazde and had gone directly to the Canton and Municipal Affairs people. There was a real commonality coming out – and it was all bad. We Brits continued to report our findings up to the UN and asked again, 'Look, could you try and get some satellite imagery?' Over the next few days some fresh imagery did emerge, showing large areas of disturbed earth. That was never going to be a good thing. Unfortunately, with our conservative Western view, the thought that thousands of people had been taken away and just killed, right under the noses of the UN, was still too much to take in. It sounds terrible but there were massacres, in the way we understood the word... and then there was Srebrenica. And, while our gut feeling was that Mladic had done something very bad, we didn't think he'd done it on such a scale. Who would really have thought the Serbs were going to carry out a massacre of 8,300 people with the UN close by? Though thousands had died in massacres much earlier in the war and before Western intervention, this figure of 8,300 surpassed anything seen so far.

How had the Dutch allowed Mladic to trap his victims, without offering more than fleeting moments of token resistance? Why couldn't they have stood up to the Bosnian Serb Army like we did? Surely they could have done more? I should emphasise that I wasn't at Srebrenica and it is very difficult to imagine what the situation must have been like.

But it was clear that the Dutch had based themselves in the town of Srebrenica and had very little depth to their positions. You've got the town and then the hills around it. At Gorazde we'd produced an 'air-gap' by putting observation posts around the town, like a ring of steel. By having those eyes and ears, we'd bought ourselves and the town some precious time when we came under severe threat.

It seemed to me that the Dutch didn't have enough positions out of town so, by the time things started happening, it was almost too late. Also, they'd approached this tour in a different way to us from the very beginning. We'd trained for war fighting (though originally we'd planned to step back from that if we could). We'd trained for the worst case, which always underpinned the philosophy of the British army. We'd trained in Canada and the UK under live fire in high-intensity operations. We believed firmly in General Rose's philosophy that to be a good peacekeeper you've first got to be a good war-fighter. While we knew we couldn't expect an easy tour, the complacent Dutch foresaw classic peacekeeping and prepared accordingly, training less intensively in the Netherlands. It's fine to settle for being a peacekeeper when there's peace to keep. But in a country like Bosnia, peace is a relative concept. And you can have peace in one area while there's fighting in another. The reality of peacekeeping is not always as tidy as the Dutch had probably hoped for.

We learned very quickly that consent from either side in this war could and would be withdrawn at little or no notice. So you had to be ready to step up and flick the switch and go hard on war fighting and then step back down. I don't think the Dutch had that mindset. I think they believed in the

UN mandate and they believed it was sacrosanct. But in the Bosnian War both sides operated with extraordinary levels of guile, cunning and deceit. We were from the naive West and we were susceptible to falling for those tactics if we weren't careful. The Dutch, in particular, seemed gullible and they were caught out. Thom Karremans has a lot to live with for the rest of his life and he must be in a horrible place during his darker moments. The poor Dutch carry Srebrenica as a national burden – and I know it hurts.

What did the emerging picture from Srebrenica mean for us? I thought, 'Thank God we held on in Gorazde.' I thought of the townspeople we knew and what might have happened to them, particularly now there really did seem to be no limit to the war crimes the Serbs were capable of perpetrating when they got hold of any Muslim enclave. If we'd had any doubts at all, Srebrenica confirmed to us that we'd done the right thing in Gorazde, even though it had taken us out of our role as peacekeepers and we'd killed a lot of people. Srebrenica gave us added justification for having defended our OPs with force because you can never lightly take a human life. I reflected back to B Company's battle on Mala Biserna and concluded that we hadn't done badly. We'd held for a few precious hours and Gorazde hadn't fallen. We were still here and so were most of the town's population.

A disturbing thought also sprang to mind though. Would the Serbs take heart from what they'd been allowed to do in Srebrenica and come again for Gorazde? I wasn't really sure that we'd get out of Gorazde at all if that happened. Would the Serbs use overwhelming force this time, take us all hostage and then use us as human shields to stop NATO air from blasting their 'Ethnic Cleansing Brigades' as they carried out a Srebrenica-style massacre in Gorazde? I didn't like to think too much about how Srebrenica might impact on us before the summer was over. One thing was for sure: we were going nowhere for the moment.

But what else could we achieve while we stayed? In purely practical terms, as British soldiers, the fact that the Serbs had switched their focus to Srebrenica in July had given us a chance to recapture our physical fitness, after weeks dodging shells in cramped conditions. That was important to all of us because fitness could yet be the key to our own survival. And naturally, the SAS men wanted to show they were fitter than the rest. Their Team Commander, Wez Harris, began to take his men to an athletics track just outside our camp. Sometimes you'd see local civilians, even blokes in suits and shoes, going for a run there too – it was quite bizarre. They tended to steer clear while Wez and his men did long-distance work on the 400-metre track though. And Harris soon set an impressive long-distance record of seventy two laps of the track in the heat.

A couple of days later, Wez and I were sitting in the canteen together. Although the shelling had stopped, we still ate in separate sittings of little groups, never all at the same time, in case the bombardment started up again without warning. One direct hit on the canteen could have wiped out everyone, so it made sense to stagger the sittings. And, even though we were slowly starving, it was hard to feel impatient to sample the slop on offer. By now we'd become used to a ghastly concoction called 'Drina Mash.' This was powdered potato mixed with water from the River Drina, which had been chlorinated.

It tasted disgusting but it was our only regular meal, so we scoffed it anyway. (If only Selma had been able to cook pizza every night!)

While we were eating our Drina Mash, Shady Kent walked in, freshly showered. 'All right, lads?'

Wez was in a friendly mood, so he asked, 'What've you been doing?'

'Just did eighty laps on the athletics track,' Shady replied.

'You what?' Wez suddenly didn't look so friendly and he quickly put his knife and fork down. 'I'm off to do ninety,' he announced. With that, he left. Wez had been right in the middle of his meal but, for him, that meal was now over. He had a more serious matter to deal with. As far as he was concerned, the honour of the Regiment was at stake.

I was with Ronnie Collins, his Second-in-Command, when Harris joined us a few hours later.

'All right?' said Ronnie. 'How many did you do?'

'I stopped at eighty-six,' said Wez.

'Eh? Thought you said you were going to do ninety?'

'Got bored,' admitted Wez.

Ronnie might have been just below Wez in the SAS pecking order but that counted for nothing now.

'Don't come back with that,' said Ronnie. 'I don't want to talk to you – fucking loser.'

Collins delivered his verdict as though he really meant it. It was typical SAS banter. Harris had failed to achieve his stated objective, so he was in disgrace. It was all a joke, of course, and Harris didn't take it to heart, not least because he was usually the first to indulge in such banter. Even so, this was just the sort of exchange that kept SAS men on their toes, determined to maintain the extraordinary standards that usually set them apart from normal men.

That same level of professionalism helped the SAS to make contact with planes high in the skies above Gorazde later that week. I saw Wez, Ronnie, Billy and the boys sitting on the stadium steps, looking skywards in the bright sunshine, talking into their radio. Someone even took a photograph of them doing so (included here, though with the faces of the men blacked out to protect their identity). I followed their gaze and saw a small speck in the ionosphere. We could only ever see one plane at a time but that was enough to lift our spirits. The SAS were simply checking that their communications still worked, ensuring that their capacity for talking to planes remained as strong and as effective as ever. But it was still good to see because you never knew when that SAS talent for guiding in air might prove vital for all us who were stuck in this place. And this still represented a significant show of strength, presumably organised by General Rupert Smith over in Sarajevo; a pre-arranged NATO exercise that would send both sides in this chaotic war a clear message: with potential air cover, we besieged Gorazde-Brits were still in the game, whatever pounding we had taken.

It was a positive scene, yet it couldn't fail to remind me of all the times the Royal Welch Fusiliers had asked for close air support to get us out of trouble, and how those pleas had fallen on deaf ears. Those 'Blue Sword' requests had gone to the UN, not NATO, and there was no reason to believe that the UN would suddenly become more helpful to us now. But in an emergency I sensed that NATO would come good; the climate was changing. And, even without air support from the UN, the very organisation we were trying to represent, we Royal Welch Fusiliers were still determined to salvage anything we could of our mission. We weren't yet ready to abandon our responsibilities in Gorazde. Was the situation around the town becoming stable enough for us to reinstate a tenuous truce and then start to keep the peace? We didn't know. Consent for our operations was always a relative concept. But it was just possible that we might be able to do some more good in Gorazde. And, despite the obvious danger, the mission still came first.

If I'd prioritised the safety of my men over the mission, B Company would have turned tail on 28 May without fighting. We'd made an important stand instead. And the more we heard about what had happened in Srebrenica, just sixty miles up the road, the more we felt we'd helped to save thousands of lives in Gorazde. As the weeks went by, Srebrenica gave up more and more of its secrets, every bit as grim as Ahmad the farmer had first warned me they'd be. Mladic had completed his work there with ruthless efficiency. In time the massacre was to be given the worst label of all: 'genocide'.

Would Mladic now feel confident enough to send his forces back to Gorazde, where he had so far been frustrated, and commit more genocide? It seemed to be the next logical step for a man with such a warped mind. And we weren't the only ones to feel concerned that atrocities on a similar scale could still happen in Gorazde. On 21 July John Major issued the following warning to an International Meeting on Bosnia, held in London: 'There is a clear risk that Gorazde and Sarajevo will be the next targets of Serb aggression.' He also stated a clear objective for the meeting he was hosting: 'We must find a way of deterring further brutal aggression and, in particular, the imminent threat to Gorazde.'

Major added,

UNPROFOR cannot stay if its personnel are to be attacked, captured, threatened and humiliated. It cannot stay simply to be abused as a shelter behind which the armies attack each other. It cannot stay if its movements are impeded. It cannot operate if the parties do not provide the necessary level of consent and cooperation.

So, if we wanted to stay, as I do, we must seek to agree realistic objectives. Then we must provide the means to achieve them... Today we must spell out in unmistakable terms the consequences of further attacks – against UNPROFOR and against areas designated by the United Nations. And we must mean what we say and be determined to carry it out. In particular, we must face up to the threats to Gorazde and to supply routes. Bosnian Serb leaders have threatened Gorazde directly. I believe we should decide today that they would pay a very high price if they tried to carry out those threats. Our response to an attack on Gorazde should be very severe. United Nations Resolutions already provide for action. Air power is available. We need to decide how it could best be used to support our objectives.

Given what we had already done for the Muslims, and the strong likelihood that Major's very public words of warning to their enemy, the Bosnian Serbs, were picked up by BiH Intelligence, it seems strange that elements among Gorazde's

## OPERATION INSANITY

Muslim forces were getting ready to turn on us. But then again, we had learned very early on to be ready for anything in Gorazde – especially the unexpected.

# CHAPTER EIGHT

# THE RANSOM

**H**ow did I come to be carrying millions in cash in my bergen, creeping out of Gorazde in the middle of the night, ready to pay a ransom to save sexual abusers of children and drug-pushers from a fate they probably deserved? Such was the madness of life in the 'Safe Area', where morality had been turned on its head to allow the worst of humanity to thrive.

The sexual abuse of children is horrific, wherever you are, whoever you are. But when the perpetrators were operating in Gorazde, where the kids were already living in fear of their lives, you just wondered how much lower the human race could sink. And when the organisers of this sexual abuse were United Nations soldiers from Ukraine, wearing uniforms that should have represented decency, stability and trust in all the chaos, it just made the sense of betrayal complete. The Ukrainians destroyed the credibility of anyone wearing a blue beret – including us. They were the worst-led troops imaginable, discipline among the ranks had broken down entirely and all they thought about was making money out of the misery to which they were contributing. No wonder the goodwill of the local community rapidly evaporated.

Among so many other vices, greed was at work within the Ukrainian contingent – and it was partly the fault of the UN. The British soldiers received a dollar a day; the rest went to the government. So, in essence, we were on the same pay we got back home. But a Ukrainian soldier received a massive $150 dollars a day. And, if you left him for six months in a place where he had no real chance of spending that money, his savings quickly became astronomical. With that sort of money to go home with at the end of his tour of Bosnia, a soldier could afford to leave the army, buy a car, even build his own house in Ukraine, where life cost next to nothing. He could happily retire on what he earned in a matter of months in Bosnia! Ukrainian soldiers certainly weren't going to risk their lives for the local population by fighting the Serbs; not when all their financial dreams were about to come true if only they stayed in one piece. Protect the kids at the school in Vitkovice, right next to their base, from a fate like Adem's? No chance. When the UN was already halfway to making you a millionaire back in your own country, were you going to put yourself in harm's way and risk taking a sniper's bullet for a Muslim kid? Of course not. With the opportunity of a lifetime to be exploited to the full, it was much easier to explore ways to make even more money on the black market. The UN mandate meant nothing to them. The UN uniform was useful though – as a means to an end.

When British UN soldiers befriended children in their early

teens, it was because they felt sorry for them and wanted to improve their life somehow. When Ukrainian UN soldiers befriended children in their early teens, there was a chance they might want to groom them and sell them for sex. And child prostitution wasn't the only black market money-spinner the Ukrainians went in for, though it was certainly the ugliest and worst. More money was to be made from the sale of drugs. If there was morphine coming in on UN trucks, why give it all to the hospital for free? Why worry about the sick and wounded when you could sell morphine and other drugs to addicts among the civilian population instead? Many Bosnians had money and were willing to pay silly prices. It wasn't money that was in short supply; it was something to spend their cash on. So the Ukrainian soldiers, hardly believing their luck and losing all sense of right and wrong, boosted their retirement funds in the worst ways imaginable.

They thought they could do what they wanted around Gorazde and that included neglecting to pay their rent on the large factory complex that formed part of their base in Vitkovice. Naturally enough, the local community leaders demanded that the Ukrainians pay up. Equally naturally, since they were a law unto themselves, the Ukrainians refused. They were the UN, they were doing the locals a favour just by being there, or so they thought. The Ukrainians thought they could get away with paying no rent. They thought they could get away with selling local youngsters for sex. They thought they could get away with depriving the wounded of morphine and lining their own pockets instead. Perhaps they saw the Bosnian Muslims as a subspecies, just as the Serbs did. They assumed there would be no backlash. They were wrong.

# OPERATION INSANITY

The flashpoint in the Gorazde 'Safe Area' came during the Srebrenica massacre sixty miles away, ironically enough. Between that first SAS radio warning of an attack on Srebrenica on 11 July and the appearance of the Muslim farmer with blue lips in our vicinity on 18 July, I'd certainly had my hands full dealing with anti-UNPROFOR feeling. The Ukrainians' situation had begun to deteriorate on the night of 13 July. Five BiH soldiers, led by a Commander 'Osmir', arrived at the Ukrainian camp and ordered them to hand over their helmets, body armour, weapons and vehicles for their own security.

Colonel Batalin, the Ukrainian UN Commander who had told us we were all going to die at the hands of the Serbs, refused to comply with the 'illegal' demands of the BiH. Osmir threatened to blockade the Ukrainian camp until he got what he wanted. The British were alerted and started negotiating with the local BiH authorities. This resulted in the BiH soldiers leaving the Ukrainian camp at 4am on 14 July ... for all of an hour. A Colonel 'Admir', claiming to be Colonel Bhato's number two, soon arrived with a well-armed force and started setting up rocket-propelled grenade-launchers (RPG 7s) all around the perimeter of the camp, while BiH snipers positioned themselves on the factory roof. By midday there were eighty or ninety BiH soldiers surrounding the Ukrainian camp and ready for action.

Our Operations Officer came on the radio to tell us what was happening over in Vitkovice. Riley wasn't in Gorazde; he was off somewhere making provisional plans for our extraction. Senior Major Stephen Hughes, Riley's second-in-command, called me in for a briefing. The dramatic developments in Vitkovice had come as no huge surprise to us, because we knew how the BiH held the Ukrainians in utter disdain. The question was: what should we do about it? We discussed the possibility of launching a strike operation against the BiH if the Ukrainians came under serious attack and sustained casualties. Hughes agreed it was an option but, for now, he wanted to keep our powder dry and see what happened next. Even so, I took the Senior Major's willingness to keep the strike option on the table as a Warning Order. Therefore, I told two of my platoons to get their vehicles 'bombed up' and made sure we'd be ready to go.

Meanwhile, five BiH soldiers broke into the Ukrainian camp early that evening and tried to take away their armoured personnel carriers (APCs). Although they were confronted and removed from the compound, the danger clearly hadn't passed. Batalin had alerted the Ukraine's UN commanders in Sarajevo, who told him to immobilise his vehicles and remove the machine guns in case a fresh attack resulted in their capture. The BiH moved in again at 8.30pm and set about towing some of the Ukrainian vehicles out of the front gate of their base.

Just after midnight, the BiH attacked in numbers. It was later claimed that Ukrainian officers on the top floor of their building returned fire, though this sounds to me like an attempt to create a face-saving version of events because I certainly didn't hear of any significant Ukrainian resistance at the time. The BiH landed a light mortar round in the Ukrainian Mess Hall, which they probably knew to be deserted. The shooting went on for ten or fifteen minutes, with RPGs flying over the building, probably deliberately aimed high as a further BiH warning to the Ukrainians. The local forces soon ceased fire to find out whether the Ukrainians had changed their minds about handing over their weapons. They had, not least because they were ordered to do so by their Sarajevo masters in order to avoid casualties. By sunrise on 15 July the BiH had what they wanted. We were soon told there had been some sort of removal of equipment in the Ukrainian camp but we had no idea how extensive this operation had been. The BiH had blockaded a checkpoint outside our base, presumably to prevent us rushing to the Ukrainians' rescue. If necessary, I was prepared to drive straight through it; even fight our way through it if we had to do so.

That night the BiH were back at the Ukrainian camp to remove anything they had left behind. Colonel Batalin was told he had precisely two minutes to comply. When he protested, he was dragged over the perimeter fence by six armed BiH soldiers and given a good pistol-whipping. He was warned in no uncertain terms that he would be shot if he didn't comply with every BiH demand. Powerless to prevent the inevitable, Batalin watched as his camp was stripped of anything useful. The Ukrainian soldiers were stripped too – right down to their underpants. They were relieved of their body armour, their uniforms and their personal stashes of money, which amounted to a tidy sum in most cases. It was total humiliation. Batalin felt so powerless that he shaved his head in shame. The Ukrainians were now near-naked hostages in their own camp. And given what many of the Ukrainian soldiers had been up to, it was easy to conclude that justice had been served.

However, it wasn't as simple as that for us. The Ukrainians were UN soldiers; part of UNPROFOR just as we were. We couldn't just stand back and watch them suffer indefinitely, even though they had done so much to ruin what we were trying to achieve. We were all part of the UN forces in Gorazde and it didn't reflect well on us that a UN camp had been overrun in this way. If the BiH thought they could shove the Ukrainians around, how long would it be before they tried the same kind of raid on our camp? We had to restore order; we had to show that UNPROFOR was not prepared to be treated in this way. That's why, despite my personal feelings about the conduct of disgusting elements within the Ukrainian force, I urged Senior Major Hughes to let me take B Company into action to free our trapped 'colleagues' in Vitkovice. He asked me if I was sure I wanted to do this and whether I recognised the risks involved. I assured him that I understood exactly how this might unfold.

I had two platoons and a small reserve with my Tac HQ. That meant about fifty of us in total were ready to go into battle. I had every intention of trying to over-face the Muslim forces with my vehicles; fire warning shots and demand the release of all UN personnel and property. But I knew that, if that didn't work, we'd have to assault the camp. We would have to strike quickly and use only enough force to get the Ukrainians out of their camp and across to ours. But the BiH blockade of the checkpoint near our camp had been lifted and we sensed they might have let their guard drop for a while. If we could get into Vitkovice swiftly and move the Ukrainians out with equal speed, casualties might be limited. The BiH would know that we were not seeking an all-out battle against them; they would realise we were simply trying to look after 'our own', however unpalatable the association was. The BiH had no reason to hate us in the same way they hated the

Ukrainians – quite the reverse. We had helped them to save their town only weeks earlier. Perhaps they would fall short of trying to hit us as hard as they could, even if they attempted to prevent our rescue operation. Whatever the strength of the BiH response, I felt we could avoid annihilation, even though there would, almost inevitably, be a price to pay.

If we had to clear all those buildings around the Ukrainian camp in Vitkovice, I anticipated 10–20 per cent casualties. In human terms, I estimated that five or ten of my guys would either be badly wounded or killed before we achieved our objective. Still, I felt it was something that had to be done, otherwise UN credibility around Gorazde would be destroyed once and for all. As far as I was concerned, the same principle was now at work as had dictated our actions against the Serbs in spring and early summer. I still hated bullies and, unfortunately, the BiH were now the ones acting like the bullies. Whatever terrible things the Ukrainians had done, our own authority was now being undermined and challenged directly by the heavy-handed behaviour of the BiH. So I prepared my men for a mission that would put their lives at risk. Did I do so with concerns? Certainly. Was I aware of the risks and probable repercussions? Absolutely.

There was every chance we would now have to go and kill some of the very people we had fought alongside up on the mountain. My friendship with Salko Osmanspahic would be destroyed, and what of Selma? Would she ever work with me again? The very people we had come to protect and save would soon regard us as their sworn enemies. It was ridiculous, but the BiH had taken now effectively hostages and that was no better than what the Serbs had done to our own soldiers in the aftermath of 28 May. This time there was a difference though; this time we had a chance of releasing those hostages by force.

Privately, I cursed the Ukrainians for all their illegal activities, for their complete lack of morality, for putting the reputation of the UN in the gutter. But the British were not going to stand back and let anyone be pushed around for long. It just wasn't in our nature. It certainly wasn't in mine. So we went through the plan several times.

Glyn's platoon would form the assault force. Sergeant Mutlow's platoon would get into a fire support position, ready to suppress any BiH positions that might try to repel us. I hoped we would present a sufficiently formidable force to bring them out to negotiate. If not, I'd give the order to commence the attack. Perhaps the destruction of one BiH position would show our intent and give them the opportunity to withdraw or surrender. Otherwise we'd use as much firepower as necessary to achieve our objective: seize the Ukrainians and move back to an Emergency RV; bring forward extraction vehicles, load them up and head for our camp in Gorazde.

All we could do now was to wait for the green light. The BiH were going to get a hell of a shock. They thought they had shown they were top dogs around Gorazde now; they thought they had put us quietly back in our place. But they didn't understand our brand of peacekeeping. It involved us showing our teeth every time our authority was challenged, making it clear to both sides that we could be the baddest boys on the block if they messed with us. Otherwise there was no respect. And if there was no respect for the peacekeeper, the peacekeeper was nothing. He would be ignored, as had happened to the Dutch that very week in Srebrenica; or else abused, as the Ukrainians had been that same week just outside Gorazde.

My men were ready. You could see it in their eyes. They had taken a pounding from the Serbs all June, they had taken disrespect from the BiH ever since they had emerged from the bunkers; now they were ready to do something. I was in my vehicle; all the crews were ready to go. Senior Major Stephen Hughes radioed Sarajevo to get the final okay – only natural with Riley absent. We were like coiled springs inside our own compound. I soon saw Hughes marching towards my vehicle and waited for the thumbs up. There was none. Sarajevo had told the Senior Major we couldn't go – at least not with the use of force in mind. The UN top brass had negotiated an agreement with the BiH, whereby we were going to be allowed to guard the Ukrainians against further humiliation or revenge attacks. We would also be able to feed and water them to keep them alive. Oh, and we were going to give them some clothes too, so they didn't have to walk about in their underpants anymore. But they would still be under overall BiH control; they were still essentially BiH captives – they were still going nowhere.

I couldn't believe it. So now we were effectively going to act as guards for the hostage-takers in Vitkovice, the only consolation being that no renegade elements would be able to take the lives of those hostages. It wasn't what I'd had in mind and I felt frustrated, to say the least. Along with that strong sense of frustration, however, I quickly felt something else: relief. Relief that it appeared we were not going to have to kill some of the people we had come to save, relief that friendships made in extreme hardship would no longer have to be destroyed, relief that some of my own men would no longer die trying to free poor excuses for men who had been involved in child prostitution and narcotics. But I also knew that the compromise negotiated in Sarajevo was only a temporary solution. Sooner rather than later, some kind of agreement would have to be struck for the extraction of the Ukrainians from their 'house arrest' and their removal from the scene of their crimes. Otherwise a precarious peace would be vulnerable to the same festering ill feeling. However, it wasn't lost on me that babysitting the Ukrainians would give me yet another task, placing even more strain on our limited manpower. That was going to tie up a platoon of mine indefinitely, just when tensions with the Muslims were at their highest. Weren't we already stretched enough?

Next the UN set about doing some more of what they do best – perhaps the only thing they do well – talking. They were hopeless operational commanders of peacekeepers in a war zone. By the time the slaughter stopped in Srebrenica at about this time, few could have argued otherwise. The UN was not good at preventing genocide; that much was clear. However, the UN was far better at finding negotiated solutions to deadlocked situations, and they weren't averse to compromising internationally accepted principles in order to find the answer. Principles such as not paying hostage-takers a ransom, for example, because that only encourages future hostage taking, and, therefore, jeopardises more people's lives in the long run. That was the way the British had always viewed hostage taking anyway. But the UN wasn't going to abide by that principle, especially when Russia seemed to feel that the plight of the Ukrainians somehow reflected badly on them. Ukraine had achieved independence from the Soviet Union in 1990, yet there were still cultural ties, particularly in eastern Ukraine. Russia was also aligned with the Serbs in the Bosnian War, so the idea of the BiH calling the shots – and holding Ukrainian UN soldiers captive – did not go down well in Moscow.

You might have thought the Russians would have laughed at the Ukrainians and thought it served them right for breaking away from the 'mother country'. But any BiH success was a slap in the face for the Serbs and, therefore, an insult to the Russians by proxy. They wanted the Ukrainian hostage crisis solved quickly. So the Russians decided to send in the troop-carrying trucks to get the hostages out. And it seems that they were prepared, temporarily at least, to put up the money to bring about the desired solution – not least because they were sure to be reimbursed by some secret UN fund somewhere along the line.

This was the background to the raising of the ransom, as I understood it. When the Serbs finally allowed a UN convoy through to Gorazde with much-needed supplies in mid-August, that convoy included in its cargo a container carrying 4 million Deutschmarks in cash. This was the astronomical sum agreed with the BiH behind the scenes; this was the ransom that would allow the Ukrainian contingent to be taken out on that same convoy, in total disgrace but mercifully in one piece. It would go some way to compensating the Muslims for months of unpaid rent around the factory complex and more than a year of exploitation, sexual and otherwise, of some of the more vulnerable members of their society.

Someone had to be selected to ensure that the ransom

money was delivered safely to the BiH local government before it lost its way. This would have to be done in secret, under cover of darkness because the ransom was not supposed to exist, let alone be paid. Indeed, to my knowledge, this is the very first time that any details of the ransom offered up for the Ukrainians by the UN have come out. The secret has been kept for more than twenty years because it was, in many ways, a shameful solution to a shameful episode. Why am I in position to reveal that a ransom was, indeed, paid? Because I was selected to be part of the three-man team that paid it, partly because I knew the side streets of Gorazde so well.

But while that little plan was starting to come together, with the lasting freedom of the Ukrainians the objective, another plan was being formed – with our own lasting freedom on the table for discussion. By the second half of August, the big question mark didn't concern whether or not the disgraced Ukrainians would make it out of Gorazde alive. The greater threat was to us, the Brits, and it was coming from both sides in the war being fought around the town, for both sides now seemed quite happy to see us trapped indefinitely. The Muslims felt our continued presence would help to prevent a massacre in Gorazde if the Serbs launched an all-out offensive. After all, we were supposed to be the eyes of the world and no one would stand for another atrocity so soon. Meanwhile, the Bosnian Serbs felt we might come in handy as potential hostages and human shields during any such offensive.

It was hard to see how they could both be right. And General Ratko Mladic probably had more reason to value us at this point than the Muslims did. We could warn the world what was happening but it would be harder for the world to do anything about it with us stuck in the firing line.

Ever since the genocide at nearby Srebrenica, Mladic had been left in no doubt about what would happen if there were any more atrocities. If Mladic gave the big Western powers the slightest excuse, swift NATO retribution would rain down on strategic targets. The London Conference had effectively authorised widespread NATO air strikes against the Bosnian Serbs if there was any further provocation. What could Mladic do about that threat? He couldn't fight NATO in the sky; he didn't have the means. But there was one thing he could do. If he knew a fresh atrocity was likely to spark a NATO attack, he could capture fresh UN hostages and use them as human shields to thwart that NATO aggression. So did it really make sense for Mladic to allow the British UN peacekeeping force to go home? No, it didn't, even though we had been a thorn in his side ever since we had arrived. It would take some very cunning diplomacy to convince Mladic, the master of betrayal, that it was in his best interests to do the honourable thing where we were concerned, when it so clearly wasn't in his best interests at all. Was there anyone who possessed such powers of persuasion?

General Rupert Smith, the British Commander from Sarajevo, was already on the case, with a view to taking control of this extremely tricky situation. He had turned up in Gorazde on 10 August, to assess our predicament for himself. The Serbs and Muslims had 'familiarised' Smith with the way things were done around Gorazde by kicking off as he innocently tried to cross their confrontation lines. Smith had been pinned down for hours. Once he had come through that welcome in one piece, the general wanted me to brief him personally on the events of 28 May and B Company's last stand on the mountain. I gave him all the relevant details and concluded by stating my belief that we had helped to save Gorazde because there had been no doubt in my mind that the Serbs had intended to take it.

Riley was with us and Smith asked him, 'What do you think the Serbs are going to try to do next?'

I'll never forget Riley's reply. 'You tell me, you're the fucking general.'

I was gobsmacked. This may have been Riley's way of expressing frustration at the way he and his men had been left in the shit for months, with precious little support from Sarajevo, London or anywhere else for that matter. Even so, it's not the sort of thing you say to a general. Smith raised an eyebrow. For a split second, it seemed this was going to end very badly for Riley. Luckily for him, Smith knew what Riley had been through and had retained a sense of humour. He broke into a dignified smile.

I had already warmed to Smith and did so even more now. He got it. He knew we had spent a summer in hell and yet he had still wanted to come and see for himself because he knew it was the right thing to do. That was the measure of the man, as far as we were concerned. He was an engaging commander. He'd had a little flavour of life in and around Gorazde already and he didn't have to be a genius to imagine what the place did to people in the long run. So he wasn't going to pull rank or create a stink just because of some tension-fuelled reply from a subordinate – especially one who had done a great job under immense pressure.

However, General Smith's chance to experience our predicament first-hand may have convinced him that it had to come to an end as quickly as possible, never to be repeated. Whatever he thought the Serbs might try to do in response, he'd be determined not to let them. We had achieved all we could in Gorazde, he felt, and now there were three possible ways out for us. One was by air, without Bosnian Serb consent. It would be an extremely high-risk operation, with the likelihood of casualties among the airmen and us. Some aircraft might well be downed by the Serbs in that scenario.

The second was to try to fight our way through those Serb lines with the help of close air support from the UN and/or NATO. We thought that might just be possible but not without heavy British casualties. We were sixty-five kilometres behind Serb lines! The third way also meant leaving by land but going in an organised convoy, with all our equipment and our heads held high, national face intact, the same way we had come in. For that to work, we would need the co-operation of General Mladic. Whichever way was to be chosen – and it was clear we all favoured the latter option – Smith and his superiors had decided that we were leaving.

On 18 August the British Government publicly announced that we were to be withdrawn from Gorazde in September and not replaced. No one bothered to tell us the announcement was coming. We heard the news on the BBC World Service like everyone else, which came as a shock because we suddenly found ourselves having to explain to both sides in the war what was happening and how it would happen – when we didn't have a clue ourselves as to the mechanics of our extraction or indeed what the impact might be on the local population.

Naturally, we were pleased, from a personal point of view, that the end might be in sight for us – but not at any price. I, for one, wanted to be convinced that, if we were leaving, NATO was finally going to back up its threats and bomb the Serbs to hell the first time they tried to attack Gorazde in our absence. But, of course, I was well below the level whereby anyone was going to give me that kind of personal reassurance. I just had to trust that what I was hearing was correct and that the UN were finally going to allow NATO to take some decisive action against the Serbs once we were clear of the area. Understandably, many of the Muslims were less than confident this would be the case and, therefore, less than thrilled with the idea of allowing us to leave. In short, the public announcement of our proposed departure went down like a lead balloon – and we still had to work out how it might actually happen.

On 20 August General Smith and Riley went to meet General Mladic in a place called Boreke. However distasteful it may be that two top British officers saw fit to dine with the devil, to pow-wow with a man very recently guilty of genocide, this simply had to happen. Generals who are war criminals sometimes still respect generals who are not war criminals. If the war criminal is given some semblance of respect in return, business can be done. Whether we liked it or not, we needed the blessing of the Butcher of Bosnia if we were to travel unimpeded from Gorazde through Bosnian Serb lines and then cross into Serbia itself, where we were confident we'd face no threat.

Was it worth losing people just so that we could say we didn't deal with Mladic? Of course not. Smith had refused to deal with Mladic while British hostages were being held back in June. That was no longer the case; there was no gun being put to our heads by the Serbs anymore. Therefore, by far the easiest option was to do things the peaceful way, if only Mladic could be persuaded to co-operate. The ends would very much justify the means – especially if Mladic could be fooled into leaving himself open to NATO air attacks once we were clear.

However, it was one thing to grit your teeth, smile and do the necessary in the best interests of your men. It was quite another actually to enjoy the experience of being in the company of Mladic, as it appeared that Riley did. Perhaps Colonel Jon was such a good 'method actor' that he actually convinced himself it was fine to be impressed by a man who had just murdered thousands of innocent Bosnians. Maybe the stress he had been under numbed Riley to more appropriate feelings about coming face to face with Mladic. But then again, who am I to judge my Commanding Officer and his personal feelings? A cordial atmosphere was required for the key meeting and that is exactly what was generated, with Riley playing his part.

Riley later described it as 'one of the most significant experiences of my life' to see 'two great commanders together, men of contrasting styles and philosophies...' Surely he wasn't putting Smith in the same category as Mladic? Yet Riley also said of Mladic that 'it was easy to see why his own men adore him and his enemies fear him... he was charm itself.'

Was Colonel Jon still suffering from the after-effects of the 'deluge of plumb brandy' he said came with a 'magnificent lunch of barbecued lamb', as he wrote those remarks in his diary? Perhaps not because he subsequently made no secret of what he had written – even though he appeared to have been in awe of a mass-murderer that day. Was Riley suffering from a version of Stockholm Syndrome – that strange psychological state in which captives take the side of their captors in a crisis? No, I think he just wanted us out and felt a kind of euphoria when he sensed our escape was possible. And yet there was certainly no earthly reason to hero-worship Mladic, even if he was among the world's most experienced combat generals at the time. Whatever the reason for his temporary blindness, Riley seemed to be struggling to take in what had happened at Srebrenica barely a month earlier. The full extent of the horror had still not been uncovered in all its stomach-churning detail and yet we already knew enough to warrant revulsion at the thought of such a massacre.

I don't know whether General Rupert Smith shared Riley's enthusiasm for the day they spent with Mladic, though somehow I doubt it. Indeed, I heard later that Smith's bodyguards had enjoyed taunting the bodyguards of Mladic, as they all waited outside the main meeting room. The Butcher's chief bodyguard was well known to all in Bosnia because he was a giant of a man nicknamed 'PJ'. He didn't intimidate Smith's men though – quite the reverse. One of Smith's bodyguards couldn't resist taking the moral high ground when he saw his opposite number, a stand that may have hinted at the true feelings of his boss, the British general.

Smith's bodyguard said, 'Evening, PJ, how's it going? Where are you going for your holidays this summer? Oh no, you can't go on holiday, can you? In fact, you can't go abroad ever again, can you, because you're a war criminal, aren't you, PJ, just like your boss!'

Whether PJ understood these taunts is open to question and, if he didn't, his bemused expression probably only increased the British bodyguards' amusement. Fortunately, tempers did not flare outside the meeting room in Boreke; the bodyguards remained professional enough to refrain from coming to blows, and the generals inside the hall managed to develop enough of a rapport to get the business of the day done without a hitch.

When Riley came back from Boreke that evening, I had the chance to speak to him.

'How did it go?'

'Couldn't have gone better. Mladic isn't against us leaving; he won't oppose it.'

'That's good!'

'His only condition is that we take everything with us – all our weapons and equipment.'

'Seems reasonable,' I suggested.

Indeed, it did. Mladic didn't want our equipment falling into the hands of his enemy – who would? It had always been our intention to take everything with us, so we weren't going to have a problem meeting that demand.

'Oh, by the way, I've got something for you,' Riley said.

With that, he gave me a cardboard tube – one of those containers used to protect maps and the like. I thanked him and went back to my command vehicle to do my evening conference, assuming he had just handed me an initial outline for our extraction plan, or some more mundane orders in the interim. But, when I opened up the cardboard tube and unfolded the contents, I got quite a shock.

Inside was a photograph of Ratko Mladic, looking very pleased with himself and just a tiny bit mad. When you examined his sardonic smile closely you found it wasn't a smile at all, more like a sneer. Similarly, the hint of a smile in his eyes barely masked their cruelty. Mladic could almost have been trying to smile at some of the citizens of Srebrenica, telling the women and children to get on the busses that had been laid on for them, because everyone would be safe as long as they did as they were told. In the photo-portrait, a head-and-shoulders shot, Mladic was wearing a Bosnian Serb Army cap, with gold braid and crest. The collar and lapels on his green army tunic looked slightly crumpled but no one was going to tell him, were they? Not if they valued their own career and safety. And, just in case anyone had any doubts about Mladic and his sick egomania, there was something else about this photograph. I spotted something scribbled in the top right-hand corner, which had been crumpled as Mladic wrote on it. What had the Butcher written? His name! He had autographed the picture, perhaps for Riley himself, because it looked as though he had done so in a hurry.

What was I supposed to do with this odd gift from Riley? I couldn't just throw it away. So I thought I'd keep it and offer it to the regimental museum if ever we got home, as a kind of macabre war trophy. I know what you're thinking: I should probably have used it as toilet paper. But I didn't. And that's another reason why I shouldn't go overboard in my criticism of Riley. When you write a book, you tell everything from your own point of view. Who is to say some people were not appalled by some of the things I did in Gorazde? We are all human, we all have our faults; we were all under incredible pressure, trying to do the best we could, and not always getting it right. Most of the time Riley got it right, and that was partly why we were all still alive, against the odds. If a lack of taste and judgement on a single, boozy day was all he was guilty of during a summer like this, he had done okay in my book. And in his defence, let us remember that Riley was not the first or last to be taken in by the charms of General Ratko Mladic, a man of undoubted charisma. That didn't make me feel any more comfortable as I put the Butcher of Bosnia's signed photograph back in its protective packaging, hid it away discreetly and quietly asked myself whether my own moral compass was still working. I thought it was. But then again, within a couple of days I was to be involved in the slightly sordid payment of that ransom for the Ukrainians.

I couldn't help but feel furtive as I sagged under the weight of the ransom cash that was stuffed into my bergen as part of the three-man delivery team on 22 August. Alan Finn, our Military Information Officer (you still couldn't be called a Military Intelligence Officer while you were working for the UN), was in charge of the ransom handover. He brought along another non-commissioned officer from his department to help carry the load and the three of us were to undertake the nervous journey to the handover point in the middle of the night. It was the Muslims who had stipulated that everything should be done under cover of darkness, at a time when no one would notice us coming in or out of the specified government building in Vitkovice. They probably feared the Serbs might hit anything that looked like an unauthorised convoy in daylight hours, or maybe they worried that someone on their own side might try to hijack the operation if they knew what huge amounts of money were involved. It would be wrong to assume that the Muslim community was entirely united in adversity; like every other community in the world, there were lawless elements ready to exploit the chaos of war in their own way. So the handover of the ransom cash was done in the early hours, on a need-to-know basis on both sides. What was the local government going to do with 4 million Deutschmarks – about a million pounds? Again, that was something of a mystery. My understanding was that they wanted the money in German currency because it was suitable for depositing in an undisclosed Swiss bank, where it could be called upon for arms deals or for any other purpose at a later date. But surely it would have been far easier and far more secure for the Muslims to insist upon a wire transfer to a Swiss bank? That would also have saved 'Finnbar' Finn, his assistant and me from the physical strain and danger of carrying backbreaking loads of wonga through the night on our backs!

For whatever reason, the Bosnian Muslims didn't want a paper trail of any kind – not even when it was well known that Swiss banks were experts in discretion and confidentiality when it came to all transactions. Perhaps those due to receive the vast sum at that government house in Vitkovici were going to take a 'transaction fee' of their own from the 4 million Deutschmarks before passing it on? There could have been any number of complex little arrangements planned, each one untraceable as long as the money came in ready notes.

Vitkovice was twelve kilometres from the camp. Mercifully, we weren't expected to carry the cash all the way on our own. The first part of the journey was to be done in UN trucks, both driven by men from the Military 'Information' Section.

Finbarr was in the lead vehicle, I was in the back of the rear vehicle, my SA80 rifle and pistol at the ready. This leg of the trip wasn't without dangers of its own. There was no way you could turn on headlights and drive through Gorazde at night without attracting all the Serb gunfire imaginable from the other side of the river. It would have been like an invitation to bored marksmen to open up with everything they had and we wouldn't have lasted more than a few seconds. So the only solution was to drive with no headlights and that meant driving very slowly and deliberately to avoid hitting something we couldn't see. With my knowledge of the town and its side streets, I'd still be able to spot in an instant if we had taken a wrong turn and tell the lead vehicle what to do next. Fortunately, it didn't happen.

And then came the really nervy part, from our point of view. On the outskirts of Gorazde, where the roads became impossible to negotiate in total darkness, we had to get out in our UN uniforms and start the hike to Vitkovice. We still had five kilometres to do on foot with our very unusual cargo and, of course, we also had weapons, ammunition and a radio to carry too, in case we were ambushed and had to call for assistance.

Alan Finn had the brief; his assistant and I were pack mules. Now we just had to hope this wasn't one big set-up, which might see the three of us attacked, robbed and murdered, leaving the onus on the United Nations to explain away what we might have been doing out there in the middle of the night, and still under an obligation to pay the right people all over again.

We were almost buckling under the weight as we marched

as briskly as we could through the night. If anyone thinks it must be a thrill to carry millions in cash, they should have been there. It was uncomfortable and it was dangerous. I was soaking with sweat and so were the others. In the still of the night, every step on the road clatters like an invitation to criminal elements, your heart is thumping and even your breath sounds too loud. Every bark of a dog in the darkness sounded like an alarm, reason enough for locals to pick up their weapons – and they all had them – to investigate. The three of us pressed on as best we could in the intimidating silence. The only certainty was that we were going to march out to Vitkovice just as quickly as we could and get this four million Deutschmarks delivered. Then we were going to sneak back into Gorazde and hide up until daybreak, at which point some of my men would come out, pick us up and get us back to camp, hopefully before anyone realised what had been going on.

Even after we were well clear of Gorazde, our conversation was limited to a few light-hearted remarks to break the tension.

'Who was the bright bastard who thought this one up?' I asked Finn.

He said nothing. Perhaps he'd planned every detail of the operation himself, once he'd been told we had to hand over a crazy amount of money to the Muslims. But, now that we had the money, a mischievous thought entered my head: why give it to anyone?

'Let's find a bridge and leg it for the Maldives!' I suggested enthusiastically.

Finn wasn't biting. With 4 million Deutschmarks to

account for, you could understand why he wanted to keep the atmosphere business-like. But the absurdity of the situation couldn't have been lost on any of us.

It took us two hours to reach the village, the scene of Adem's murder and the scene of the Muslim attack on the Ukrainians. The government building we were heading for was only five minutes round the corner from the school we'd tried to protect from the Serb snipers over the water. I put the memories of the boy on the bike to the back of my mind. This was no time to allow anything to distract me. I had to live in the present and stay very alert now. Any number of things could go wrong if the wrong people had been tipped off about the cash delivery.

Alan Finn and his assistant were going to knock on the door of the government building and enter while I waited outside for any signs of unwanted attention. I was going to give them a maximum of five minutes to do the handover. If they didn't come out after five minutes, I was going to go in – and I wasn't going to wait for an invitation. Not that I could have gone in with all guns blazing because that might have sealed the fate of Finnbar and his mate. But I knew I'd have had to be ready to kill if, by killing, I could free them and get us all somewhere safer to radio for assistance.

As it turned out, the door was already ajar and three men who had clearly been waiting for precisely this moment quickly stepped outside to meet us. Finbarr already knew the contact, a BiH Intelligence Officer, but he wasn't taking any chances in the darkness and checked his ID. After that, he gave us the nod and we handed over the three bergens. Alan and his assistant stepped inside the building for a while. I waited outside. The formalities didn't take five minutes. In fact, Finnbar and his assistant were back out in two, carrying a piece of paper to confirm the delivery, the relief written all over what I could see of their faces in the gloom.

We headed back towards Gorazde, our loads significantly lighter than they had been on the outward journey. Gone was the possibility of losing millions in UN money. By the same token, the chance to make a break for the Maldives had also passed us by and we realised, reluctantly, that we were going to have to survive on soldiers' pay for a little while longer. The first rendezvous point was the old UNHCR building in Gorazde. Then we headed for the bank, which was base for Alan and his Military Information Detachment, just as it had become home for the SAS lads when they could stay in one place for long enough. At dawn I called out my vehicles to take us back to our camp. We were safely in before the sun had risen properly: it was over. I was still trying to get my head round what we'd done. It wasn't for me to judge the rights and wrongs of it. Would the Muslims keep their word and release the Ukrainians? We were going to look pretty bloody stupid if they didn't.

Sure enough, on 24 August 1995, the Ukrainians were allowed to leave Gorazde. They probably thought the UN had spent all that money well because it enabled them to complete the first stage of the journey home. And, once the Muslims had given the green light for their initial extraction, there was never going to be a problem with the Serbs, who virtually regarded the Ukrainians as their cousins. Back in Ukraine, those UN soldiers who hadn't been robbed of all their wealth by the BiH could live the lives of rich men. Only Colonel Batalin seems to have taken the blame for the terrible things the Ukrainians did in Gorazde in the name of UN peacekeeping. I believe he had to serve a prison sentence.

How did I feel about this unfortunate episode? Though I was glad there was one less problem to think about, I had no time to think about the rights and wrongs of the UN ransom. With the Ukrainians gone, the BiH prepared to set their sights on a new target... us.

# CHAPTER NINE

# MUSLIMS ATTACK

'You don't understand, Major Richard,' Selma warned me when we were at one of my liaison meetings with Salko down in the basement of the bank one evening. 'The men in the town can't just let you leave; they have to show they are in control of all this. Everything has to be done their way. That's how they think. And many in the town fear the consequences of you leaving. They won't let it happen.'

'We can handle it,' I said.

Selma's expression told me I still didn't quite get it. 'Major Richard,' she said, 'please listen to me and try to understand. People in the town are saying they will lie down in front of your vehicles in order to prevent you from leaving. It's not just about fighting your way out. You will have to run over civilians if you want to get out. Are you prepared to do that?'

I didn't answer. But the simple truth was that we were not prepared to do that. In that scenario, we would have to climb down from our vehicles and remove the people lying in our way. Gorazde's civilians didn't know that though. Were they really desperate enough to risk being run over and crushed? I came to the reluctant conclusion that some might well be.

That BBC World Service announcement on 18 August really hadn't done us any favours. Going public like that had warned everyone of our intention to leave, meaning that those who wished to obstruct us had time to dream up all kinds of ideas about how they could do it. And, by then, there were plenty who were determined to stop us.

I needn't have been there for the crisis that was about to unfold – one that would attach itself to me personally and threaten a major diplomatic incident inside a few days. I could have got out a month earlier, not long after Srebrenica.

Towards the end of July I'd been due some Rest and Recuperation but I'd refused to take it because there was no guarantee I'd be able to get back in again. Srebrenica hadn't influenced my thinking. In fact, I'd decided as early as June. I wasn't going to leave my blokes in someone else's hands, someone whose capabilities I didn't know. It just wouldn't have felt right, not in this place.

Riley claimed later that he should have ordered me out, but he was more than okay with me staying at the time. My wife, Jane, was less enamoured with my decision – and understandably so. She had one demanding toddler to look after and another on the way. Breaking the news to 'the boss' back home that I was going nowhere hadn't been easy.

'Jane, you've got to understand this. I can't come back. Not now.'

She understood all right; she'd known me since we were teenagers, so she realised how stubborn I could be. But this time she sounded very worried and unhappy about it. I tried to lighten the mood.

'If I came home, Jane, the first leg of the journey would be a UN flight in a Tupolov 155. I'd have more chance of being killed in that old plane than by staying in Gorazde, believe me!'

Stony silence.

'Safer on the ground!' I forced a chuckle at my own little quip and that didn't impress her either.

More silence.

She knew my motives for not coming back and understood they were the right ones. She knew I could not, would not, leave the blokes in Gorazde under anyone else's command because, if anything went seriously wrong in my absence, I'd never forgive myself. It's a personal thing but, morally, I could not come home on R and R while my blokes were still in the shit. Jane got all that but it didn't mean she had to like it. Perhaps she suspected that, if I didn't get out soon, there might not be another chance.

Others left because their tour was over; people I'd grown close to. Wez had taken the original SAS team out on a convoy at the start of August, leaving behind Billy and Mick, the Forward Air Controllers, for continuity. I was sad to see Wez go and the warmth of our handshake just before he left told me we'd be friends for life.

'See you back in the UK,' he told me.

'Keep your head down,' I said with a smile.

Wherever he'd be taking his team next, it had to be better

than this, I thought. But I was determined to see our tour out to the bitter end. The trouble was this: the locals didn't want to give us an end. Why should there be an end to our ordeal while they were still going through theirs? You could see their point, even if they had analysed their situation and probably come to the wrong conclusions.

Brigadier Bahto, the head of the local Muslim forces, certainly wasn't planning to allow us to leave. Not unless it happened under his terms. Bahto's open resistance to our plans didn't go down too well with our Gorazde boss, Colonel Jon. When a routine liaison meeting took place down at the 81st Division headquarters in town, both men knew they were reaching a critical phase in their complicated relationship, and the conversation soon became heated.

Backed by public announcements from the Bosnian government, Bahto was refusing to contemplate British departure from Gorazde unless we placed all our weapons, vehicles and equipment in a 'weapons control point'. In other words, hand everything over to the BiH. We were never going to do that. Some of our stuff was British government property and, besides, there was a principle involved here. From the outset, we had resolved not to allow ourselves to be pushed around by either side and, after all we'd been through, we weren't going to let that happen now.

'You will only be allowed to leave if you hand in your weapons first,' reiterated Bahto.

'That's not going to happen,' Riley insisted once more.

'Then you will stay,' his opposite number repeated, almost casually.

'Don't be so naive!' said Colonel Jon – and, at this point,

Riley actually grabbed Bahto by the arm. I suspect this wasn't a technique recognised by any school of diplomacy but Colonel Jon was frustrated and determined to get his point across.

'You'll never get air strikes against the Serbs by keeping us here,' Riley warned. 'The UN will be too worried about Serb retaliation against us. Think about it, Brigadier! Do you really think you're going to get what you want, the way you're behaving? How can NATO hit the Serbs with us still stuck here? Everybody knows the Serbs will try to use us as human shields against air strikes. But, if we're out of the way, it all changes, don't you see? The next time the Serbs try anything against you, NATO will be ready to attack them. The Americans and London won't have to worry about us anymore because we won't be here. Give us what we want and you'll get what you want. We leave, the Serbs get bombed, the siege ends, the threat to Gorazde goes away. You win.'

Bahto had been listening carefully and he seemed to get it. He looked at Riley, who had by now released his arm. 'I will think about what you have said, it is good,' the Brigadier replied.

'Yes, you think about it,' said Riley. 'And, while you're at it, think about this too. Some of your men have been trying to get into our camp. What are you going to do about it?'

It was true. Over the previous seventy two hours, armed men had not only moved into checkpoint positions around the British camp but some had even been trying to raid us at night, probably in search of fuel, supplies and weapons. Stealing from us was nothing new. Once, when the daily shelling back in June had been at its worst, we had emerged after a brief lull in the barrage to find that three of our bergens, which we'd left strapped to the Saxons, had disappeared. They hadn't been blown away by the force of the explosions, so Muslim infiltrators must have risked getting their heads blown off by Serb shells to pilfer basic bits of British kit. We'd only left those bergens unattended during the height of the shelling that day, so either those thieves must have been pretty fearless or pretty desperate – probably both.

The perimeter wasn't impregnable – not if the raiders were determined enough to find a point in the wire that wasn't being observed at the time. But the idea of having armed men creeping around our camp and helping themselves to our equipment was totally unacceptable and, if we wanted to maintain our security and authority, then pretty soon we were going to have to start shooting them. We didn't want to do that and I'd already tried to persuade Bahto to help prevent unnecessary bloodshed.

'This has got to stop!' I'd warned him.

'Okay, I'll make it stop,' Bahto had assured me but it hadn't stopped.

Things had the potential to turn very nasty. And, frankly, it was a good job that Riley hadn't ordered me out a few weeks earlier because we were running short of commanding experience by the last weeks of August. We'd been thinning our people out by sending them away on convoys for 'Rest and Recuperation', including Senior Major (second-in-command) Stephen Hughes, Riley's deputy and the other experienced company commander, Phil Jones. They were due their R and R and they had thoroughly earned it but they weren't going to be brought back in once our intended departure had been announced.

Martin Leader was unlucky in that sense. He had already been out on R and R earlier in the tour so he'd come back in again. I was pleased to have him around but he wasn't as senior as me. He was an acting major, just as I was, and he had been a captain before this tour too. But he was way off being made a substantive major because he was about four years younger than me. He only had the Recce Platoon and Assault Pioneers under his command – both comprised of fine men but only two platoons in total. Besides, they were autonomous and reported directly to Battalion HQ. So there was always going to be more responsibility placed on my shoulders than Martin's.

I wanted to make our camp a fortress but we just didn't have enough defensive equipment available to strengthen every point in the wire, as much as we would have liked. Though the concertina wire wasn't exactly inviting intruders in, it wasn't always keeping them out either. If one person held down the wire, another could crawl through. We tried to compensate for any materially weak points in the perimeter by putting extra manpower there. But, if an alert sounded, warning of sustained Serbian shelling, our men sensibly found cover, which was the cue for the Muslim raiders to risk their lives by snipping away at the wire, crawling under it or getting over it, coming through by whatever means they could.

Since it was now common knowledge that we planned to leave soon, the Muslims must have decided to fill their pockets with whatever they could, while they still could. Nine times out of ten we'd spot them and challenge them with the traditional 'Halt! UNPROFOR! Who goes there?' Often they'd be scared off by a warning shot. But most recently they'd managed to get in twice in three days. We'd had to send up flares to stay in control of the situation because warning shots alone hadn't initially deterred them. It was clear that, the closer we came to our proposed departure in September, the more daring the raiders were becoming. Desperate people, desperate times, and it looked as though we'd soon become targets too. Were they also testing our defences so that one night they could try to come through the wire in enough numbers to try to subdue or capture us? That way, they could take anything they wanted.

Or maybe they reckoned they could earn themselves a few more rucksacks full of cash if they held the Brits captive. After all, if the Ukrainians had been worth 4 million Deutschmarks in cash to the UN, what might the British contingent be worth? The Brits were bigger political players on the world stage, significant allies of the Americans. Maybe the Muslims could ask for three or four times the ransom to let the British go. That's the problem with paying ransoms: they tend to lead to further, greater ransom demands at some point in the future. Not that the UK or US would have paid a ransom because it was totally against the policy of the UK and US to do so. But the Muslims didn't know that and, besides, maybe the UN would have paid anyway if the British and American governments could be persuaded to turn a blind eye. Under those circumstances, the ransom would be huge. The Ukrainians were only 70-strong, whereas we were 300 blokes in a sports stadium. The demand would be closer to 12 or 16 million Deutschmarks, which equated to about £3 million or £4 million.

Whatever the BiH were hoping to achieve through these night raids, we weren't going to back down and we weren't going to be overrun. Maybe Bahto wasn't in full control anymore; but if he was deliberately allowing these raids on our camp to happen, as a precursor to a full-scale attempt at capturing it, then he had to get one thing clear in his mind.

So Riley seized the moment to make a little threat of his own. He looked Bahto straight in the eye and said, 'If you think you can do to us what you did to the Ukrainians, you are making a big mistake. That's already lost you a lot of sympathy within the international community. But if you try to attack our camp, something else is going to happen. There's going to be a fight. Do you understand? We will meet any attempts to take our camp with force. So, before that happens, you had better think about the consequences.'

'Okay, I will think about all you have said and talk to my superiors,' repeated Bahto. And that was as much as we could hope for. Bahto's hardline stance against our departure seemed to be softening before our eyes. But this was Gorazde and things were never quite as they seemed.

After Bahto left that meeting, I believe he did call for calm and was apparently supported at a much higher Bosnian governmental level, so the situation should have improved in the following days. But it didn't, either because Bahto and his superiors were trying to fool us or, more likely, because elements within his own command had decided to do things their way and placed Bahto and the town authorities under huge pressure to let them do so. Influential people in the town may even have been sympathetic to the hardliners. Losing face was a huge thing for Muslim men in Gorazde and they were not going to be part of any softening that could be construed as losing face, even if their pride was pushing them towards lawlessness.

Bahto might personally have wanted to do a U-turn and let us go but it appeared that he wasn't going to be allowed to climb down. He had already publicly announced that the Brits would only be allowed to leave if they put their vehicles and weapons in toll points. It's likely that an element of his command told him, 'If we're just going to let them go, after what you said before, we're going to be seen to be weak.' You could see their point. Bahto had said, 'You'll go when I say.' We had said, 'No, we'll go when we feel like it.' If Bahto subsequently caved in and told us, 'Er... Okay then, do what you want,' it would amount to a loss of face among the Muslims at senior level. Influential people in the town had probably been trying to hold Bahto to his original word from the moment he began to waver. 'I thought you said they couldn't go? Are you letting them go?' And, of course, the citizens of Gorazde, in general, wanted us to stay.

Although Bosnian civilians had been let down by the UN before, horribly so in Srebrenica, it was only natural that Gorazde's inhabitants were going to feel even more vulnerable without any UN presence there at all. They didn't have a cast-iron guarantee that NATO would save them if the British were allowed to leave. For all they knew, the British departure would send a signal to the Serbs that Gorazde was up for grabs and that no one would try to intervene this time should Mladic start to do what he had always wanted to do there.

Despite the recent events at Srebrenica, many people thought that while British UN soldiers were still in Gorazde, the Serbs wouldn't attack because we'd resisted so strongly before. At the very least, the locals believed we'd be able to report quickly on any atrocities and fuel sufficient international outcry to prevent another full-scale massacre. The alternative – a Serb takeover of the town while the world looked the other way – was too painful for them to contemplate. The British simply couldn't be allowed to leave. If Selma was right in her interpretation of the mood in the town, therefore, Gorazde's civilian population had come to some dangerous conclusions about what needed to be done and why. 'If the British UN soldiers are leaving, this is going to be another Srebrenica. Let's lie down in the road and stop them at all costs.'

Some BiH elements clearly didn't intend to let things get that far. They had already started trying to restrict our movements around the town. That didn't go down well with us. We'd stood by and fought the Serbs on 28 May, we'd given the BiH time to get into position; we'd shown our worth. But the BiH were still strutting about as though it had all been down to them. We had never disputed the fact that they'd done a cracking job during that battle and we couldn't have held our positions up on the mountain for much longer because we were running out of ammunition. But the fact that they were now acting like 'Big-time Charlies' grated on us. They liked the idea that they were restricting our movement, because to them it showed that they were in charge. We weren't going to accept that.

We just carried on preparing for our departure, keen to reinforce the message that it would happen on our terms, regardless of BiH intentions. They responded by blocking our low-loaders, our prime movers or DROPS (Dismounted Rack Offload Pick-Up Systems) vehicles, which have a flat deck and a crane. These vehicles had arrived to remove 'heavy plant' – our industrial-style diggers, JCBs and other vehicles. The

JCBs were very expensive – they cost about £250,000 – and we weren't leaving them behind. They'd been lifted onto the low-loaders, strapped down and made ready to be moved out. The BiH and their blocking tactics made for a tense stand-off.

They wanted what was ours. If the British were going to try to leave, the BiH thought they had better get hold of everything they could, in preparation for a fresh Serb onslaught. I could see their point of view. But we didn't want to be accused of giving heavy equipment to one of the warring factions, not at this delicate stage in the game. And, besides, we wanted to leave Gorazde with our national pride intact, and to abandon equipment simply because we had been bullied into doing so wasn't part of the game plan.

We were locked in a dangerous stalemate. And, whatever assurances Bahto tried to give us that all would be well in the end, we saw no sign on the ground of a shift in policy or attitude towards us. At least the Ukrainians had been allowed to leave on 24 August. But the local forces weren't prepared to extend the same co-operation to us. Worse still, the following afternoon and early evening, armed men in military uniform began to probe the perimeter of our camp afresh. Bahto was either prepared to turn a blind eye or else these had ignored him. I still didn't want to believe he was authorising this, not after the conversations we'd had. So I sent a radio warning to Bahto.

'Tell them to stop this. Now!'

But it didn't matter who was pulling the strings behind the scenes anymore because the intimidation didn't let up. We surprised two more armed men who had broken in through the camp perimeter; our guards fired warning shots and the intruders slipped away again. But the frequency of these raids suggested to me that they were getting familiar with the layout of the camp and preparing for something bigger. As the pressure increased, we were faced with the very real possibility of a battle. You could feel it in the air that they meant business and there was potential for something bigger to happen. Warning shots clearly hadn't been enough to deter the raiders from trying again another night. We'd hoped they would be but, in reality, they had probably just made us look weaker. Perhaps the BiH thought the fight had finally gone out of us and we'd be there for the taking if they showed up with some firepower of their own.

As the only experienced company commander left, and because B Company always seemed to be at the sharp end of Tactical Command issues, I was made Tactical Commander to deal with any situation as it unfolded. That allowed Riley, who had come back in after the Ukrainian crisis, to base himself in the Ops Room, where he could receive reports and gain an overview while maintaining contact with the BiH command.

I told Second Lieutenant Charlie Brand-Porter to take his platoon down to the northern end of the camp, where I thought any big attack might come from. Aggressors could use the natural cover of an orchard, which stood just outside the northern and north-eastern boundary of the camp. The closest trees in that orchard were too near the perimeter wire for my liking and there were bushes even closer to us. You wouldn't see anyone before they entered the orchard either because the land on the other side dropped steeply down to the River Drina. It all made for a good covered approach for anyone who wished to make one. So Charlie was told to hold the fort there and place his standing patrol in an over-watch position.

Brand-Porter – known as 'BP' – was quite a character. He had let his hair grow and, with his tan, he looked more like a surfer than a soldier. In fact, he really was a surfer and he even used 'surfy' language at times. BP was not like many people I'd met before. He had a horrible Japanese car with an engine packing no more power than a pathetic 1000 CC. He called it Jackie Chan – no difference between China and Japan in his eyes, apparently. Absurdly, it had a little overdrive button on the gear stick. He'd be driving around in this shitty little estate car with a surfboard in the back and then he'd make a big show of getting ready to press the button. 'Brace yourselves, the overdrive is going to kick in,' he'd say, before hitting this button with his thumb. Nothing ever happened.

He was so eccentric that he painted stripes on his rifle and called it 'Tiger'. Sometimes he almost talked as though Tiger was the talisman that really commanded his platoon instead of him. As long as he did his job, I wasn't going to come down hard on him over the length of his hair or the way he spoke, not in this environment. A bit of individualism was fine in my book, as long as the team came first when it mattered. And that evening he knew that he and his team might have an important role to play, because I'd warned him it could kick off. That didn't mean it definitely would though – and his watch became a waiting game.

It was approaching 11pm, BP had been at the northern wire since 6pm and the evening had been dragging on. I couldn't stay in a helmet all night; I had things to do, such as get round all the other blokes to make sure they were all right. Having done that, I went down to A Company's end of camp; the southern end. I was in constant radio contact with Charlie, who had been reporting back: nothing much was happening and I sat down next to my Saxon, still monitoring the radio. My signaller was monitoring the net as well. Everything seemed to be covered, so I felt relaxed enough to walk over to the new SAS lads, who had replaced Wez and his men. The new troop was just chilling out on the stadium steps – it wasn't their job to guard the camp.

Les Dixon was the new SAS Team Commander. A cigarillo-smoking cockney covered in tattoos, he was just as unflappable as Wez had been. Les was a mountain climber in his spare time and, when he went for a run, he did long distances in army boots, carrying a bergen on his back. Dixon couldn't have been any fitter if he tried and he was always ready for action.

'Mac' was the most memorable of his men. He was known as 'Obediah', after Obediah Hawkmore, the intimidating character in *Sharp*, a popular TV series starring the British actor Sean Bean. I had another nickname for Mac – 'Dr Death' – because there was so much death in his eyes. Mac was granite-hard and had a reputation as an outstanding sniper. He looked scary, even by SAS standards, but I got on well enough with him. Another of the 'JCOs' was a Para called John, a veteran of the First Gulf War. And the fourth man in the new SAS troop was another mountaineer called Paul, who was a quieter, a wiry bloke with ginger hair and a moustache. (Billy 'Pig Man' Walters had stayed on with Mick Ramsden as the Forward Air Control Party, to give the SAS handover some continuity).

Mac had been given a bottle of slivovitz by one of the

interpreters. Dr Death decided to treat his mates to a nip of this plum brandy on the steps and I was invited to join them and take a swig. Mac was first to taste the slivovitz but screwed up his face immediately.

'This is minging,' he said. 'What can we mix it with?'

Somebody produced some boiled sweets and a metal bowl, and Obediah began to heat the slivovitz over a little stove, putting the boiled sweets in to try to make it taste better. As he tried to sweeten this evil brew, we were all taking the odd sip and laughing out loud. He kept stirring as we chatted away but the potion was still rancid. Anything from our ration packs that we thought might take the edge off the taste was thrown in too. There was nothing to say we couldn't drink on operations but we had what's called a two-can rule because two cans won't affect your judgement. All I'd had was one or two sips of the slivovitz and my resistance was pretty high because I'd been offered slivovitz on almost every patrol and at every meeting I'd done since arriving in Bosnia. People practically lived on the stuff around Gorazde.

I was talking to Mac about a couple of new sniper positions he'd identified, places where he could get better coverage of the hills. So he was planning to go and build up those positions the very next day. That way, if anyone started to shoot into the camp, he knew the perfect place from which to respond. Dr Death was talking enthusiastically about one of those positions when, in the background, I heard a voice on the radio saying something about 'movement in the bushes'. Not long after that, an almighty burst of fire rang out from down at the bottom end of the camp.

As soon as it went noisy, I grabbed my rifle, webbing and

radio and set off towards the sound of the gunfire. As I did so, I listened to Charlie Brand-Porter and told him I was approaching from the south. By now a big burst of gunfire had ripped into the camp and hit the Medical Centre or, to be more precise, the first bullets had hit the vehicles around the Medical Centre. Our doctor, Mark Coombe and the guys inside the building had been clearing up and doing their prep for the next day when they heard all hell unleashed just outside. Luckily, they suffered no casualties.

I don't know if the attacking force had directly targeted the Medical Centre but they must have known where it was because it had a big bloody red cross on it. If this burst had been a deliberate tactic to distract our people, so that some of the raiders could get close enough to the wire to crawl under it, they had chosen a pretty stupid target. The assault on the wire perimeter appeared to be taking place almost directly below the position from which the burst had come and near the Medical Centre itself. The BiH had clearly set up a fire support position on the high ground overlooking the north of our camp. Meanwhile, an assault force had crawled through the trees and bushes to get to the wire.

I was getting closer to BP but I didn't want to go running into a fire-fight in the dark. At the same time, I couldn't turn a torch on either because there could still be people in the wire or beyond, watching and capable of shooting straight at the light. So I was constantly calling Charlie on the radio, telling him where I was and what direction I was coming in from, to make sure he didn't shoot at me. Then I heard another burst of fire, just as I was getting quite close to them. There had been some more movement in the bushes. BP had reacted instinctively because more noise in the bushes seemed to signal a fresh attempt to attack. So Charlie and his guys had fired some more rounds in the direction of the movement they had heard. At that point, the BiH on the high ground began to lay down more suppressive fire to try to help their people.

'Shit? What the hell was that?'

I felt like I'd been whacked in the shin with an iron bar; that was the sort of force that hit me, except the pain was sharper.

'Fuck! I've been shot.'

I went down on one knee and tried to peer at the wound in the darkness to assess it.

'No, hang on, I can't have been shot. There'd be more damage.' The impact was right on the shinbone. A bullet would have shattered it. 'What the hell has just happened?'

Then I saw a fragment of metal in the wound. It must have been shorn off something by a bullet aimed roughly in my direction. The bullet itself hadn't ricocheted into me as far as I could tell. But the fragment of metal had caught me right there in the shin. Who had fired the bullet? Probably some BiH rifleman trying to cover his guys as they were moving back, rather than the men in the bushes. It was pretty inaccurate stuff but, for me, there had been this unfortunate knock-on effect.

'Crack on,' I thought. 'Fuck it.'

I had to get to the rendezvous point BP had sent me over the radio. Bullets were now pinging off various surfaces around me as the BiH fire support position did its job. But I had to press on if I wanted to be where my men were in this contact.

Then, after about twenty seconds, the incoming fire seemed to stop. Had the Muslims in the bushes sustained more casualties? Had they told their mates on the high ground to stop provoking the British any further? Both were very possible.

As I neared the RV, I heard shouting.

'They're in the wire, they're in the wire!'

It was Charlie Brand-Porter. Did he still fear he was about to be overrun by forces coming out of the bushes and trees? No, that couldn't be so: it had gone too quiet.

I arrived at the RV, hobbling slightly and treading carefully, as my men were excited and adrenalin fuelled. I was acutely aware that sudden movements to the rear of pumped up soldiers were unwise. I crouched down next to Brand-Porter. He was trying to contain his agitation as he shone a torch into the low wire. That was when I caught my first glimpse of a white face, arm twisted back, his camouflaged shirt rucked up. The man looked dead, his body trapped in the wire, but we couldn't be sure.

'There's another one, at least one more, behind him – and another crawling away,' BP said. He turned the light off, still aware of the potential threat from a sniper. We moved back, watched and listened.

'Make sure everyone's got a safety-catch on now,' I said.

I asked Charlie what had happened. He told me he had issued the standard challenge. 'Halt! UNPROFOR! Who goes there?' He'd followed that up with 'Stoi!', which is Serbo-Croat for 'Stop!'

If people don't mean any harm, they'll stand still. But BP's challenge had only prompted further movement, so he had opened up, dealing with what he saw as an immediate threat to the security of the camp and the safety of the people inside.

He had no choice but to try to whack some rounds into them, as he saw it; anyone would have done the same. The BiH fire support had opened up at that point and the fight had become more intense.

It seemed to me that part of the attacking force by the wire had taken cover after the first two men had been killed. The rest of them had probably decided it was time to get the hell out of there, so they had tried to take advantage of a lull in the firing by attempting to turn around and move away. But in the darkness, it's hard to tell if the sound of movement means retreat or fresh attack, so the rustling noise had provoked another burst from BP and his men.

I got on my radio to the ops room and told them to send the Muslims a message: 'Stop this. We have casualties.'

The BiH quickly denied all knowledge of the attack, dismissing it as a piece of independent, renegade madness. I instructed the Ops Room to send them a new message, telling them again to stop, therefore making it clear that we didn't believe for a moment that they didn't know what was happening.

We waited two or three minutes and, when we were convinced the area was clear, we got the torches out again and inspected the perimeter wire. BP was right. It looked like one body in the wire and another on the far side of the wire. I moved forward to the first casualty we'd seen. He was warm but there was no immediate sign of life.

By now, two of the SAS guys had come down to the scene of the shooting. One was the new Team Leader, Les Dixon. The other was 'Pig Man' Billy, who always liked to be in the thick of it. They had arrived at the perimeter a few moments after me because I'd had my kit ready, right where we'd been sipping the slivovitz. The SAS men had needed to go and grab their kit once it went noisy but they'd still joined us not long after I got down to BP.

Les came up behind me.

'Dead, boss?'

'Looks like it, mate.'

We got hold of some wire cutters and cut him out. We were pretty sure he was dead, though Les grabbed his weapon just in case. The mystery man was heavy – well fed for a citizen of Gorazde.

I said, 'Les, can you and the lads sweep the wire outside? We'll get this poor bugger into the Med Centre in case the Doc can do anything for him.'

'Roger that.' We were all business-like, focused.

With a couple of others, Charlie and I carried the casualty face down towards the Medical Centre. We were all still tensed up, not knowing whether the firing would start again. The moment we got the casualty into the Med Centre, we saw Mark Coombe waiting there with a stretcher, oxygen and medical equipment at the ready. I told him to do his stuff but he didn't need telling. I was the company commander but we were all now in Mark's domain.

'Get him on the stretcher. Stand clear. I have control,' he said.

Mark checked very thoroughly for vital signs, while I took the opportunity to start co-ordinating the follow-up action. As I started to talk into the radio again, I glanced back at the casualty and was greeted by a gruesome sight; one that made me realise how futile Mark's actions were going to be.

There was an obvious entry wound to the soldier's upper arm, which he could have survived. But he also had a small entry wound in his forehead and the bullet had made a mess by the time it had reached the back his skull. Blood and brains were dripping onto the floor and the canvass stretcher. He was very dead and, after only a few seconds, Mark confirmed what I knew already.

'No way, man, no fucking way! I've fucking killed him and there's fucking head jam all over the place.' It was Charlie Brand-Porter. He didn't like what he'd done and 'head jam' was his expression for brains.

I took BP back outside and tried to focus his mind on the task in hand because there was still work to be done. We found the other casualty, with a rifle, by the wire. He had clearly been shot too and he wasn't moving. He was wearing camouflage trousers but his torso was bare. Somebody had been trying to administer first aid. 'Pig Man' grabbed his weapon and we put him onto a stretcher and carried him to the Medical Centre too. The casualty had fair hair, protruding teeth and what we could now see was a gaping chest wound. He smelled of booze, which was no surprise, because most of them were on it, especially before an attack. Mark did his checks straight away, tried everything, and you couldn't fault his professionalism. But, even to a layman like me, it was obvious this poor soul was already on a journey too. Mark confirmed that the fair-haired man was dead, just like the other one.

As the adrenalin began to subside, I felt strangely detached from these unfortunate sights. My thoughts had turned to the lads outside, who were still presumably sweeping the perimeter for any more nasty surprises. With my mind mostly elsewhere, I found myself absent-mindedly lifting an eye-lid belonging to one of the casualties. I'd opened the left eye of the man whose brains had been leaking onto the floor. The eye transmitted nothing, though the lid was still warm.

My radio told me all call signs were in firm, safe positions. I took stock of the situation. We seemed to have it under control. There had been no more firing, we had the bodies and we also had their weapons. That was key because, at some point, we were going to have to explain why we opened fire.

The new Ops Officer, Ian Cave, had come down to see what was going on for himself. He was visibly shaken by the sight of the bodies. He was one of the coolest characters I knew but this was very close, very direct. He went back to the Battalion Headquarters vehicle and got on to the BiH liaison officer at their headquarters. Again, the message was crystal clear. 'You need to stop this or any thought of repeating it. I've been down there myself, there are bodies, we're going to get them down to the gate and that's where you can collect them.'

Mark Coombe was going to clean the dead up a bit, so that the sight of them wouldn't spark any more fury than was already inevitable. Having seen the bodies in their messiest state, however, Charlie Brand-Porter didn't look much better than Cave had done. He'd been the one forced into inflicting the damage and, though he'd had no choice, that didn't make him feel any better. The state of the first man and all that 'head jam' seemed to have disturbed him most.

I decided it was time for one of the SAS men to have a

firm but considerate word with BP, to sort him out before he fell apart completely. I was still too busy to do the job at the time, so I needed someone with gravitas, someone who had been there and done it. In short, I wanted BP to speak to a man who was well versed in the ugliness of killing. Any one of the 'JCOs' could then assess if BP was just a bit rattled and shaken up or if there was anything deeper to worry about psychologically.

I said to Les, 'I'm going to send BP up to you. Can you get one of your guys to talk to him?

'Yes, good idea.' Les replied. Then he chose Doctor Death.

'Look, he's a bit shocked,' Les said to Mac. 'He's never killed anyone before so can you have a chat with him?'

Obediah would be able to talk about killing with Charlie and make him see how it came with the job sometimes. There was another reason why Mac would be a good choice – he was free. I heard he was still up at the northern end of the camp, stirring that pot full of boiled sweets and slivovitz over a stove, as though he were auditioning for a part in *Macbeth*. No doubt Doctor Death would have sprung into action if he'd been called upon to do so but he hadn't been needed because the attack had been thwarted and was over fairly quickly. So Mac was ready and waiting when Les sent BP up to him, hoping the more experienced killer could settle the nerves of the novice with a chat over a sweet, boozy brew.

Everything was calm at both ends of the camp. And now my body realised there was no more need for adrenalin: pain took over. My leg hurt.

Mark looked down and said, 'What's happened to you?'

# MUSLIMS ATTACK

My trouser-leg was soaked in blood but I couldn't rest easy yet. I knew I'd have to answer to Bahto for this because the dead men were in uniform. Then I noticed the insignia on those uniforms. They were from the Manevarska Brigade – and that was the 81st Division's Special Recce Force. This was the kind of Special Forces Brigade used for deep reconnaissance and disruption, so I don't know why they had made such an obvious mistake as to attack from the same direction as a bungled diversion. And why had they attacked in the first place? Who, if anyone, had told them to do so? Although they were commanded by a major called Ahmed Sedic, he answered directly to Bahto. Sehdic had a certain amount of freedom compared to other commanders but he still had to clear anything of importance with Bahto. Something of this nature, against a UN mandated force? Bahto would have known about it. He didn't necessarily order the attack but he surely knew. What had been the motive? Were they simply trying to steal supplies from us? Perhaps they had simply gone one step further in testing our defences and our resolve, as a precursor to launching all-out attack in the next forty eight hours. If so, we had shown we meant business, just as we had promised to do, and that ought to act as a deterrent.

Back in the Medical Centre, I got back on the radio and began to transmit a formal Situation Report to Riley. I was calm by this stage but I still had to command the incident. While I was transmitting my report, Mark Coombe made me sit down and stick my leg up in the air. While he was cleaning and stitching up the wound, I contacted the Muslims again, asking them to come and pick up their dead.

'We have no dead,' they told me. 'This is nothing to do with us.'

The Muslims continued to insist that this had been some kind of renegade assault for which they couldn't be held accountable. But the Manevarska Brigade were fairly disciplined Special Forces by Bosnian standards and the attack had been co-ordinated, so it must have been planned, albeit without any tactical acumen.

Although the BiH repeatedly denied they had been involved, they did agree, since no one else had any appropriate vehicles, that they would come down and pick the bodies up. Meanwhile, Mark told me, 'You're going to need something for the pain. And I'm going to give you a massive shot of antibiotics.'

He wasn't kidding. He produced a syringe the size of a fire extinguisher and began injecting me. Then I saw a big bright flash. It was nothing more sinister than one of his blokes taking photographs of the bodies for evidence. He took a photo of me while he was at it.

We bagged the bodies up and they were taken down to the main gate for collection. Sure enough, within the hour, I was to be told that the men who had lost their lives had been picked up, presumably by their comrades.

Back in the Medical Centre, meanwhile, Coombe told me I looked as though I could do with a Jack Daniels. Before I could say, 'If only,' he presented me with one. Where he'd got the booze from I didn't ask. He had obviously been bartering somewhere and it was great to have a morale-boosting nip of JD with him.

Even by the bloody standards of Gorazde, this had been no

ordinary evening. Not that my mate Mark was particularly anxious to give me any peace of mind.

'Your wound could turn quite nasty,' he warned me.

'Oh. Great,' I replied.

# CHAPTER TEN

# THE WAR CRIMINAL

'What does it feel like to kill a man? Be honest. Feels good, doesn't it?'

Mac seemed to want Charlie Brand-Porter to connect with his inner animal.

Since I'd done all that was needed for now, I'd limped back up to the part of the camp where the SAS troop had originally been gathered. That's when I saw Mac's face: Doctor Death, illuminated by the glow of his cooker. BP sat opposite him, looking uncomfortable and holding a glass of slivovitz. Half an hour had passed since BP had been sent up to see Mac, so it was time to check on how the pep-talk was progressing. When I reached them, I saw the boiled sweets floating in their cups to sweeten the evil brew.

'How do you feel now then?' Mac continued, undeterred by the silence. 'It's a good feeling, isn't it?'

'No, it's not fucking good Mac, this isn't what I want,'

was the reply from Charlie, since he had been forced to say something.

I'd wanted Mac to be a bit more subtle. I thought he might say, 'Look, Charlie, it's always an unnatural feeling to end someone's life at close quarters and we need to talk about it. How do you feel?'

But Mac was empathising too much, almost trying to appropriate an experience with which he was all too familiar. Whereas BP wasn't familiar with this experience at all and he hadn't particularly wanted to be, not if he could help it. Mac, on the other hand, seemed to be savouring the whole thing. Added to that, I almost thought I detected a hint of envy in him. There shouldn't have been any envy, of course, not least because Mac had killed so many people himself.

Mac should have been saying, 'You're going to have to put this to one side, son. You did your job and, if you hadn't engaged them, they might have killed you or your soldiers. What you did was the right thing. Your training kicked in and now you're doubting yourself, and that's a normal reaction for a first-timer but you absolutely did the right thing.'

Instead, Mac was appealing to a baser human brutality. Poor BP was shaking and, when he saw me. he sent an imploring look in my direction – one which said, 'Actually, I don't want to talk about this with Mac because he scares the shit out of me.'

I realised this chat wasn't going well so I said, 'Thanks, Mac,' and I sat down to talk to Charlie myself about what had happened. BP was still a young kid really. And he'd just realised the enormity of what he'd done.

I said, 'Charlie, what you did was right.'

'Yeah, I knew Tiger wouldn't let the side down,' he replied.

Tiger, his rifle, had done the killing, not him. He was disassociating himself from the whole thing. This told me he was still completely fucked in the head and might need a bit of time to get back to normal. Les and the others came and sat down and we talked late into the night about it. I focused on debriefing BP and got him to concentrate on what he had seen prior to opening fire. I just wanted him to talk about it and go through what he had seen, heard and done.

He said he'd been in position, seen some people moving and reported it. I knew this was true because the Ops people had confirmed he'd reported, 'Movement out there.' I hadn't had my ear piece in at the time but the radio had been right next to me and I had heard that myself. There was no response to his challenge and so it had all kicked off.

BP said, 'At that moment, I just went for it. Gave them a good squirt and then a couple more for good measure. I heard one short grunt – like 'uugghh'. They were only about fifteen or twenty metres away from us. The guys wanted to get some torches and shine them into the wire but I was worried that would make us targets for their fire support position. I went forward in the dark and saw a body in the wire. I came back and realised I had to refer this up the chain of command.'

I told him again, 'Charlie, you did absolutely the right thing and I'm going to back you totally on this. People tried to come in, they were armed, there was only one reason they were armed and that was to do no good. You've told me you issued a challenge and they failed to comply; you did your job.'

I didn't want to worry him, or make him think that we were looking at a Board of Enquiry here. It wasn't going to be an easy one to deal with though. I sent a message to the BiH to say that I would come down into town in the morning to talk to their Liaison officer and any other officials from their Brigade about what had happened. I didn't expect that to be a comfortable meeting but we had right on our side. We had been attacked and were forced to defend ourselves. We had warned Bahto that we wouldn't be a soft touch like the Ukrainians. That warning had been ignored.

I wasn't going to go down that night because I thought feelings would be running too high. We'd dealt with the incident, we'd locked down and we'd deal with the aftermath the next morning, if nothing else happened before that. We couldn't be sure this would be the end of it for the night. Would they try again? Personally, I thought they might wait for the early hours if they did intend to have another go.

I got the rest of my Situation Report written up and sent it to Riley in the Ops Room. Then I told him I'd promised to see the Muslims the next morning to explain what had happened. I also sent a quick message up to the interpreters, to say that I'd need one of them for the job. Already I was hoping that interpreter would be Selma. This was going to be a tough assignment and she was just the woman to have by my side.

Would the Muslims understand that we had been left with no choice but to take down the men who had made the bizarre decision to attack our camp? I hoped so. I planned to do everything I could to make sure this was handled sensitively. The meeting with the officials from the brigade in town was set for 9.30am. That would be my chance to explain what had happened. The Muslims seemed just as keen as I was to have the meeting and that was a good sign. The interpreter, whoever that might turn out to be, was arranged for the following morning at 9 a.m., and that's when we'd go down to Muslim headquarters and face the music.

I snatched a few hours' sleep, knowing I'd be woken the moment there was any fresh hostility around the camp perimeter. Since there was none, I woke and got up at dawn. The mist still clung low to the River Drina, embracing both riverbanks, and that was just the way I wanted it. A couple of the SAS boys were ready to leave camp with me. We knew what we were after – as many clues as we could find to determine how many casualties the Muslims had sustained. I tried to ignore the pain in my leg from the minor wound I'd sustained the night before and suppressed the need to limp as best I could. We followed a trail of blood from the camp's perimeter fence, through the bushes and into the orchard, then down to the river. The mist was going to provide precious cover from any vengeful snipers already in position on the high ground over the river.

Using that natural cloak of invisibility to good effect, we calculated that, in addition to the two dead, two more BiH Special Forces must have been seriously wounded in the attack. Were they dead by now too? Or had they been rushed to hospital and successfully operated upon during the night? I hoped they had lived, though it certainly wouldn't have been the fault of my men if they hadn't.

By the time we returned to the camp, Selma was waiting. I hadn't known for sure that it was going to be Selma, though something told me it would be. I'd have to explain this one to her and I felt apprehensive; these were her people we'd been forced to hurt, after all. Mercifully for me, she already seemed to know all about it.

She came up to me and said, 'Is this about last night, Major Richard?'

'Yes,' I said a little sadly.

Either she had heard the gunfire herself or else the story had reached her from someone who knew. But the main thing was that she didn't look at me reproachfully and, immediately, I knew we could maintain our professional partnership for what might prove to be a tricky meeting.

'What do you want to do?' she asked.

'I just want you to come down and help me explain exactly what's happened.'

I got changed and shaved while she waited outside. Then she jumped into my vehicle and we were driven down to the municipal buildings in the centre of Gorazde by the Sergeant-Major. My official driver, Corporal Bird, was in the vehicle too, but the Sergeant-Major never let himself be driven by anyone else – he hated it.

My mind turned once more to the meeting. It was going to be important to keep things factual, so I had my notebook with me, and I was ready to tell them exactly what had happened. I hoped they would appreciate my openness and honesty. My approach was going to be sympathetic, up to a point, because people had died. But the Muslim authorities were going to have to be told in no uncertain terms what a big mistake they had made by allowing these Special Forces to attack us. These raids had to stop in order to avoid more loss of life. They had to get this simple message too.

When we arrived at the municipal building where the

Mayor Rasic was based, right next to BiH headquarters, we saw he had sent out a menial to greet us. I just had time to leave my rifle with the Sergeant-Major, as you always did for this kind of meeting. A big show of arms wasn't helpful to any diplomatic conversation and the Muslims wouldn't have allowed it anyway. The Sergeant-Major and Corporal Bird were told to wait outside. You never went into these occasions mob-handed.

'This way,' the Mayor's menial said, and even Selma looked surprised when we were led round to the side of the building, a route we hadn't taken before, and found ourselves in front of some huge mahogany doors. They opened, as if by magic, and we were ushered into an elegant room, beautifully adorned with wooden panels and ornate carvings. As we walked in, I was amazed. 'I didn't even know this building existed,' I thought, 'let alone how grand it looks inside.'

I realised it must be the Obstina, the Mayor's headquarters, but all the liaison work with Mayor Rasic had been done by Riley, which explained why I'd known nothing about this hall. It was quite something to see this stunning interior, such a formal setting in such fabulous condition, hidden away in a suffering town so pockmarked by war. Not that there was much time to admire my surroundings. Something about the scene ahead of us didn't feel right.

The door was quickly closed behind us and we were faced with a strange sight: there was big bench and five men dressed in bright red robes, who were just sitting there, looking stern. They stared at me solemnly. Rasic wasn't among them.

'What the fuck is going on here?' I sensed I'd been tricked in some way and this formality had a threatening feel to it.

It was time to take control. I took my beret off and walked towards them but they didn't like that and one of the men in robes spoke up strongly.

Selma translated, 'You're being told to stop, you haven't been told to approach the bench.'

'You tell them to fuck off,' I said.

'I can't say that, Major Richard,' she replied.

So I said it myself – 'Jebi se!' It was crude but a sixth sense had told me I needed to issue a direct challenge to their authority and seize the initiative if I was going to have any chance of gaining the upper hand here. Predictably, there was absolute outrage from the bench at my insolence.

'To hell with them! Keep walking,' I told Selma.

I pulled up chairs for Selma and me and we sat down. I tried to look confident and at ease. The central man of the five, who wore the robe with the fanciest-looking embroidery, stood up and began to talk in a very grand way.

I whispered, 'Selma, what's going on here?'

I could feel her shaking as she replied, 'You're being tried for war crimes because they say you commanded the murder of two innocent men last night.'

'You're joking.'

'No, this is serious,' she warned.

In truth, I'd realised something bad was happening the moment we walked in. But war crimes? Maybe it was time to turn round and leave while I still could. I glanced over my shoulder but there was a BiH guard on the door and he had a gun. I tried to stay as relaxed as I could under the circumstances. The head judge in the robe was still on his feet and making his grave pronouncements. Selma was trying to translate for me but, by now, I was only half-hearing what she was saying.

'I'm being tried?' I could still hardly take it in.

Selma was saying, 'You are charged on 25 August with the murder of Tetlic Ahmed...'

Murder? That stunned me so much that I didn't even hear the name of the other attacker we'd had to kill. But I knew I couldn't show any hint of panic. Potentially, that would be fatal.

'Try to look bored and disinterested,' I told myself. This was now a high-stakes game of bluff.

When my accuser had finished and sat back down, I asked Selma, 'Could you ask his lordship if I might have a word?'

Loftily and rather reluctantly, permission was granted from the bench. I stood up, all the time trying to convey a sense of control, and began. 'I've never been so insulted in my life. I came here to protect your town. The thanks I get is to be attacked in my own camp as a UN peacekeeper by your renegade, ragtag army. I come down here, out of courtesy, to say, "Isn't it a shame this happened?" And you have the audacity to put me on trial in this kangaroo, kindergarten court.'

As I spoke, I started to get genuinely angry. And I could feel Selma shaking next to me. She was holding onto my wrist and she was trembling as she tried to translate all this. The insults to the court were mine not hers, yet they were coming out of her mouth and she was going to have to live there if she survived the war and couldn't get away to start a new life for herself in somewhere like Spain.

Still I continued my verbal barrage, until, after about

five minutes, the judges looked almost as shaken as Selma. I suddenly realised I'd been admonishing them as I would admonish my most junior fusilier for getting drunk and pissing his bed. It was time to put an end to this and make good my escape but I wanted my final gesture to be as dramatic as possible, to mirror the setting somehow. I put my beret back on, saluted the coat of arms behind the bench and then turned to look at the guard on the door and his gun. He was between twenty eight and thirty and he already had some teeth missing. His gun was on a sling down by his side.

I strode purposefully towards him and felt Selma still at my side. Adrenalin was by now overriding any limp I should have had from the shrapnel wound the night before. With every pace I took, I looked the guard harder in the eye, almost daring him to defy me. And all the time I wondered, 'Is he going to level his weapon at me? I've left my rifle outside but I still have my pistol with me. Under what circumstances, in the next few seconds, will I be prepared to use it?' Is he going to refuse to step aside? Am I really prepared to shoot him?'

Mine was a Browning 9mm pistol. Although there was a magazine in there, the pistol hadn't been cocked. (It's not the sort of thing that you cock unless you're going to fire it because the safety on a Browning is not great). I had to think quickly. 'I don't want to fire it unless I really have to. So, if the guard gives me any trouble and I'm already close enough, I'll whip the pistol out and rap him firmly on the nose with the handle. Then I'll give him a sharper dig straight in the sternum for good measure and push him aside.'

Selma was still keeping up alongside; she wasn't going to get left behind. I sensed she was excited and agitated all at once but, most important of all, she was still right there with me. I kept walking and deliberately increased my pace. This was going to be the climax to our game of bluff. 'Come on, guard, make your move.' Just before I reached the door, he began to step to one side. I assume he must have received a signal from the bench because otherwise he would have stopped me, but I didn't care why it was happening; I was just relieved he was making way. I was able to open the door and walk out before they changed their mind.

Selma was beside herself. As we stepped outside into the sunlight, part of me was still trying to make sense of what had just happened. In some ways, it was the most outrageous thing I'd ever been through. I had thought I'd come down to attend a meeting with them, to explain what had happened, and to tell them why they shouldn't continue to try and break into our camp. I'd ended up on trial and I was still reeling from that. Part of me was incredibly angry that they had placed me in that farcical situation; part of me was still relieved that the guy had moved aside and we'd got out; there were any number of feelings racing through my mind at the time. Outrage, fury, surprise and relief all fought for control inside me as I walked briskly to my back-up vehicle. The sergeant major was still inside with Corporal Bird, my signaller, and they were parked up no more than twelve paces away from the front of the building. I was still half-expecting something else to go wrong and a belated attempt to detain me. Too late! I got into the passenger seat next to the sergeant major, while Selma climbed in the back next to 'Birdy'.

'You will not fucking believe what I've just been through,' I told them.

A wry grin of anticipation spread across Mark Adams' face as he said, 'Go on.'

'I've just been put in front of a panel of judges.'

'What?'

'I'm telling you, I've just been in there and they've pulled some kind of kangaroo court on me for killing those blokes last night.'

The grin on the sergeant major's face had quickly been replaced by anger. 'They did what? Do you want me to go in and have a word with them?'

He may have had a little more than 'a word' if I'd let him, knowing Mark Adams, but what use was that now? I'd said what needed to be said. And I'd got out in one piece – a free man.

'No, no, Sergeant-Major. I don't think so. Let's just head back and I'll tell the Ops Officer what's just happened.'

Poor old Selma was plaiting her legs in the back because she needed to relieve herself so badly. She insisted we drive round the corner to her house so that she could sort herself out. When she climbed back in, looking a bit more comfortable, I told her, 'Selma, I need you with me, so I can verify this for the Ops Officer – you are my witness.'

Our camp had rarely felt like a more welcome sanctuary. I dropped my kit off back at my portacabin and then went up to see Ian Cave, to tell him what had been going on. His mouth dropped open as he took notes. Having given Cave the heads up, I found Riley, who was sitting with his head in a book.

I said, 'I think you might be interested to hear what happened down in town.'

As I gave him the details, his eyes widened and then he

broke into a grin, shaking his head as if to say, 'What do you expect in a place like this? Expect the unexpected.' But then, as the implications started to sink in, he began to look angry on my behalf.

'What do I need to do?' he asked me.

'Nothing,' I said. 'The point has been made.'

He said, 'I'll be mentioning it in my next meeting with Rasic.'

I looked at him with an expression that must have conveyed my true feelings. 'You know what? What's the point anymore?'

Back in my portacabin there was a chance to sit down and reflect on my morning. 'What a fucked up world,' I concluded.

And my world was about to get just a little bit crazier, if that were possible. On 26 August, the day after the Muslims had attempted to try me for war crimes, I had to take a trip over into Bosnian Serb territory for a meeting at the Kopace wire factory, their local headquarters. It was all about judging the mood, keeping the Serbs sweet for long enough to get our men away to safety when the right moment came. Our first convoy was almost ready to leave Gorazde, so good communication was going to be important. We wanted to make sure our boys wouldn't receive an unnecessarily hostile welcome as they headed towards Serbia on the first leg of their journey home. I was hopeful that a reasonable working relationship had been restored but I also wanted to see for myself that the vibes were business-like over there.

The Bosnian Serbs' tactical commander for the town of Gorazde was still Lieutenant-Colonel Fortula. (He had been a major when we first arrived but, suddenly, one day he made himself a lieutenant-colonel). The way to reach him was through the latest Bosnian Serb liaison officer, whoever had succeeded the odious Captain Kepic. We, in turn, had put our own liaison officer back into Kopace as soon as things had settled down with the Serbs. His name was Rob Kirkup, he was a TA officer and I think he had been attached to one of the Wessex regiments. After first light, he used to cross the confrontation line to the Serbs in Kopace because he had an office there. And then, as he grew more confident, he started to stay down there for a couple of days at a time. I wanted to assess the situation with Rob's help. It was important to make sure Rob was happy that the Serbs were going to play ball on our extraction.

From the moment I arrived, one thing was clear: the meeting with Mladic – the one Riley, among others, had recently attended – certainly hadn't done relations any harm. It was tempting to believe they were almost back to normal – if anything could be called normal in this place. If you hadn't known better, you would hardly have suspected that the Brits and Bosnian Serbs had fought one another in May and that British soldiers had been taken hostage. In fact, the Serbs had even contacted Riley during the Muslim attack on our camp to ask, 'Do you want a hand?' I hadn't heard that offer first-hand because I'd been too busy dealing with the attack at the time but I'd heard about it since. Naturally, Riley had declined the Serb offer, just as they had probably known he would. But the Serbs must have struggled to hide their amusement at our plight that night. After all, we had taken sides for a while earlier in the summer and, no doubt, the soldiers of Kopace felt we had backed the wrong horse.

Rob soon told me there had been a lot of smugness over there about the Muslims attacking us.

'Bet you're really glad you defended Gorazde against us, only to be attacked by the very people you were fighting for.'

That was the kind of jibe Rob had to put up with. He told me he had played a straight bat and told them it was just renegade stuff.

'We believe this was the work of local criminals, not the BiH.'

The Serbs had a very good electronic warfare capability and they were listening in to all our radio messages by then anyway. I think they managed to piece together what had happened, so they probably knew that the attackers were of a higher calibre than local criminals. But they wouldn't have blamed Rob for sticking to his line anyway.

Having been briefed by Rob, my next task was to meet some of the Serb liaison people. The wire factory was quite a big area, all fenced off, and they had an office area where such meetings always took place. I went into one of these offices to talk about our extraction and make sure the Serbs would be focused on doing their bit to get us through when the time came. 'Reception procedures,' we called it. I didn't see Lieutenant-Colonel Fortula; they said he was busy, which sounded a little strange because this was supposed to be a significant meeting. Otherwise all went well and it was a relief to see that the Serbs were, indeed, ready to play ball, as far as I could tell. So, when I came out of the office, I was in a buoyant mood. Then I noticed that all the Serb soldiers were snapping to attention. Surely they weren't doing it for me?

Someone else was coming out of another office; somebody quite big on the Serbian side, it seemed. Presumably the self-important Lieutenant-Colonel Fortula himself. I saw part of a uniform and looked at the man's face and thought to myself, 'That's not Fortula. Isn't that...? No. It can't be.'

But it was. General Ratko Mladic was still deep in conversation with some of his officers and Fortula. I had almost bumped straight into the Butcher of Bosnia. His head was bare; he wasn't sporting the distinctive military cap he'd worn in the photo Riley had given me. Mladic was wearing a green top and camouflage trousers, looking relaxed and confident. He hadn't spotted me yet. How would he react?

Shit. Mladic was the last person I'd expected to see. I'd assumed he'd be long gone after losing a tactical level battle around here relatively recently. But then it dawned on me. He was here to make sure he could finally see the back of us. He had come down to make sure that the arrangements for us leaving were all in place. He'd probably just told Fortula, 'Right, let's not fuck this one up. We know the British are leaving, so let's make sure it goes smoothly. After they've gone, we can think about taking Gorazde.'

Strangely, given all that he'd done and all the misery he'd caused, some of which I'd witnessed at close quarters, I wasn't conscious of feeling immediate revulsion, as I stood there and stared at him in that moment of recognition. Here was a man who, to my mind, summed up the whole polarity, desensitisation and dehumanisation of the Balkan War. He had helped to bring about a situation whereby people living in the same town, who had married across the ethnic, religious and social divide, suddenly turned on each other and committed atrocities on a scale I couldn't previously conceive. There had been atrocities on both sides and yet

Mladic, more than anyone, seemed responsible, as head of the Bosnian Serb Army. He was a terrible man. So why couldn't I feel any hatred as I stared at him? I just felt numb. So how close was I to becoming desensitised and dehumanised too?

He turned slightly and saw me. Strangely, I felt compelled to acknowledge him, so I just said, 'Evening, General.'

He sneered at me. That was his way of acknowledging the presence of a British officer in this Bosnian Serb headquarters just outside Gorazde.

'Fine,' I thought. 'You just sneer away.'

He didn't seem to know that I'd been responsible for the deaths of a hundred of his soldiers just three months earlier. Or maybe he did know. Mladic obviously knew I was from the British battalion in Gorazde. He also knew from my uniform that I was a major, so he could have worked out that I was a company commander. The sneer remained on his face. He was a general and I was a lowly major; he was letting me know that... or was it something else?

'What else do you know, Uncle Ratko? Has the penny dropped? Do you know I'm the bloke who beat the shit out of your men earlier this summer? Hope not!'

Mladic might have been working it out as he walked past me, still wearing that sneer. And all the time I was wondering, 'Will he stop and come back? Our safety currently depends on his co-operation. How will I react if he comes over and starts prodding me in the chest, as he often does to people he wants to intimidate? It won't help anyone if I show open contempt for the man. But how will I react?'

Here was the butcher who had walked into Srebrenica,

as friendly as you like, smiling at the women and giving the children sweets, while all the time plotting the murder of those children's elder brothers and fathers. He had looked into the eyes of the women, knowing he was about to take the lives of their husbands, and he had told them all would be well. This disgusting man had been, at least indirectly, responsible for the casual murder of children in Gorazde such as Adem. He was the main reason my soldiers had suffered so much in Gorazde all summer, all driven to the limits of their endurance. And I was letting him walk away. My hands were tied, just as they had been tied all summer, except for in that battle in May and the skirmishes that smoked out the worst of the Serb snipers for destruction.

General Ratko Mladic did not turn back or provoke me. At least he didn't ask for money in return for what we'd done to his precious 'Ethnic Cleansing Brigade', as Captain Kepic had done after we'd hit the Butcher's child-murderers across the river from Vitkovice. Mladic didn't call for any recompense. And neither could I as I watched him disappear.

It had been a strange two days. On the first day, I had been put on trial as a war criminal, even though I wasn't one. On the second day, I had met a man who was surely the greatest war criminal in this entire bloody mess. And no one was parading him in front of judges in red robes. No one was trying to call him to account for the very real atrocities he had inspired and committed. He strutted around like some kind of untouchable god of war. And, for the time being at least, that's precisely what General Ratko Mladic was.

For all the so-called might of the United Nations and NATO, Mladic was still pulling the strings, to the extent that our lives still depended on his goodwill. And, as the poor citizens of Srebrenica had discovered to their dreadful cost, you could not depend on the Butcher of Bosnia for goodwill.

# CHAPTER ELEVEN

# THE SARAJEVO FACTOR

I couldn't believe what I was hearing. On 27 August Riley gathered his commanders together and told them, 'We're leaving very soon and I'm planning to take some of our interpreters with us. They have expressed their strong desire to get out of here and, if we can help them, I think we should. You have the right to object if you wish to do so.'

I objected immediately and explained why. 'Point one: we're going to be searched by the Serbs – and, if we're found with Muslin interpreters, it will jeopardise our chances of getting out. Point two: what's going to happen to them once they're found? They'll be taken away, gang-raped and murdered. And we won't be able to do a thing about it.'

The SAS Commander, Les Dixon, backed me up and Riley said he'd give it some thought.

It wasn't as though I was being disloyal to Selma, because she didn't want to go anyway. We'd touched upon this subject several times. She didn't want to leave her sister Samira, who was pregnant and had a husband in the BiH. And that was a relief because I was then able to explain to her that to try to smuggle any interpreter out would pose such a terrible risk and the consequences could be so catastrophic that it was almost suicidal. Selma could enjoy being an auntie for a while and then build her new life in Spain when the time was right.

After the meeting, Riley told me that Sabina and Adiata were the two interpreters due to be smuggled out – but it wasn't just them. The future of Sabina's baby hung in the balance too. There was even talk of the baby being sedated, so that the Serbs weren't alerted by the sound of an enemy infant crying at precisely the wrong moment. To me, this was all madness but I waited to see what Riley would decide.

Meanwhile, the first convoy was ready to go out and Padre Tucker was going to be on it. He'd stuck out the tour, strengthened by his faith. He'd continued to be pleased at the numbers attending his services and never had been told they were mostly there for the wine. I still didn't have the heart to disillusion Padre Tucker. But now, as he prepared his kit for his exit from the scene, he came to me with a complaint.

'I had a little Bible and I lent it to Fusilier Powell and he won't give it back.'

I said, 'Well, maybe he just draws great comfort from it. But what does the Bible look like?'

'I've got a few left. It's one of these,' he said, showing me a small Bible.

I noticed that the little Bible was made up of a certain type and size of paper. It was time to find Fusilier Dave Powell.

'Turn out your pockets,' I told him. He did so. 'That's rolling tobacco is it?'

'Yes, sir.'

'And what do you roll your rolling tobacco in, Fusilier Powell?'

'Paper, sir.'

'What kind of paper?'

'Whatever I can find, sir.' Powell was starting to look a little uncomfortable.

'Whatever you can find?'

'Yes, sir.'

'Show me your Bible, Powell.'

'Sir?'

'Show me your Bible. The little one you borrowed from Padre Tucker.'

Reluctantly, he pulled the Bible out of his kit bag. Let's just say it was incomplete.

'And let me take three guesses at what your tobacco has been rolled in lately, Fusilier Powell.'

Those three guesses weren't necessary because Powell confessed.

On closer inspection of the Bible, Padre Tucker decided he didn't want it back after all. Neither was Fusilier Powell granted permission to continue to dismantle it for his own practical purposes. I had no option but to throw the mangled remains into a bin.

There wasn't much time for smoking anyway because things were moving fast now. The medical station mobilised and went out with an advanced party before the first convoy left. The advanced party was commanded by Sergeant Richard

Mutlow, from my company. Mark Coombe and a couple of medics joined Mutlow's platoon and put up a first-aid dressing station, in case the worst came to the worst and the first convoy took casualties. Three or four vehicles in that advanced party also set up a checkpoint and were able to confirm that the confrontation line was not active when the first convoy started to roll. Those vehicles also acted as a guard position so that, if anything did happen, they could respond. If, on the other hand, the convoy passed through without incident, the advanced people would shut up shop and come back in to Gorazde camp.

There was so much to think about that I barely remember the first convoy leaving. There were only a limited number of fighting troops on it; members of the A Company platoon that had come under my command for the last few weeks of the tour in order to guard the Ukrainians. The first convoy consisted mainly of low-loader vehicles, admin people and a basic protective escort. It was made to look as much like a normal convoy as possible, although, with so much heavy equipment being moved out, suspicions were bound to be aroused. The locals were only too aware that there were no particular plans for us to be replaced and there was always the potential for feelings to spill over, even at this point. Yet, at the same time, there was perceived to be little obvious threat to this convoy, as the rest of us were still in the camp in numbers. Ours, the final convoy, was always likely to be the trickiest part of the extraction. If the locals were going to panic over the final UN pull-out, it would happen then because we sensed they would make their stand right at the end.

Mercifully, our hunch with regard to the first convoy was

correct and they made it through to Kopace. It was Rob Kirkup's job to make sure everything was in order for their final trip across the border and he played his role to perfection. Having seen the convoy pass by without local resistance, our medical station collapsed itself and came back into camp along with the guys who had set up the guard position. Unfortunately, by the end of the day, the medics would be needed within the camp itself.

That evening I was relatively close to the front gate and on my way to see Mark Coombe, the doctor. There was no particular reason for going to see Mark; it was just that he and I had got quite close and liked to spend quite a bit of time chatting to each other when nothing much was happening. He had been moved into what was like an ISO container that had been sunk into the ground. That made his Medical Station quite well protected from explosions. You had to go down a ramp to get into it but that was easy enough if anyone needed him. Inside, he had set up a temporary inspection room.

I was somewhere between my portacabin and Mark's ISO container when I heard a really sharp crack and then someone yelp in pain and shout, 'Fuck!'

For a moment I thought, 'Shit, is this the start of another attack?' But no more shots rang out and so I was able to glance across to the front gate without too much urgency to see what had happened. A young lad, Fusilier Jones 35, had just been shot between his thumb and forefinger. A corporal next to him, Griffiths 03, didn't appreciate the fuss he was making.

'Shut up and let me have a look at your hand,' he said. Then he began to bandage it. The corporal with the casualty was also looking to see where the shot could have come from. He seemed to have the impression it had been fired from a block of flats that overlooked the gate from a distance. The fusilier and corporal didn't look keen to hang around at the front gate longer than they had to. The shooter might be lining up another attempt.

Since the casualty was obviously going to be taken across to Mark Coombe, I carried on in the same direction. The situation looked under control so I thought, 'Might as well crack on and see Mark anyway, give him a heads up, because this bloke's going to be brought in at any moment.' It wasn't a company commander's job to go running to his men's assistance every time any incident happened. This hadn't been a sustained contact; they were big boys and they could handle it.

'Was that a shot?' Coombe said when I reached him.

'Yes. You've got some trade coming your way,' I warned him.

'Bad?'

'No, just a minor wound to the hand, I think.'

We had all seen so much worse over the course of the summer; this incident seemed to be little more than routine, though it clearly wasn't a typical occurrence for Fusilier Jones 105, who had received a nasty shock as much as anything. And, although the bullet didn't seem to have done much damage, the fact that the locals were angry enough to attempt to kill one of our blokes while they stood guard on the front gate was worrying. I was pondering the implications as Mark started clearing things away and getting himself ready with his team. Jones 35 arrived on cue with his hand bandaged over the first field dressing.

'Do you want me to clear off?' I asked.

'No,' Mark said and we carried on talking while he dealt with the casualty. Jones 35 was all right; the bullet had gone straight through his hand. Coombe stitched him and patched him up in no time. But our chat was interrupted when my Second-in-Command came in to tell me there had been another incident, just a minute or two after the first.

'We now have an unexploded grenade outside the main gate,' he said.

'How the fuck did that get there?' I asked.

'A Muslim brought it with him. He was drunk and, when he was challenged, he dropped the grenade – with the pin still in it – and he scarpered.'

Whoever the drunkard was, it sounded as though he was extremely lucky not to have been shot.

'I'd like to order in the UXO team,' my Second-In-Command said.

'Yes, do that straight away,' I said.

UXO was what we called the Engineer Unexploded Ordnance team. They'd clear the grenade and put an end to a potentially nasty incident. I thought I'd better go and tell Ian Cave what had happened. Somebody was making a point.

The next day, Selma came up to the camp and I asked her, 'Do you know anything about this?'

She said, 'I hear the man who fired the shot was a member of one of the families, Major Richard. You know, one of the two men killed here the other night.'

Over the next twenty four hours a message came in through intelligence that the culprit had, indeed, been one of the relatives of a raider shot dead at our perimeter fence. His family had wanted a bit of retribution by shooting one of my gate sentries. Fusilier Jones 35, it emerged, had been shot from a block of flats where Tetlic Ahmed had lived – Selma confirmed as much. I'd never known Tetlic Ahmed; the first time I'd seen him had been when we examined his body and found out who he was. Our paths had crossed under very sad circumstances, and a member of his family, probably in great pain due to that same sadness, had tried for a reprisal killing.

I could see why Tetlic Ahmed's family would hate us, even though he had been the aggressor. What felt strange was that the local community partly hated us and partly wanted us to stay. If we respected the views of the local community, we were supposed to stay so that we could be attacked by them. No way was that a sustainable situation. We could do the locals more good in the long run by leaving – we knew it, even if they weren't so sure.

'Selma, I believe we've outstayed our welcome,' I told her when we had a bit of free time in the camp together later on.

She stared at me unusually and said, 'There might be people in the town who don't want you to go.'

I said, 'We have to go.'

'I've told you before, Major Richard,' she said, still looking me in the eye. 'Maybe they won't let you.'

Her expression suggested she knew we'd be prevented. I thought, 'What's going to happen? Are people going to lie down in front of our vehicles so we can't drive out?' That would prove problematic. We couldn't just drive over them. They might be ordered to lie down in front of the vehicles by the BiH or the people running the town. In that case, it wouldn't even be their fault that they were obstructing us. We'd still have to get out of our vehicles and rip them out of the way at gunpoint though. And that would leave us vulnerable to sniper fire. Were we going to be attacked again? I tried to explain to Selma once more why such stubborn gestures of defiance would be against the best interests of the townsfolk.

'We're not making you any safer by being here now. The only factors that will make you safe now are your own soldiers, who have control of the high ground, and the continued presence of military observers and forward air controllers after we've gone. In fact, stay in your basement once we've left, Selma, because there's every chance our Forward Air Controllers will bring in air strikes against the Serbs, almost as soon as we're out of the country.'

I wanted her to take that message to anyone in the town she could. I wanted to convince her that I wasn't abandoning her. Yet, as I spoke, our eyes didn't really meet.

Deep down I was thinking, 'What's going to happen to you?'

And all the time the expression on her face suggested, 'You're just like all the rest. You come in and do your best but now you're going home and I'm left here.'

She was right about one thing. We were going home. At least we were going to try, while we still could. It was a very tense time, even by the insane standards of Gorazde. More and more Muslims were patrolling the high ground around the camp. There was menace in the air. Riley got on to Bahto and told him to stop the escalation before something even worse happened between two sets of soldiers who had fought almost shoulder to shoulder against a common foe a few months earlier.

'Get a grip of your command, Bahto. We've agreed we're going, you're going to get a good deal out of it.'

Bahto listened and said he would do what he could. But we knew by now that he couldn't guarantee us anything. Would the simmering resentment we could feel all around us explode into violence once more? Or could we get out in time? It was now or never. We were the last convoy. Now we were just sitting round, waiting to go, and all the vehicles were packed.

Riley gathered us together. In an effort to try to restore some normality to the camp, we'd started using the old headquarters briefing area – the one we'd used when we had first arrived a lifetime ago, as it seemed. This briefing area wasn't by the bus station but at our end of camp instead. So the commanders met and sat down at a location just inside the main gate on the left. Given what had happened at the main gate relatively recently, this may have seemed unnecessarily risky but, to us, it was a way to show that we weren't going to be intimidated. The spot was also convenient for Riley because it was right next to his accommodation.

'We're definitely leaving in the next twenty four hours,' Colonel Jon began.' Probably in the early hours of tomorrow morning. We'll make it as subtle as possible when we go. I repeat, let's not make it too obvious, otherwise they may try to oppose us.'

Riley certainly hadn't made a big song and dance of his extraction plan. I wouldn't go as far as to say that it had been written on the back of a cigarette packet but not far off.

He had actually scribbled a sketch of the formation on the back of an old ration pack! He'd drawn the formation in the way he thought it would most naturally and effectively stay mobile and, if necessary, defend itself as one. When he gave us all a good look, it sort of made sense. So no one argued about how the convoy was going to be formed up when the big moment came. But what about the more controversial issue of the interpreters?

'One more thing,' added Riley. 'Having given your objections due consideration, I've decided to respect your wishes. The interpreters who wanted to come with us will no longer be doing so.'

Although I was relieved, I also suspected this late U-turn wasn't going to go down well with the interpreters, not least because I knew that Mark Coombe had already sedated Sabina's baby.

I bumped into Selma near the briefing area, just after we had left the meeting with Riley. The interpreters' hut was quite close by and, when I came out, there she was, standing outside. She must have come out of the hut only seconds earlier but it almost felt as though she or someone else had been secretly listening to our briefing. She was a little downcast, her brown eyes not yet able to meet mine. There was some uneasy shuffling. She was still looking at her feet, rather than looking at me.

'Hi, Selma. How are you?' I said, as easily as I could manage.

She looked up slightly and then back down again, before muttering, 'So, you're leaving.'

'We were going to have to leave at some stage,' I pointed out.

'And none of the interpreters are going out with you?'

I suppose I'd been waiting for this. 'Listen, Selma, it's just not safe. I have no doubt that, when we get to Kopace, the Serbs will want to do a number of things. They'll want to exercise control over us, show who is boss in their eyes. They'll do the sort of humiliating stuff they're used to doing. We'll be told to get our rucksacks out, the Serbs will go through every personal possession to make sure we're not smuggling anything out. And then, above all, they'll make a point of searching our vehicles. Thoroughly. And, if they find that we're smuggling people out from the town, any number of things could happen. First, they'll probably impound us. And that would be extremely embarrassing for the UN. Then they will take away the civilians they have discovered. And you and I both know what will happen to them.'

Selma didn't seem to want to accept this explanation, perhaps because she had talked to the interpreters who were ready to leave and saw how desperately they wanted a new start for themselves and, in Sabina's case, for her baby. Selma wanted a new start too and, even though she was prepared to wait for her own chance, she completely understood those who could take life in Gorazde no more and wanted out immediately. I understood too. But we weren't going to be able to help them like this. In fact, I thought it would be tantamount to killing them.

It was awful to have this atmosphere between us, Selma and me, so close to the end of our time together. Even then, I didn't think it would be our last meeting because we didn't think we'd be going until the early hours. So there was no sense of goodbye in that conversation; there was no finality. It felt a bit embarrassing to have bumped into her, in all honesty. There was no farewell. I thought I was going to see her again within a few hours. Departure wasn't so imminent that I wasn't going to have the chance to go round a bit later, clear the air, give her a final hug, look her in the eye and say, 'Selma, look after yourself. Thanks so much you for everything you've done and for helping me to stay strong.' For now, we just went our separate ways and the only thing we had in common during those moments was our growing sense of awkwardness.

Selma had conveyed her sense of betrayal mostly in silence and that is often the hardest thing to handle. But Sabina was unlikely to be silent, probably because she had reason to believe there could be no going back. After all, her baby had already been drugged by our doctor. That way, the hope was that the little one would sleep once hidden in the back of a wagon and, without the baby making a sound, they might get all through. That obviously wasn't going to happen now because Riley had listened to me and changed his mind about taking interpreters with us. I suddenly saw Sabina come storming towards me. I realised that somebody must have told her that I'd been the most vocal opponent of the plan – probably Selma.

'Why are you stopping us? Why?' she screamed.

'Because you'll be discovered,' I replied, trying to stay calm.

'No! We'll hide well! What's the matter with you? We're not scared. Are you? Why are you doing this?'

'Listen to me. Sabina, listen. They'll search the vehicles at Kopaci and they'll find you. When they find you, they'll take you away and rape you and then murder you. And they'll murder your baby too. I'm not going to let that happen.'

It was true. Sabina was very attractive and the Serbs would

have enjoyed their sport. The baby would have been silenced as an inconvenient distraction. I wouldn't have been able to influence events because the British would have been seen by the Serbs as the villains of the piece, for treacherously trying to smuggle 'the enemy' through. They would have been raping and murdering for fun but they would still have seen us as the bad guys. That's how messed up this place was. I didn't want the consequences of any discovery of the interpreters on my conscience. The sight of Sabina being dragged out of a vehicle with her drugged child and led away to be used as a plaything before slaughter would have haunted me forever. It would have destroyed me.

'Give me back my baby,' said Sabina, calmly and coldly, as though we had just given them both a death sentence. She looked at me as though I were a traitor, a coward and a murderer all at once. It hurt but I held onto reality and the knowledge that, whatever she felt right now, she was probably going to live through this, and so was her baby. With that perspective, I could just about live with the way she looked at me before she left the scene in disgust.

This was Gorazde. The Serbs hated us and had fought us and we'd had to kill some of them. The people we had tried to save now mostly hated us and we'd had to kill a couple of them too. Those we hadn't killed felt we were as good as killing them anyway by leaving, even though the opposite was true. Gorazde was a madhouse and we had to get out, for everyone's good and for our own sanity too.

I went to see my sergeant major and we went through the basic extraction plan once more, making sure we hadn't overlooked anything. A Muslim commander had already warned us that it wouldn't be safe for the British to stay another night in Gorazde anyway. On that basis, it didn't seem logical to wait until the early hours before we left. More and more it was starting to feel as though it was now or never.

Another of my occasional interpreters, Hassan, came up to me. I thought he was going to give me more grief but he just wanted my Nike training shoes. If I was leaving, he reckoned it was only fair.

'Okay, a hundred dollars,' I joked.

'A hundred? I don't know.'

He seemed to be considering it. And that meant he was a desperate guy because these were the training shoes I'd been running in just about every day for six of Bosnia's hottest months, so they truly stank! And he was still thinking about paying me a hundred dollars for them?

'No, Hassan, it's a joke. You can have them.'

He'd been annoying me for months and all I really wanted to do was to cuff him around the head. But I wasn't going to let one of my last acts in Gorazde be to rip off one of the locals. That's what the Ukrainians had done, not the Brits. I pulled the pair of trainers out of my kit bag and handed them over. He was still thanking me when a runner came down and interrupted us.

'Sir,' he said to me. 'The CO wants you with him immediately. He's in the Ops room.'

'Oh God,' I thought, 'What now? How many more problems can we have? This is the last convoy. Has something happened to prevent our departure? Will we be stuck here forever, until we desensitise and dehumanise so completely that we lose the basic morality and humour that is holding us together as a group?'

I'd soon find out because I saw the urgency written on that soldier's face and there was clearly no time to waste. I dashed up to the Ops room to join Riley and find out what was going on. I got there just in time to hear General Rupert Smith, the British UN Commander, convey some alarming news on the TACSAT radio from Sarajevo.

Smith said, 'We've got a problem. There's been a mortar attack in Sarajevo. We have thirty local people dead in the market.'

Riley looked skywards and I said it for him. 'What the fuck next?' We knew the Serbs were already on a final warning from NATO. We realised the potential ramifications straight away. But Rupert Smith spelled them out anyway.

'Listen, this could be a bit of a game-changer for you people because we believe this mortar has come from the Serbs. We're not a hundred per cent sure at this stage. But fairly soon the UN is going to have to make a statement condemning it. We'll try not to point the finger until we have to. Because once the UN points the finger at the Serbs, the word will go down their chain of command to that effect. And, just because they can, the Serbs will stop all movement. And then you won't get out.'

What else could go wrong? It wasn't the first time the Bosnian Serbs had shelled the marketplace in Sarajevo and caused innocent casualties but why do it again now? The senseless butchery was horrendous enough in itself, even in a place where civilian deaths had become commonplace. But this time there were likely to be extra consequences. The climate had changed and, if it was shown beyond reasonable doubt that the Serbs had been responsible for this atrocity, it was clear that NATO might initiate instant reprisals against the Serbs through air strikes. It was hard to argue against the fact that air strikes were, by now, the right way to go; in fact, the Americans had been pushing for this no-nonsense outcome for a long time. The trouble was that, if we were to avoid being seized and used as human shields by the Serbs again, we had to get away immediately. We had to follow the outline of our agreement with Mladic before he had time to realise how useful we might be if captured. And that meant escaping as quickly as possible over the border from Bosnia into... Serbia.

Yes, it sounded ridiculous. To escape from Bosnian Serbs into their spiritual homeland, Serbia itself. But Slobodan Milosevic, Serbia's leader, had distanced himself from the battle in Bosnia. He could see the way it was going, so we weren't going to be taken hostage by Milosevic in Serbia itself. And Mladic had granted us safe passage out of Bosnia, as long as we unloaded all our weapons at the border for the final journey towards Belgrade. Would he stay true to his word this time?

Mladic was his own man. He wasn't a puppet of Slobodan Milosevic, or even the most respected political leader, Radovan Karadzic, for that matter. Mladic realised he had to have political masters but that didn't mean he always had to bow to them; indeed, he had even told Karadzic to shut up during meetings, according to many accounts. When it came down to matters military, Mladic was the man – he was all-powerful. So it was still conceivable that Mladic could yet turn, particularly in light of the latest atrocity in Sarajevo and the likely reaction of the civilised world.

No one knew any of this better than General Rupert Smith, the British UN Commander.

Smith sounded anxious when he said, 'Jon, listen, how soon can you be across the border?'

Riley said, 'Thirty five to forty five minutes.'

# CHAPTER TWELVE

# THE RACE
# AGAINST TIME

General Rupert Smith paused for a moment. There was a big decision to make and no time in which to make it. 'I'm not sure how long I can keep the lid on this,' he admitted with disturbing honesty. 'But get going. And tell me when all of your Fusiliers are across the border.'

But how was Rupert Smith going to 'keep a lid on it', as he put it? As we prepared to leave, the fact remained that there had been an explosion in Sarajevo's market place and civilians had been killed. You couldn't keep that a secret. But Smith and the UN in Sarajevo had decided, at least for now, to say that the origin of the lethal shell was unknown. And that was much better from our point of view than if the UN pointed the finger at the Serbs straight away. A direct accusation of 'you did it' would likely set off a chain of unfortunate events that would put us in even more danger.

The biggest immediate threat to us posed by those tragic events in Sarajevo was that the Western media would broadcast something about the atrocity immediately and spark a storm of protests and demands for action. Then Mladic would rightly suspect that the international outcry was going to result in an instant backlash and he would issue the order we dreaded: 'Right. Freeze all movement. If NATO's thinking of hitting us, we've got British hostages here to use as a bargaining chip.'

The Americans were getting impatient with the Serbs and NATO was ready for action. Once they had proof that the market-place atrocity was the work of the Serbs, they'd be sure to say, 'Right, you've had your last warning – we're going to smack you now.' And as soon as the Serbs knew they had a NATO strike coming their way, they would try to seize us as human shields. General Mladic was a butcher but he was also a shrewd customer and he would know how to protect himself in a crisis. We were hoping that Mladic hadn't been the one to order the Sarajevo shelling and that no local commander had told him what had happened yet. Of course, Mladic would have to be told straight away if there was unequivocal UN condemnation of the Serbs. We were hoping that condemnation wouldn't come too soon for us.

The longer Smith could say, 'We're not sure who did it,' the more time he bought us. We only needed an hour or two of any kind of measured statement – anything but a knee-jerk reaction. Smith might only need to say, 'This could have been a Muslim misfire for all we know, or it could indeed have been a deliberate Serb shell attack. We're investigating before we jump to any hasty conclusions.'

But the atrocity was probably already causing such outrage among the Muslim authorities in Sarajevo that we could well imagine the intense pressure Smith and his colleagues must have been under to condemn the Serbs from the outset. That's why General Rupert had admitted to us that he wasn't sure how long he could keep a lid on the situation. We knew he'd do his best. But we had to leave now, while we still could. We had to get ourselves together quickly enough to give ourselves a chance of getting through.

Within ten minutes we had assembled the tactical convoy. It was fast work, to say the least, but, in theory, it also left the potential for errors.

Riley looked at me searchingly and asked, 'Have you got everybody?'

'There's nobody outside the camp,' I replied. 'We're all here.'

But a little voice in my head was telling me, 'There's always one. I bet there will be one. "Fusilier Fucknasty" from Rhyl will have spotted the local prostitute and decided to have a quick one before we go.'

That's why my next move was to tell Sergeant-Major Mark Adams, 'Go and check every man.'

Adams came back a few minutes later and said, 'Sir, I can account for them all.'

But he hadn't been gone long and I still wasn't convinced. 'Sergeant-Major, don't get angry with me,' I said, 'but go and do it again.'

Adams gave me one of his disapproving looks and I felt he was owed an explanation.

I said, 'I've got to be sure. My biggest nightmare is that

we're driving out and we suddenly realise we've left a bloke behind.'

The sergeant major doubled round, went off again and came back to give me his news. 'Sir, I can absolutely confirm, one hundred per cent, that every man is in their vehicle, bombed up, weapons made ready, waiting to go.'

As Tactical Commander for our extraction, I felt a huge weight of responsibility. We'd come so far during this harrowing summer and, under the circumstances, we'd achieved more than we could have hoped for. Gorazde had not been taken. Not that Gorazde was looking particularly grateful. In such a hostile atmosphere, how was this going to play out? I felt a deep nervous tension but couldn't show it. I needed everyone to see that we were in control of our own destiny, and there was no room for any trace of doubt in a leader. We'd planned for this and we were ready for anything.

We'd been through all the possible outcomes and there were a number of them. As with the first convoy a couple of days earlier, we had sent forward an Advanced Guard Platoon and a mobile Medical Station, in case we had to fight our way out and had casualties. We thought there might be some serious opposition from the locals and, should that materialise, the advanced platoon was going to lock them down with fire while the main convoy came through. Then the advanced platoon and medics would eventually rejoin us at the back of the convoy. Any problems during a fire-fight might be compounded by the breakdown or partial destruction of a vehicle, of course. But once we'd established superior firepower – and we had to believe we would – we planned to hook up any vehicle that had broken down or been immobilised and then drag it out of there. Under extreme pressure, we still hoped we'd get air support to help suppress enemy positions. That would give us time to deal with any casualties or other problems as best we could. Nobody was going to be left behind, absolutely nobody. So, if we had to fight a bit longer to get those casualties out, that's what we would do. My company would provide the final rear-end guard. No one was going to get picked off at the back. Not on my watch.

Of course, we could plan all we liked but that didn't mean we wouldn't be surprised in some shape or form. It was always a case of 'expect the unexpected' in Gorazde, so we were going to have to be ready for anything. I thought back to Selma's recent warning: that people might try to throw themselves in front of us to prevent our departure. My position hadn't changed. If we encountered civilians lying in the road like that, we'd have to get out and shift them. That would expose us to potential sniper fire. Would snipers be willing to risk killing their own people in the chaos as well? They just might. Would Selma's concerns prove well founded? We'd soon find out.

As for Selma herself, there was going to be no time to say goodbye. No time to mend the tension between us. No time to hug her in shared recognition of the horrors we'd been through, or even shake hands and thank her more formally for all she'd done in the most trying of circumstances. Selma had translated the casual words of the callous Captain Kepic, as he told me that Gorazde's children were fair game for his snipers. She had endured all the Serb threats of rape and murder at the confrontation lines; she had interpreted for me when the delirious Srebrenica survivor had come over the hill and told us of the massacre there. She had interpreted at the start of my trial for war crimes and she had remained at my side even as she shook with fear. Dear, brave Selma. Would I ever see her again? No time to wonder because I'd just heard the order over the radio.

'Charlie Charlie One this is Zero Alpha move now, move now.'

I ran to my Saxon and climbed towards the turret, ready to move. Then, bizarrely, I heard my sergeant major say, 'What are you doing?'

'What does it look like? I'm getting in the turret,' I said.

Mark Adams was adamant. 'You promised me I could command the vehicle on the way out.' Shit. I had, indeed, promised him that. When any vehicle was on the move, he just hated not being in control.

'For fuck's sake, have it!' I said.

Then we heard a noise. I could hardly believe my ears when I heard the sweet sound of a plane in the skies above. And the irony was that air support had finally arrived just as we were leaving. They never had before, no matter how many times we had requested 'Blue Sword'. I had personally been refused air support six times in six months. Not that I was complaining now. For the first time, apart from that SAS exercise in mid-summer, we saw an aircraft above us.

That's when I thought, 'This might just work.'

Although it was just one aircraft, we knew that no one really flew alone in this environment. Each pilot flew in his respective orbital but there might have been five or six aircraft in the area and then perhaps another four or five in a nearby orbital. Rupert Smith had managed to arrange this little surprise as a show of force, even though the aircraft were NATO, not UN. Who cared what they were? Even if one aircraft screams in low, it's generally enough to shock and scare anyone into getting their heads down. If we needed air power to dig us out of trouble, we were now confident it would.

We started to move out. But, as we did so, I heard a couple of shots fired into the air and they certainly weren't taking pot shots at the plane. It was the BiH warning people we were on our way. I thought, 'Right, this could get cheeky now.' At every turn, I was expecting to see a roadblock and knew we'd have to smash straight through if they offered any resistance. We had to keep moving. Had we done enough preparation with the local population to make this work? Although we'd done our best, I was well aware the Muslims were still feeling betrayed. Had they belatedly bought into our reassurances, or were pride and resentment about to get the better of them?

'It doesn't matter that we're going because we're leaving behind Forward Air Control parties and UN Military Observers.' Riley had told Bahto this repeatedly and Selma knew it too because I had told her so. But most of the locals probably still didn't know that a group of Forward Air Controllers would remain to operate in the area covertly, ready to guide NATO air strikes down onto the Ethnic Cleansing Brigade if the Bosnian Serbs so much as threatened Gorazde again. Most locals probably saw UN soldiers trying to desert them, just as UN soldiers had deserted their Muslim neighbours in their hour of need at Srebrenica.

Our first destination, the Kopace wire factory, still seemed a long way off as we headed for the outskirts of Gorazde. If someone was going to jump out from behind a gravestone in the Christian cemetery west of Gorazde and have a go at us with a rocket-propelled grenade as we left the town, we'd have no warning. However, it was going to take a very ballsy person to expose themselves for long enough to set their sights and fire an RPG, when we'd have a twelve-ton Saxon with a machine gun on top of it and a trained soldier ready to open fire. Any attacker with an RPG would need to be a minimum of about three hundred metres away, otherwise the missile wouldn't have time to arm itself. But that sort of range wouldn't pose a problem for our machine-gunners. While the enemy fanatic was trying to take aim, he'd more than likely be killed before he pulled the trigger. Of course, there was always the possibility that he might get lucky and get his shot off before we could take him down. But we felt the chances of that were slim. There were six to twelve of those Saxons and each machine-gunner was covering a set arc. If it happened, the vehicles were protected by armour, so we'd be unlucky to suffer a fatal hit.

The SAS were also with our convoy and no doubt ready for anything. It wasn't their job to confront attackers in this situation; the instant reaction would have to come from my men. But it wouldn't do us any harm to have the SAS on board if we were faced by a determined and fearless enemy launching a sustained assault. Were they about to hit us with something we hadn't foreseen? We braced ourselves as we continued our journey towards the confrontation lines. We waited for the Muslims to launch some foolhardy attack, just as they had when we were still in our camp. And we waited some more, every one of us thinking, 'It's too quiet, something's wrong, this is the calm before the storm, it must be.' We were almost out of Gorazde, reaching the end of the cemetery, and still there had been no opposition. Nothing. Just people staring.

Still I was thinking, 'It's got to come... they're going to hit us somehow... it's got to come.'

We met up with the Advanced Guard Platoon, which was waiting for us up the road. Sure enough, the medical station was up and running nearby, all ready to tend to our casualties – but we didn't have any. So the medics collapsed their mobile base and joined the back of our convoy with the advanced platoon as planned. Keep moving. Just keep moving because this is too good to be true.

We left Gorazde and all its recently dug graves behind, following the main road along the Drina towards the Serb liaison officers at the wire factory. For all our differences, the Muslims had left us in peace when it mattered and placed their trust in our promises instead. A fragile, belated trust maybe but they had apparently decided to believe what we had told them about imminent air strikes against the Serbs once we were clear. I imagined Selma putting her personal anger to one side and assuring all who asked her that it would be so. I believed she had done so, for, with the painful exception of our necessary U-turn on taking interpreters out with us, we had been as good as our word all summer – and Selma knew it. Salko Osmanspahic knew we had acted with honour too, as did Bahto, above him in the BiH chain of command. The five grave men in their red robes must also have known it, even as they tried to sit in judgement on me a few days earlier, for we had warned we would fight off any further raids on our camp using all available aggression. So the Muslims had put their trust in us and listened at the key moment for us and they had let us go without a fire-fight, or the kind of organised delays that might have ended our hopes of winning our race against time. I wasn't sure what it all meant. There was no time even to allow myself to think that it might represent hope for the future.

All I consciously hoped was that NATO and the UN would keep their promises to protect the people of Gorazde. We had to. After all they'd been through, Selma and the others deserved that much. Personally, there was nothing more I could do for them. It was their enemy who represented the next immediate threat to us and then, perhaps, to Gorazde once more.

We could still hear air cover somewhere above us. But would those planes be able to stop the Bosnian Serbs from taking us hostage when we reached Kopace, if that's what they intended to do? Hostage-taking was almost a national sport for these Serbs. Could NATO stop the pursuit of that sport from high in the sky? It was doubtful. If the Serbs snatched us, planes couldn't hurt them without hurting us too, so the NATO pilots would be powerless to prevent our seizure. All those aircraft would be able to contribute, if the game suddenly changed, was a show of strength. It had worked with the Muslims, which was something. But, if the summer had taught us anything, it was that General Ratko Mladic and the Serbs didn't always respond to Western strength in the way the West wanted or anticipated. So, with the Muslim threat all but behind us, we began to switch our focus back onto the race against time, to get through all the Serb lines before they could turn hostile on us again.

We reached the confrontation lines and passed from the

Muslim world we had inhabited for so long into the Bosnian Serb world at Kopace. There was no time to look back on all the suffering we had just left behind or to assess what we had or hadn't achieved. The Serbs, who had caused so much of the misery we had witnessed, were waiting for us – and in force. Was Mladic himself among them? He had been here two days ago; I'd seen him with my own two eyes. Had he stayed to oversee our departure personally? I sincerely hoped not; his mood could change like the wind if he suspected he was being played in any way.

This was undoubtedly going to be the greatest period of risk. Had we beaten the Serb passage of information? Did this particular bunch of commanders know about the Sarajevo market atrocity and the outrage brewing in NATO? Had the media already broadcasted something? Or would they tell the world about what had happened while we were still effectively trapped under the perpetrators' control, in their own back yard? If the Serbs were being publicly blamed already, I didn't think they would hesitate to block us. If they sensed they were once again public-enemy number one, the Serbs would react angrily, like the bullies they were.

It might not take the Butcher of Bosnia to order our detention either. Even if Mladic was no longer at Kopace in person, Colonel Fortula, the local commander, would probably issue the same order if he foresaw an imminent NATO backlash for the Sarajevo slaughter: 'Freeze all movement.'

That was the three-word directive we dreaded. Fortula could then tell Mladic what he'd done.

'Don't worry about that news bulletin, sir. If NATO's thinking of hitting you on Mount Igman, or wherever those shells into Sarajevo were fired from, we can make them think again, sir. I've got at least fifty British hostages here to use as a bargaining chip.'

These were the thoughts running through my mind as we were processed into a car park and subjected to the kind of intense scrutiny I'd anticipated.

'Get out of your vehicles!'

We had to oblige, so that they could be searched and we could show we weren't smuggling anything or anyone out.

'All your kit out!'

We had to follow that instruction too. Every item of our kit had to be laid in front of us. The Serbs were searching everything.

'Christ,' I thought, 'this is going to take time.'

Numbers of people were checked off by the Serbs. The clock was ticking. Meanwhile, as an officer, I had to ignore this heavy-handed treatment and go through the UN protocol of smiling and saying hello to the Serbs, even while our vehicles and kit were practically being taken apart. I searched for the sneering face of Ratko Mladic. I couldn't see him. Where was he?

News travels fast. Was it going to travel too fast for us? One journalist and one mention of the Sarajevo markets could prompt our encirclement by tanks, accompanied by the pronouncement, 'You're going nowhere.'

Much earlier in the year, a British unit had been kept in this area for fourteen days because of some Serb-manufactured reason for a delay. It didn't take much to come up with an excuse, not if it meant satisfying the latest whim of Ratko Mladic. Never mind a fortnight; we felt we had no more than an hour or two at the very best. And yet, despite the tension I was feeling inside, I was still casually strolling around, trying to look relaxed; still trying to smile at the Serbs. We hoped and prayed Rupert Smith had done a good enough diplomatic job to get us into Kopace and out again the other side before the penny dropped in the Mladic camp. Smith had practically said himself that it could all go 'tits up' at any moment. That was hardly reassuring.

The Serbs were still practically dismantling the British vehicles by now, as if looking for something. And I couldn't help thinking, 'Thank God we didn't bring Adiata, Sabina and her baby with us, as Riley had offered. I'm so glad I opposed that.' The Serbs would have found the interpreters and the infant in the back of one of the vehicles, however well we'd hidden them. I could have been stood there, at this very moment, watching helplessly as the Serbs took them away to rape the women and then murder all of them – I was even more convinced of it.

As it was, they found no offensive item and we were told, 'All right, put your kit back in the vehicles.'

Did that mean we were free to go? Maybe Mladic hadn't even heard about the shelling of Sarajevo yet; maybe he hadn't personally ordered that atrocity and no one wanted to tell him about it, because it was widely known the Serbs were on a final warning and he might fly into a rage. Whatever the reason, this was going as well as I dared hope for. But nothing in Bosnia had ever been simple or smooth and, at any moment, I expected a shout of 'Halt!' to tell us the game was up. As we followed our kit into our vehicles and prepared to set off again, the border with Greater Serbia felt so near yet so far away. Then, perhaps inevitably, we encountered a complication – one Riley should perhaps have anticipated.

He had been laughing and joking with Colonel Fortula, trying to keep him sweet. I always wondered whether the Bosnian Serbs would go for a PR hit if they weren't authorised to do anything more forceful. The obvious target was Riley, Commander of British UN forces in Gorazde, a town besieged by the Serbs for so long; a siege that had caused mayhem among Gorazde's innocent civilians, as we knew all too well. Riley was chatting away merrily with Colonel Fortula, who commanded the Serbs in Kopace and Visegrad and was, therefore, responsible, on a local level at least, for those same horrors in Gorazde. The scene was ripe for exploitation. What Riley should have done, when the time came for him to say goodbye to Fortula, was to salute him formally. Unfortunately, that's not quite how it happened.

I can imagine exactly how Riley was feeling and what he was thinking: 'Nearly there. Let's just keep these people sweet for a few minutes longer. I'm going to get all my men out of here and, right now, I don't care what it takes. This thing is still right in the balance: the warmth I demonstrate now might yet make the difference – especially if news of the Sarajevo atrocity reaches this place and Fortula is suddenly left in two minds about what to do with us.' And, to that extent, no one could blame Riley for what happened next.

He and Fortula ended up giving each other a little kiss on each cheek, and the Serb TV cameras were rolling. It wasn't clever from the British point of view. This was a real PR ambush and surprisingly easy to achieve. This was what the Serbs needed, in their eyes, to demonstrate to the world that what they had done around Gorazde had been acceptable. How could it be otherwise if the British who had been stationed in the town were saying farewell with such warmth? Perhaps Riley decided that the value to this PR hit would only be very temporary and what the world really thought about the Serbs and their activities along the bloody River Drina would become clear soon enough. For now, like the rest of us, I'm sure Riley just craved our freedom – and it felt tantalisingly close.

Whatever the rights and wrongs of the friendly farewell, the Serbs finally let us leave the Kopace compound, which came as a considerable relief to all of us. Riley was given a Liaison Officer by the Serbs – a guy called Brahni Suker, who joined the convoy in his own vehicle. In theory, that increased our chances of getting out, though Suker's presence wouldn't necessarily deter any rogue elements in the Bosnian Serb military who might be intent on making one final statement about the unwanted effect we'd had in the middle of their war zone.

The next half an hour would decide everything. By now, the sun had set, it was dark and difficult to see where we were, as we set out on the last road towards freedom. Not that the limited visibility had much effect on me. I was closed down in the back of my Saxon because Mark Adams had once more insisted on doing the driving in the cupola (turret). I had no problem with that because it allowed me to follow our progress on the radio, making sure I could chart stuff on the map too. I probably knew where we were better than Adams, and someone had to because a tricky part of the journey was coming up.

Once we were clear of Kopace, the idea was to press on with best speed to Visegrad. But there was one stretch we'd always worried about because we'd be driving along the road with hills on either side of us. These positions on the high ground were just right for launching an attack on anything moving down our road blow. As we entered this treacherous stretch, we hoped we could rely on friends above, whom we couldn't see. If the Serbs had set up an ambush, we trusted our air support – assuming it was still up there somewhere – to have spotted the enemy moving into fire positions on the high ground. Then, we hoped, they would swoop down and suppress those people before they had time to dig in and get comfortable. That way we'd be left to make use of the clear roads and get out as quickly as possible. A few minutes of driving through this potential death trap was enough to sharpen the senses though. We still had to be battle-ready; there could still be a very nasty twist to an increasingly hopeful evening. We drove on as fast as we could, always wondering what the next hundred yards would bring. But we soon realised we'd put the danger of the hills behind us and we'd encountered no resistance. Were we actually going to do this?

Almost before we knew it, we reached Visegrad. We certainly drew some strange stares from the early-evening drinkers there. Some voiced their disgust for UNPROFOR and the UN in general, spitting on the ground or throwing stones as they cursed us. As long as they didn't offer a more potent threat than that, we couldn't have cared less. On we drove, through the town and away, before anything more substantial could be organised against us. If they didn't have a roadblock set up already, we weren't going to give them time to do so.

We left Visegrad behind, a convoy growing in confidence with every passing moment, believing we were nearly there.

And then we approached the border and dared to think, 'We might just have made this.' We wouldn't believe it fully until we were over the border though. Suker, the Serb Liaison Officer, had gone ahead to the border crossing. Riley had then gone forward to meet him and the border commander. By the time we reached them, it looked as though they were locked in an intense conversation. Had something changed? Had Sarajevo altered everything at the last moment and denied us our way out? Then I saw something glorious – smiles. They suggested we weren't about to have our hopes dashed after all. In fact, there seemed to be some kind of formal signatory taking place and that could only mean one thing – we were leaving for real. And still I didn't want to let myself believe it entirely, just in case the dream was shattered.

Riley sent back the order to unload our weapons, which we were duty-bound to do as part of the agreement because we were crossing a sovereign border. That didn't mean we were leaving the weapons for the Serbs to use against the Muslims – far from it. They were still ours to hand over to whomever we wanted and we intended was to give them to the Royal Regiment of Fusiliers in Belgrade. It seemed fitting because they had been due to replace us in Gorazde – until it was decided that no one should have to do that. Now the RRF was due to be redeployed elsewhere in Bosnia but we knew they would still find our weapons and equipment useful.

We were at our most vulnerable once our weapons had been unloaded. There was a nagging thought at the back of my mind, hard to dismiss despite our promising predicament:

'Was this all a trick?' General Ratko Mladic had tricked so many men, women and children in his time – and very recently too. When Riley began to walk back from his little conference, I was standing at the back of my vehicle; we had stepped out of our vehicles in case we were going to face another search. Then I saw people closing in on Riley and that made me anxious. I walked briskly towards my boss, knowing that, as his Tactical Commander, I ought to be right there with him if there a problem. After all we'd been through, were these people about to deny us the chance to take the final step to freedom? As I neared Riley, I saw that he seemed unconcerned by the border officials around him though.

'That's it. All signed!' he said with a smile. 'Gather round.'

Riley called in all his company commanders. He was very emotional and, at first, there were no words. He instigated a team hug, as though we were some kind of basketball team. It made me feel a bit uncomfortable. It shouldn't have had that effect because this was his way of saying we'd made it by reaching the border. We were still just inside Bosnia but we were about to cross into Serbia. We'd done it!

Even then, Riley fought back his tears to warn, 'We are so close. So close! Stick tight for the last push!'

Like me, he almost didn't want to believe we'd made it either. And yet I felt differently to him. Why weren't my eyes filling with tears like Colonel Jon and some of the others? Why did I feel strangely detached from this happy scene? I couldn't let anything out, because where would it stop? And besides, I wanted Riley and the others to believe I was unfazed by it all, right to the end. Emotional self-protection and bravado combined, call it what you will. Deep down, I suppose I knew that there had already been so many better reasons to cry. If you're going to cry, you do it when you see a child murdered right in front of you, or when you hear the terrible scream of a mother who has just lost her baby. If I didn't cry then, I certainly wasn't going to cry now. The summer had been too terrible for tears because, if you had opened the floodgates to tears, you would never have been able to see clearly enough to survive and get your men through.

Riley was savouring his moment, he was enjoying this emotional release, and I certainly didn't blame him for that. Tears were acceptable in that circle and so there was a healthy release for some. Not me. I wasn't part of it. Physically, I was there, still in the huddle, but, emotionally, I had stayed out of it. What was I thinking? Just that I wanted everyone to be professional to the last. That thought allowed me to stay neutral and almost unfeeling, just as it had allowed me to function through the danger we'd experienced all summer. It was hard to grasp the fact that the threat to us had all but evaporated.

We crossed. Two simple words that took us from extreme danger back to freedom. Last push? What last push? We left Bosnia just like that. Serbia certainly wouldn't have been anyone's idea of freedom under normal circumstances and it was not a country that had much to be proud of, given the leading ideological role it had played in this dreadful war. But, for us, in those moments Serbia felt like heaven. The nightmare was over and even I could relax a little at this point because there was nothing more we needed to do in order to secure the safety of our men – except of course to drive them on to Belgrade.

So we drove. Sergeant-Major Mark Adams used his Walkman to play 'Nothing's Gonna Stop Us Now', that well-known rock anthem by Starship, through the speakers of our Saxon. How long had he been planning that? Corporal Bird, my signaller, was sitting there in bewilderment, probably the start of a long process of trying to understand what we'd just been through for the previous few months and how on earth we'd all got out alive. I tucked into some 'slivovitz' that Hassan had kindly given us, partly in thanks for my stinking trainers. Plum brandy. In a way, it had represented the thick, sickly-sweet taste of violence in Bosnia. It had numbed the senses of many a soldier in this atrocious war as he went about his bloody work. It had numbed the senses of the peacekeepers too, as we processed the brutality all around us and were sucked into it.

We had not killed children but we had still killed. We had fought for our principals but did we still know right from wrong? Of course we did. When we had killed, we had done so out of necessity; we had not killed for fun – not like some. And we had not killed children. We had killed adults, partly to save children. We could leave the region with our heads held high. Not that we were appreciated by our latest hosts any more than we had been appreciated in the country we had just left. But that was no big deal. By now, we were more than used to being unpopular.

What more did we have to endure? Just a few catcalls and stones aimed by Serbs along the way. The stones bounced off our Saxons harmlessly, the catcalls died in the night air. The cries of 'UNPROFOR shit!' and disdainful spitting in our general direction bothered us very little. The song was right. Nothing was going to stop us now. So we were able to arrive safely in the Serb capital of Brigade and we were met, as planned, by the Royal Regiment of Fusiliers there.

Our doctor, Mark Coombe, and I had already agreed to be 'roomies' at the Belgrade hotel that was allocated to us as part of the UN agreement with the local authorities. First Mark and I stood on the side of the road, making sure all the boys got away safely to the hotel. Then we cobbled together all the Serbian dinars we had to buy a couple of bottles of wine. When we reached our room, we saw to our amazement that everything had been laid out ready for us, even fresh toothbrushes. It was around then that I realised what a disgraceful state I was in. And even if I hadn't wanted to acknowledge it, I'd been daft enough to room with the doctor, so he wasn't going to allow me to ignore my physical condition.

The minor wound on my shin wasn't the problem – that was behaving itself, so Mark had been wrong for once when he had suggested it would become infected. It was the longer-term effects of life in Gorazde that had begun to take their toll, although you'd hardly had time to notice them while you were there. For a start, my uniform was rotting on my body; it was in a shocking state. And my body wasn't much better because I'd lost about two and half stone over the summer due to the creeping effects of malnutrition.

Then there was the question of my skin. Mark Coombe has been doing his best to treat my psoriasis. I call it that but my condition was really something akin to scurvy, caused by the deficiencies we'd had in our diet for so long. The sores had fallen off, almost unnoticed in the wider drama and tension of daily life in Gorazde. But now I'd got white dots all over me.

Sometimes you try to come up with a nickname for yourself in the army, before someone else comes up with something even crueller. I didn't know whether to call myself 'Hyena Man' or 'Leopard Boy'.

Doctors have always seen far worse and there was precious little sympathy from Mark Coombe, who thought it was hilarious that my skin was in such shocking condition. I wasn't about to feel sorry for myself and, besides, Mark didn't look so great either, as I gleefully pointed out. We just laughed at ourselves and took our bottles of wine up onto the flat hotel roof to have another drink. We basked in the knowledge that, for us, the nightmare was over. After all, the next day we were going to continue on to Croatia and, from there, we'd be flown back to home sweet home. For a while up on that roof, we took in the startling normality of a Belgrade night and savoured every moment. People weren't stuck in their homes, not if they didn't want to be; the city was alive and buzzing. Headlights and traffic. That was why the additional noise was hard to pick up at first.

We could have been forgiven for thinking that the booze and sheer exhaustion were playing tricks with our senses as we turned our attention to the night sky.

'Can you hear that?' I asked Mark.

'Hear what in particular?'

He had a point. Although we'd become used to the sound of shells and bullets in Gorazde, the nights had otherwise been largely silent. And the level of noise we were experiencing now, caused by normal city life, was almost overwhelming. But I thought I could hear something else.

'Aircraft.'

'Are you sure?' Mark listened harder. 'Hang on a minute...'

It was the mounting din of a substantial presence gathering in the air, and then we saw the lights in the sky to confirm it. Though we couldn't make out the shapes of the aircraft in the darkness, the lights were so numerous that we knew this must be a sizeable force.

'Jesus. Look at that!' I said. 'Are you thinking what I'm thinking?'

'Holy shit! Someone's early morning's going to get ruined,' said Mark.

'Even before they've woken up, with a bit of luck,' I added.

A huge Combined Air Operation was stacking up and preparing to head towards Bosnia. We looked at each other, smiled and raised our glasses to them. We'd always thought this would happen once we were clear – but maybe not quite so soon. NATO, with a quiet nod of acceptance from the UN, had decided not to waste any time in letting the Bosnian Serbs have it for what they had done to those poor people in Sarajevo market, for what they had done around Gorazde and for the massacre at Srebrenica. The Americans had been pushing for this decisive action for ages. Now it was happening fast.

There could be no doubt whatsoever that, among their many targets during the coming hours and days, NATO was going to hit Serb Communication and Logistics bases in areas around Gorazde. What did I feel about seeing those planes in the night sky, knowing what was going to happen? Happy would be the wrong word. I was not happy that the Bosnian Serbs were going to be bombed, because no one takes loss of life lightly. But I was content as a UN peacekeeper to know that, if the UN had endorsed the decision to bomb Serb positions around Gorazde, it would mean a greater degree of safety for the town's inhabitants in the long run. And if the Serbs hadn't still posed a clear threat to the town, this extreme action wouldn't have been necessary. The idea that this precision bombing was going to protect the town we'd fought for, among other besieged communities, made me very content indeed.

By the same token, if the Muslims had suddenly gone on the offensive, broken out of the Gorazde enclave and headed for Visegrad to create mayhem among the Serb civilian population there, equally I would have been content for air strikes on the Muslim forces to prevent a massacre in Visegrad. But that had not happened. Sure, the Muslims and the Croats had been guilty of massacres in this crazy war as well. But that had not been part of my experience. And, objective as I had tried to remain through all of this madness, in the end I was just a human being with natural reactions to what I had lived through.

And so, when I saw those planes fly over, destined for places I knew and perhaps for people who had murdered kids for fun and made no apology for it, was there a part of me that was pleased? I would be lying if I said it wasn't so. What was that subjective part of me really thinking and feeling? Something like this: 'That's for Selma and the living, even if she's barely talking to me anymore. That's for Adem and the rest of the Muslim dead, even if it's too late for them. Gorazde is the one enclave you won't be taking, General Ratko Mladic. And we've helped to save it.'

# POSTSCRIPT

# POST-TRAUMATIC STRESS DISORDER

The subsequent NATO bombing campaign helped to turn the tide of the war in favour of the Croatians and Muslim Bosniacks. I don't know if Nasty 1-1, the Dutch female pilot who had showed such bravery over Srebrenica, was involved but I wouldn't be surprised because some of our guys saw her later on, back at Split in Croatia. They told me she was blonde and gorgeous. Had Billy 'Pig Man' Walters known this up on the mountain as he heard Nasty 1-1 tell the SAS that she was 'coming in hot', his fantasy would have been complete. Not that anyone ever tried to make light of the events that followed. Even to this day, the world still struggles to take in the terrible enormity of what happened in Srebrenica. To think that could have happened in Gorazde too.

There were atrocities on all sides but the world was relieved to see the Bosnian Serbs effectively beaten and forced to sue for peace. That meant their worst war criminals were left without the power to realise their dreadful vision any further. Ratko Mladic went into hiding. It was intensely irritating to hear he had slipped away after all the misery he had caused. He'd destroyed so many lives and toyed with so many others. He'd played with the lives of some of my own men too, by taking them hostage. I hoped he'd be hunted down like an animal.

I didn't see Dave Parry again until I returned to the UK. It was a relief to meet all the hostages again at last. It was even more wonderful to see my pregnant wife Jane and my little son, George. But they didn't know what we'd been through. Much as my family tried to be supportive, they could never really know Gorazde, not even if I really tried to explain just how bad it had been. I didn't bother. Neither did the rest of the guys.

Her Majesty the Queen had first-hand experience of what many of our families had been going through and she was wonderfully quick to recognise our safe return. On 8 September 1995, she wrote to Riley from Balmoral:

I was very pleased to hear that every member of the 1st Battalion The Royal Welch Fusiliers who were in Bosnia had now returned safely to this country.

As your Colonel-in-Chief I have followed your deployment with the closest attention. During the last six months you have displayed exemplary courage, tenacity and resourcefulness in the face of a whole series of most exacting situations and conditions. I send my warm congratulations to each and every one of you and my best wishes to your families whose support, I well know, has been so important.

Rwy'n filch iawn ohonoch i gyd.

Elizabeth R.

'I'm very proud of you all,' she had written in Welsh. It was a heart-warming letter and thoughtfully written. She was right: support from families was still important, of course. Yet it was primarily down to us to understand what we'd been through and what we were feeling. That psychological awareness we'd been given in theatre was first class, and Captain Pete Roberts, the PTSD specialist from Gorazde, deservedly earned some recognition of his own in time because he went on to do a Masters Degree and a PHD in the United States. He called his thesis 'The Gorazde Triangles Study', or something similar. He won huge acclaim in the PTSD field, based largely on his experiences with us, I believe. He designed a new system called TRiM – trauma risk management. It was pioneered by the Royal Marines and, at the time of writing, was being used across all three British services – army, navy and air force – to reduce the likelihood of PTSD in veterans. Pete was later awarded an OBE. We were probably interesting material for him; perfect guinea pigs. There's no doubt that the man who designed that programme to keep at bay the demons of PTSD in future soldiers had developed much of his thinking in Gorazde, either cowering in a bunker under Bosnian Serb shelling, or observing soldiers who had been besieged by child murderers for rather too long for their own good. We were happy to have Pete Roberts around and pleased if we helped him arrive at many of his conclusions.

But when we got back home – and this is absolutely no reflection on Pete – there was no follow-up. The Battalion effectively went on the piss from the moment it arrived home. Those who'd been in Gorazde tended to gravitate towards one another in all situations because they felt they could talk more freely to people who'd been there. The one company from the Royal Welch Fusiliers that hadn't been there became so annoyed with our constant references to Gorazde that we had to start calling it 'The G-spot'. 'Don't mention the G-spot' was our new catchphrase.

The Gorazde bond was therapeutic because, in those days, you couldn't go to the camp doctor in Britain and say, 'I've got an emotional problem, I'm not coping with what I've been through and I'm not sleeping at night, this is disturbing me, my wife doesn't understand me and I can't talk to her about it, obviously I can't speak to my children about it and the only people who get me are my blokes.' At least you didn't think you could. There was a risk you might be perceived as 'Lacking in Moral Fibre' – the dreaded 'LMF', three cruel initials that had been used since the World Wars to describe people the armed forces often wrongly regarded as cowards.

But the blokes really didn't think it was fair to dump all their problems on their families, and those who tried to confide in friends were often greeted with a reaction that bordered on the incredulous. People who hadn't been there just couldn't get their heads round what we'd been through, or so it seemed. So you either shared it with the other blokes as you swam in a sea of booze, or you bottled it up. You soon found yourself in a downward spiral and that was classic PTSD.

By the time we got home to face the jarring normality of life in the UK, I suspect all of my company were suffering from PTSD in some shape or form, including me. Some of us might never have admitted it to outsiders or even to one another. Neither, I suspect, would the army have wanted to accept that we suffered 100 per cent PTSD casualties owing to what we saw, heard and smelled in Gorazde. There are no accurate data on PTSD casualties in the aftermath of Gorazde because, as mentioned, people feared the consequences of coming clean about how they were feeling. The army may have been slowly changing its attitude but the change had not yet hit home and that same army, you sensed, was still relieved not to be told about something it didn't fully understand. Why would soldiers be feeling so bad, even now they were home and out of danger? Where was the logic? Where was the hard evidence? Yet you didn't have to wear underpants on your head and go around with pencils up your nostrils while muttering 'wibble, wibble' in order to be suffering from PTSD. It was widespread among us, whether it was obvious or not, and, deep down, most of us probably knew the truth.

Despite the warnings from Pete Roberts, some of us had been so traumatised by certain things we'd locked away 'in the box' out there that the mere sound of a child crying loudly in a supermarket after we got back home was unbearable for us, so much so that we'd have to get out of seemingly harmless places and away from innocent tantrums while we still could, just so that we could breathe normally again. Memories of the terrible suffering of Gorazde's children, with all the accompanying horror, could be triggered so easily. Bored, screaming kids would soon cause me and the blokes to retreat from any British supermarket and regroup outside, gasping for air or puffing on cigarettes, with the trauma of Gorazde too raw inside us. One knowing look between us or a simple shake of the head said it all.

Listening to warnings about PTSD in the field is one thing. Putting what you had learned into practice back home, in order to counter PTSD, was quite another. We had been well prepared for what might happen; we knew we were carrying around an intolerable amount of emotional baggage. But unburdening ourselves was easier said than done and the consequences, therefore, inevitable. One of the doctors from our camp in Gorazde explained to me many years later that it would have been 'inconceivable' for any of us to come through our experience there and not suffer from PTSD as a result. 'Only two types of British army people could have emerged from Gorazde,' said the doctor, who had experienced problems himself back home. 'Sociopaths and people with PTSD. And we didn't have any sociopaths. We all came home from Gorazde suffering from PTSD in some shape or form. How could anyone go through the intensity and helplessness of that summer without suffering severe psychological strain?'

The mother of a friend of mine, who was in Gorazde with me, finally said to him one day, 'It's good to have you back.' That was ten months after he had returned. But that's how long it took for him to start behaving like the son who had left for Gorazde in the first place. He wasn't unusual in any way. I suspect most people had similar stories to tell.

We weren't unscathed, that's for sure, but we certainly hadn't been defeated either. If anything, we'd been successful in Bosnia, and that was recognised by the powers that be. By 1996 it had emerged that, to our surprise, the Battalion had been awarded an unprecedented number of 'peacetime' gallantry awards. Jonathon Riley won the Distinguished Service Order for his superb leadership. With his backing, we'd stood up for ourselves and yet we hadn't suffered a single fatality. Little short of miraculous, that, and a credit to his judgement too.

Colour Sergeant Pete Humphries won the Conspicuous Gallantry Cross for 'tremendous presence of mind, aggressive spirit and coolness under fire'. The Conspicuous Gallantry Cross was second only to the Victoria Cross, so the medal showed how brilliantly and bravely Pete had performed.

Dave Parry and Hugh Nightingale were awarded the Military Cross for their heroics after they had been taken hostage – a tribute to their cool leadership in the face of beatings and threats of execution. Surprisingly, I also got a Military Cross. Just deserts for the men in general, but I felt humbled at having been picked out, along with the other two recipients. Only because those who have helped me write this book have insisted upon it, I include the citation for my MC below:

It was his company which formed the rear-end guard on the last day. His personal example and leadership over a prolonged period and in the face of unprecedented difficulties, as well as his disregard for danger, were key factors throughout the operation.

I don't think I 'disregarded' danger; neither was I prepared to be a slave to fear. There is a middle way that helps you to do the right thing and I hope that balance enabled us all to do our very best and get back in one piece too.

Along with the others who were accepting their medals on behalf of all the blokes, I went to Buckingham Palace, ready to be presented with my Military Cross by the Queen. So many could have been given the medals we were to receive. Unfortunately, there is a maximum number that can be awarded within a single battalion and we had reached our quota. But there were many who either deserved more than they received, or got nothing at all.

We 'smuggled in' Dave Vaatstra as our uniformed driver. Vaatstra was one of seven to be Mentioned in Despatches, and there were also two Queen's Commendations for Valuable Service. Vaatstra had done so much with his machine gun to hold the Serbs at bay up on that mountain that we felt he just had to be with us on the big day. His wife had met the Queen at the height of the crisis; so it was only fair that Dave had a royal experience of his own.

I felt pride and humility in the same instant when it was my turn to receive my award. The Queen told me, 'We are absolutely delighted to award you this. We didn't think you'd get out of that place.'

There were times when we didn't think we'd get out either. Perhaps, in a sense, we never did. But here we were at the Palace, enjoying the moment as we knew all the lads wanted us to, for we were representing each and every one of them – nothing more, nothing less. And we took some of that mischievous battalion spirit and humour to the occasion too.

There were professional photographers ready to take portraits of medal recipients once we were outside again.

Dave Parry asked one 'pro' how much he was charging.

'Twenty-five pounds,' the photographer replied.

# POSTSCRIPT

'At least Dick Turpin had the decency to wear a mask,' Parry said, which made us all chuckle.

We refused to pay that kind of money and, besides, we had our own 'professional' on hand – Vaatstra himself. Before he'd made the Butcher of Bosnia's 'Ethnic Cleansing Brigade' wish they'd never attacked us, Vaatstra had enjoyed using a camera more than a machine gun. In his younger days, he'd spent a lot of time hiding under bushes in Northern Ireland, trying to get pictures of suspects who were up to no good. Taking a picture of a few decorated soldiers was going to be a piece of cake for Dave – and so it proved. We got quality photos without being ripped off. Pete Humphries was with us, as unfazed as ever, talking quietly to his wife in Welsh. Then, suddenly, there was pandemonium among the boys and I wondered what was going on.

They'd seen Ieuan Evans, a top Welsh rugby player at the time. Evans was there to receive an MBE and found himself swamped. It amused me, all these guys who were true heroes in my eyes hero-worshipping a rugby player on their own big day. It just showed the humility the men possessed. Receiving medals wasn't going to change them. They still contested the bill when we'd finished our post-ceremony meal in the Chicago Pizza Pie Factory in Hanover Square. They always did, they always would.

I don't know everything about how they felt deep down as time marched on but I could hazard a guess from my own post-traumatic experience. For about ten years after Gorazde, I used to wake up in a filthy mood on 28 May – the date of our battle on Mount Biserna. I'd get a call from Riley and we'd tell each other how shit we were feeling. Those feelings have pretty much passed now. Life goes on, there are always fresh challenges. Even now I find there is no time for tears, though there is certainly no shame in crying if the tears will come, and I hope many others have benefited from them.

What of the people of Gorazde, the many who survived the Serb onslaught? I still like to think we helped them and that, in the end, they appreciated it. Is it too much to hope that Western and Muslim cultures could take the case of Gorazde, for all its imperfections, and see that we can still work together, shoulder to shoulder, to beat the real bad guys in the world? Maybe that's just fanciful.

Selma? She never made it to Spain, though, mercifully, the son she raised in Gorazde would never have to live in fear of a sniper's bullet. We achieved something then.

Could we have taken much more, the men of the Royal Welch Fusiliers and the SAS, had we been trapped in Gorazde for longer? Who knows? I'm glad we never had to find out. The Butcher of Bosnia had pushed us to the limit.

Over the years, the hunt for Ratko Mladic went on. But it always appeared he was being protected by someone powerful somewhere because he evaded capture for so long. Then in 2011 he was finally hunted down and called to account for his war crimes. Perhaps political pressure had finally told and no one was prepared to make excuses for the villain of the peace any longer. At the time of writing, Mladic looks destined to spend his last days behind bars. He looks frail and broken but it's hard to feel pity for him.

None of my men – especially not the ones who had been taken hostage and led to believe their days were numbered –

were ever going to feel very sorry for the Butcher. Personally, I feel an element of revulsion whenever I hear the name Mladic. To this day, I sincerely hope he spends whatever life he has left in prison.

The men of B Company, Royal Welch Fusiliers, carry their psychological scars. That doesn't mean we don't go about our professional lives with the same determination we always had when we were together.

I often meet the 'old guard' from B Company. We talk about Gorazde. The frustrations, the excitement, the trauma and, above all, the deep, deep sadness surrounding our time there. None of it will never leave us entirely, of course. That's the price we had to pay.

Not one of us has ever said it wasn't worth it.

# ACKNOWLEDGEMENTS

I would like to thank my old friend Mark Ryan for persuading me to undertake this book and then helping me to structure and write it. Thanks also to Chris Mitchell, who commissioned the book for John Blake Publishing on the strength of the story, and to the Executive Editor, Toby Buchan, who steered the book through the editorial and production phase with such diligence and dedication. I'm grateful to all at John Blake for the invaluable role they played in bringing this book to the point of publication. Finally, a special thank you to Colonel Tim Collins, OBE, for his typically generous and insightful support from the moment I told him about the project.

COLONEL RICHARD WESTLEY, OBE, MC